ISRAEL AND WORLD POLITICS

ALSO BY THEODORE DRAPER

Abuse of Power

Castroism: Theory and Practice

Castro's Revolution: Myths and Realities

American Communism and Soviet Russia

The Roots of American Communism

The 84th Infantry Division in the Battle of Germany

The Six Weeks' War

ISRAEL AND WORLD POLITICS

ROOTS OF THE THIRD ARAB-ISRAELI WAR

THEODORE DRAPER

New York / THE VIKING PRESS

To Dorothy and Jacob Rabkin

PREFACE

The third Arab-Israeli war of June 1967 will long be studied from different points of view and in its various aspects—military, diplomatic, sociological, and so forth. For the present, so close to the event, no one can hope to make more than a modest contribution to the understanding of such a complex subject. My own interest has been mainly devoted to inquiring how and why it came about. I have dealt with the background or antecedents of the war rather than with the war itself or with postwar problems. I was drawn to examining some of the forces behind the war because I consider that, in the long run, they will prove to be the deepest and most important aspects of what has already been, in effect, a twenty years' war. If this is not the last one between Arabs and Israelis, the same forces will be responsible for bringing about another war.

A much shorter version of this essay first appeared as an article in *Commentary* magazine of August 1967. When I was asked to republish this article in more permanent form, I decided to go over the ground again and to see whether a number of points could not be told more fully and clearly. Only minor revisions seemed necessary in the first half, but the second half of the article has been rewritten and enlarged to take in much new material not previously available to me. I have tried as much as possible to base this work on documentary sources, but contemporary history cannot be written from documents alone. It has not, unfortunately, been possible to cite sources of a personal nature. I can only assure the reader that these sources were, in every case, leading figures who were able to give firsthand, authoritative accounts, often based on documentation which cannot yet be revealed.

It also seemed useful to include a number of key documents, many of which are not easily obtainable. The documents have been chosen by virtue of their close relation to my own treatment of the prewar period and have mainly been limited to the United States "commitment" in 1957 and the immediate prewar period in 1967. In some cases, their length made it unfeasible to give them in full, but I have tried to select all those passages which have a direct bearing on something in the rest of the book.

I am indebted to The Hoover Institution on War, Revolution, and Peace, at Stanford University, and to its Director, Dr. W. Glenn Campbell, for making it possible for me to work freely and independently. I am also grateful to Walter Laqueur, Director of the Institute for Advanced Studies in Contemporary History (London), who generously showed me a chapter of his forthcoming book on the third Arab-Israeli war; to Ze'ev Ben-Shlomo, of the same Institute, whose assistance was invaluable; to Howard Koch, Jr., of The Hoover Institution, and to Phyllis Freeman, who helpfully criticized the manuscript; to Lise Hofmann and Ann Richards, of The Hoover Institution, for devoted assistance.

—THEODORE DRAPER

November 18, 1967

CONTENTS

Appendices

ISRAEL AND WORLD POLITICS

A peculiar combination of internal and external forces was necessary to set off the third Arab-Israeli war. A most unstable equilibrium had, of course, existed in the area since the second war in 1956. But for all their suspicions and grievances, the two main antagonists, Egypt and Israel, had not resorted to force against each other for ten years. That a full-scale war should have erupted in June 1967 suggests that a new element had been injected into the Middle East to upset the *status quo*. And this new element could have come only from the outside.

I

The antagonisms and rivalries which led to this war crisscrossed in all directions. Some were more important than others, but no single one of them could have brought about the conflict. The Arab-Israeli conflict, deep as it was, had been held in leash for the most part since 1956 by other conflicting forces. Foremost among them were the conflicts among the Arab states themselves. They could not turn on Israel as long as they were spending so much substance and energy fighting among themselves. To the "revolutionary" Arab states, Egypt and Syria, victory over the "reactionary" Arab states, especially Jordan and Saudi Arabia, was a precondition for victory over Israel. Egyptian priorities seemed first to be Yemen, where its forces had been fighting for more than four years, and then Aden, which the British had promised to evacuate by 1968. On top of this, Egypt and Syria were busy competing for the leadership of the "revolutionary" Arab struggle, and they were also divided on the strategy to be followed against Israel.

What we know as the Middle East, moreover, has more in it than Arabs and Jews. In addition to about two and a quarter

3

million Jews and sixty million Arabs, it contains some seventy-five million non-Arab Moslems extending from Turkey to Iran. Until World War II, most of the area was essentially a British sphere of influence, with France entrenched in Syria and Lebanon only. France was eliminated by 1946. Britain quit Palestine in 1948, Iran in 1951, Sudan in 1953, Egypt in 1954–1956, Jordan in 1957, and Iraq in 1958. As the British and French retreated, the United States and the Soviet Union moved in. The Truman Doctrine, for the containment of Communism, was promulgated in 1947 in response to Soviet pressure in three countries—two of them, Turkey and Iran, in the Middle East. In 1951, the Truman administration unsuccessfully tried to organize a Middle East Defense Command, embracing the United States, the United Kingdom, France, Turkey, and the Arab states. In 1955, former Secretary of State John Foster Dulles was more successful on a more limited scale by bringing together Turkey, Iraq, Iran, Pakistan, and Great Britain in a defense arrangement known as the Baghdad Pact. The Soviet Union countered that same year with an arms deal with Egypt—the first great Soviet military and political breakthrough in the Arab world. By the end of the decade, the Chinese Communists had begun to assert themselves, especially in Iraq and Syria.

Thus there had been antagonisms and rivalries between Arabs and Israelis, Arabs and Arabs, Arab and non-Arab Moslem states, United States and USSR, Russian Communists and Chinese Communists. The war of June 1967 was not the result solely of differences between Arabs and Israelis, and it probably would not have broken out when and how it did if they had simply been left alone.

As in all such seemingly irreconcilable conflicts, the real *casus belli* was a struggle against history. This history has been so encrusted with myths and legends that there can be little hope of progress toward reconciliation until some of them have been swept away.

One of the most potent legends is that Israel owes its very existence to "Western imperialism." It is well to determine how much truth there is in this story, not only for its own sake, but because it offers a good starting point for considering the curious course of Soviet policy.

It is true, of course, that the British government's Balfour Declaration started Israel on the road to statehood in November 1917. But a good many British governments and Foreign Secretaries came between that promissory note on the Promised Land, which cost Britain nothing, and the United Nations General Assembly vote on November 29, 1947, in favor of partitioning Palestine into an Arab and a Jewish state. Ernest Bevin, then British Foreign Secretary, was so little sympathetic to the Jewish cause that he opened himself up to the charge of anti-Semitism. From the "infamous" White Paper of 1939, as David Ben Gurion called it,[1] * to 1947, the Zionists considered Britain the greatest obstacle to the fulfillment of their hopes. Britain, in fact, abstained in the vote on the crucial resolution, and did little or nothing to implement it.

If Israel owed its existence to any powers besides itself, they were the United States and the Union of Soviet Socialist Republics. The favorable United Nations vote would not have been politically possible against Soviet opposition. In fact, the Soviet representative, Andrei A. Gromyko, then Deputy Foreign Minister, defended the partition of Palestine and the establishment of an independent Jewish state with all the arguments that the Arabs then and later have considered most unacceptable. For example, he linked the birth of Israel with the Jewish past in Palestine and with the extermination of millions of Jews in Europe. In the session of November 26, 1947, he said:

> The representatives of the Arab States claim that the partition of Palestine would be an historic injustice. But this view of the case is unacceptable, if only because, after all, the Jewish people has been closely linked with Palestine for a considerable

* Reference notes begin on page 266.

period in history. Apart from that, we must not overlook—and the USSR delegation drew attention to this circumstance originally at the special session of the General Assembly—we must not overlook the position in which the Jewish people found themselves as a result of the recent world war. I shall not repeat what the USSR delegation said on this point at the special session of the General Assembly. However, it may not be remiss to remind my listeners again that, as a result of the war which was unleashed by Hitlerite Germany, the Jews, as a people, have suffered more than any other people.

No one exceeded Gromyko—once the Soviet leaders had made up their minds that a binational, Arab-Jewish state in Palestine was impossible—in the ardor with which he praised the decision to set up a Jewish state:

> The solution of the Palestine problem based on a partition of Palestine into two separate states will be of profound historical significance, because this decision will meet the legitimate demands of the Jewish people, hundreds of thousands of whom, as you know, are still without a country, without homes, having found temporary shelter only in special camps in some western European countries.

Yet, in the same speech, Gromyko made a prophetic gesture to gain the favor of the Arab states:

> The USSR delegation is convinced that Arabs and Arab States will still, on more than one occasion, be looking towards Moscow and expecting the USSR to help them in the struggle for their lawful interests, in their efforts to cast off the last vestiges of foreign dependence.[2]

The first country to recognize Israel, on May 14, 1948, eleven minutes after the new state's declaration of independence went into effect, was the United States. But the Soviet Union, the third, was not far behind three days later.* The first

* The Soviet Union even has a claim that it beat the United States to the recognition of Israel because the United States recognition on May 14, 1948, was only *de facto* (*Department of State Bulletin,* May 23, 1948, p. 673).

diplomatic representatives to arrive in Tel Aviv one after the other in August 1948 were the American and the Soviet; they stayed at the same two-story hotel, which flew United States and USSR flags on its roof. Indeed, according to a French official then in Israel, a Jewish colonel in the Soviet army helped organize the first Israeli artillery.[3] The Israeli parliament on March 9, 1949, adopted a program of basic principles, one of which avowed "friendship with all freedom-loving states, in particular with the United States and the Soviet Union."[4] For a while, it seemed that, diplomatically, the Messiah had come to bring the two great powers together again in the Holy Land. If the existence of the state of Israel was the original sin, the Soviets were as implicated in it as anyone else.

A glance at the first Arab-Israeli war yields some useful historical perspective.

The Arab guerrilla war broke out as soon as the United Nations voted for the partition plan in November 1947. When the state of Israel was established in May 1948, the regular armies of Egypt, Syria, Jordan, Lebanon, and Iraq invaded Palestine.* If arms were all that mattered, Israel should have been throttled at birth. Israel had only a small, underground defense force, the Haganah, with no artillery, tanks, or planes. The Arab armies were overwhelmingly stronger in numbers and

---

* Nineteen forty-eight was not so different from 1967: "The Arabs had to a great extent been deluded by their own enthusiasm. Fond of studying and retailing in public the story of the Arab conquests of thirteen centuries ago, they believed themselves to be a great military people, and regarded the Jews as a nation of shopkeepers. The Egyptians, the Syrians and the Iraqis, out of touch with the situation in Palestine and too inexperienced to realize the necessity to find out the facts, assumed that they would find no difficulty in defeating the Jews. The Arabs of Palestine, familiar with the Jews but knowing little of the Arab governments, were confident that the Egyptians, Syrians and Iraqis would be amply strong. The Arab governments did immense harm to the cause of the Palestine Arabs, because they encouraged them to be defiant, and when it came to violence, they failed" (Sir John Bagot Glubb, *A Soldier with the Arabs* [New York: Harper, 1957], pp. 78–79). Sir John should have known; he was commander of the Jordanian army.

equipment. At a particularly crucial moment, the Israelis managed to secure rifles, light machine guns, and ammunition from Czechoslovakia.[5] Once war had broken out in earnest, the United Nations did not know what to do. The United States wavered and suddenly switched from supporting the partition of Palestine to putting all of it under a temporary "trusteeship." Ironically, the Soviet Union came out most firmly for going through with the original plan; Gromyko severely criticized the United States for holding back.[6]

As long as the Arab states thought they were winning, they ignored the United Nations, which vainly called on them to cease and desist. When the battle began to turn against them, they agreed to a one-month truce or cease-fire on June 11, 1948. But the pause gave the Syrians and Egyptians time to rest and regroup; they refused to renew the truce, took up arms again, and fought for another ten days—with the result that the Israelis captured almost half of Galilee in the north, which they would otherwise not have had. In mid-October, the Egyptians again broke the truce and renewed the fighting—with the result that the Israelis pushed them back and gained control of the Negev in the south, which they also might not have had. The fighting in the Sinai stopped on January 7, 1949, and armistice agreements were signed separately with Egypt on February 24, with Lebanon on March 23, with Jordan on April 3, and with Syria on July 20 of that year. Each of the Arab states tried to get the best bargain for itself, irrespective of the others. The procedure may be suggestive of the future.

In terms of the United Nations' position, there is no doubt who the "aggressor" was. The Arab states' resort to force was unmistakably a defiance of the United Nations resolution of November 29, 1947. Trygve Lie, then United Nations Secretary General, wrote in his memoirs: "The invasion of Palestine by the Arab States was the first armed aggression which the world had seen since the end of the War." * The "aggression"

---

* Trygve Lie, *In the Cause of Peace* (Macmillan, 1954), p. 174. Lie confirms that the Soviet Union was "more steadfast" than the United

was halted by Israeli resistance, not by the United Nations, which stepped in only after the Arab states had lost their taste for fighting.

If the Arabs had accepted the United Nations plan of 1947, as the Jews did, Israel would have been a tiny geographic monstrosity. The plan divided Palestine into seven parts, three Jewish and three Arab, each virtually disjointed, and a seventh, Jerusalem, which was to be "internationalized." But a condition of the partition was the economic union of the Arab and Israeli parts. The largest Jewish part consisted of the Negev, then a wasteland. But this also meant that Eilat, at the southern tip of the Negev desert and at the northern tip of the Gulf of Aqaba, was allotted to Israel to give it an outlet through the Straits of Tiran to the Red Sea and the East. Thus, when Israel captured the Lower Negev in the 1949 fighting, it was able to occupy Eilat, which the United Nations had allotted to it in theory only.*

Once the Arab leaders became more interested in saving their shattered armies than in destroying Israel, they were delighted

States in support of partition (p. 164). Of private consultations in March 1948, in which the United States, USSR, France, and China took part, Lie writes: "Only the Soviet Union seemed to be seriously intent upon implementing partition; the United States clearly was not" (p. 169).

* The Israeli "right" to Eilat has been challenged on the ground that Israeli forces entered it after the Israel-Egypt armistice agreement was signed. But the Israelis were opposed in this area by Jordan's Arab Legion, not by Egypt. *The New York Times* of March 12, 1949, reported from Tel Aviv: "Israel has occupied the disputed five-mile Elath [Eilat] coastal area at the southern tip of Palestine after a minor clash with Transjordanian troops based at Aqaba, it was reported here yesterday." In fact, there were no Arabs in the area; the small garrison at Aqaba was made up of British troops (George Kirk, *Survey of International Affairs 1939–1946: The Middle East 1945–1950* [New York: Oxford University Press, 1954], p. 296). According to the Israelis, Eilat was taken on March 6, 1949; according to Kirk on March 10, 1949; and a Jordan-Israel cease-fire was signed on March 11, 1949. Eilat was originally a small Palestine police post called Umm Rash Rash. In any case, the demarcation lines of the armistice agreements with both Egypt and Jordan clearly placed Eilat outside Egyptian and Jordanian territory.

to go back to the 1947 United Nations partition plan which they had previously denounced. But it was too late. The armistice negotiations, which earned Dr. Ralph Bunche, the United Nations mediator, his Nobel Peace Prize, were advanced lessons in Oriental haggling. In the end, all parties remained pretty much where they had been when the fighting stopped. For example, the Egyptians remained in the Gaza strip, which they still held but which had never been Egyptian soil. The Jordanians held on to the West Bank of the Jordan River and the Old City in Jerusalem, neither of which had ever been part of Jordan. Though the armistice agreement provided for "free access to the Holy Places and cultural institutions," such as the Wailing Wall and the Hebrew University on Mount Scopus, Jordan refused to live up to it—and nothing was done. As for Israel, the 1949 armistice agreements left it about one-quarter larger in territory than it would have been under the 1947 United Nations partition plan. Each war has ended with the Arabs more than willing to go back to the *status quo ante*. The Arab states have always made war on Israel in the spirit of: If we win, we win everything; if we lose, we lose nothing. This was just as true in 1949 as it was in 1967.*

The Soviet Union did not object to the outcome of the first Arab-Israeli war. It did not insist on the 1947 boundaries of the United Nations plan. It did not assail the Israelis as aggressors because they had beaten back the armies of five Arab states and had forced them to accept armistice boundaries. It must be emphasized that none of these states had a "right" to Palestine territory which had never been theirs; the United Nations partition plan of 1947 had envisaged a new Arab state which never came into being. The main territorial effect of the 1949 armistice agreements was the enlargement of Israel, Jor-

* In fact, Israeli Foreign Minister Abba Eban wrote an article in 1965 that contained these words: "It is not absurd to imagine Arab leaders ardently urging 'a return to the frontier of 1966 or 1967,' just as they now urge a return to the frontier of 1947 which they once set aside by force" ("Reality and Vision in the Middle East," *Foreign Affairs*, July 1965, p. 630).

dan, and Egypt in that order. In the present crisis, Arab leaders
have talked much of going back to 1956, 1949, or 1947. Yet
the differences between these three periods resulted from Arab-
Israeli wars.

The United Nations' function was limited in the main to
providing a skillful mediator for the 1949 armistice negotiations. Once the armistices were signed and the Arab leaders had
recovered their nerve, United Nations resolutions were not
heeded any more than the famous resolution of November 29,
1947, had been heeded. In violation of the Constantinople
Convention of 1888, Egypt has never permitted an Israeli ship
to pass through the Suez Canal.* To justify this hostile act,
Egypt claimed that it was still in a state of "belligerency" with
Israel, armistice or no armistice. On September 1, 1951, and
again on October 13, 1956, the Security Council called on
Egypt to lift these restrictions. The resolution of September 1,
1951, specifically rejected the Egyptian claim of "belligerent
rights" and ruled that "neither party can reasonably assert that
it is actively a belligerent or requires to exercise the right of
visit, search or seizure for any legitimate purpose of self-defence." Neither resolution enabled a single Israeli ship to pass
through the Canal. At the end of 1949, after the armistice
agreement was signed, Egypt installed guns at Ras Nasrani near
the camp at Sharm el-Sheikh overlooking the Straits of Tiran
to blockade the Israeli port of Eilat. By the time Israel attempted to take the issue to the Security Council in March
1954, the Soviets had adopted a new pro-Arab line, and a
Soviet veto prevented the Council from doing anything about it.

Oddly, if any Middle Eastern state was created by imperialists, it was Jordan. The Emirate of Transjordan was set up in

* Article I of this Convention, which governs the conduct of the Canal,
provides that it "shall always be free and open, *in time of war as in
time of peace,* to every vessel of commerce or of war, without distinction of flag" (my italics, T.D.). Article XI directs that even measures
taken for "the defense of Egypt" should not "interfere with the free use
of the Canal." Thus this is not an issue which depends on whether
Egypt still considers itself at war with Israel.

1921 by the British, who had won the territory from the Turks during World War I. Emir Abdullah was installed in power on condition that his fief should be administered under the control of the British High Commissioner for Palestine. Abdullah's army, the Arab Legion, was organized in 1921 under a British commander and remained under British command until 1956. Transjordan's independence was proclaimed in 1923 on condition that Abdullah continue to be "guided" by the British in foreign, financial, and military affairs. The West Bank of the Jordan River and the Old City of Jerusalem were occupied by the troops of Transjordan during the Arab-Israeli war in 1948. Abdullah refused to yield this territory despite the opposition of the other Arab states, which wanted to form an Arab "Government of All-Palestine," with its headquarters at Gaza, then occupied by Egypt. But Abdullah refused to give up the spoils of war, which interested him far more than overthrowing the nascent state of Israel. As a result, Transjordan increased its territory by 2165 square miles and trebled its population because the East Bank, to which it had been formerly restricted, was over four-fifths desert. The enlarged territory was renamed the Hashemite Kingdom of Jordan on April 26, 1949.[7] Abdullah, grandfather of the present King Hussein, was the only Arab ruler who wanted to make peace with Israel, for which he was assassinated by Arab fanatics in 1951. Thus, Jordan owed its creation to British power and policy far more than Israel did, and Jordan expanded to its present borders far more as a result of competing successfully against other Arab states than against Israel. The West Bank of the Jordan and the Old City of Jerusalem became Jordanian in 1948 solely by virtue of military occupation, which happened to serve Israel's interests at the time. But the precedent could easily be turned against Jordan nineteen years later.

I have touched on some aspects of the crucial 1947–1949 period because so much of the present Arab-Israeli conflict goes back to it. To both Arabs and Israelis, their third war was a continuation of the first and second. If the issue were merely the blockade of Eilat or the status of the Gaza strip or the treatment of Arab refugees or the prevention of terrorist raids, it would probably not be beyond the wit of Arabs and Israelis to resolve. But the one, fundamental issue has always been the *existence* of the state of Israel. Once this is put in question, no lesser, immediate, practical problem can be settled in good faith or, as more often happens, even brought up for settlement. As we shall see, the third Arab-Israeli war was fought in order to return, or to prevent a return, to the *status quo ante* of the second, and if the Arabs had been successful, they would not and could not have stopped short of going back to the *status quo ante* of the first. It is only by knowing something about the first two wars that the third can be understood.

And yet, if there is one subject that must be considered off limits, it is Israel's very existence. This is certainly true for all those powers which helped to bring Israel into existence or have recognized its right to exist. The contradiction in the Soviet position is that although it was most instrumental in bringing about the United Nations decision to partition Palestine in 1947–1949 and cannot repudiate the right of Israel to live without repudiating its own past, it has nevertheless supported Arab states whose policies have been dedicated to just such a repudiation. There is a more fundamental reason, however, why nothing useful or hopeful can come out of questioning the very basis of Israel's national existence. If the Arabs have a "right" to destroy Israel by force, Israel cannot be denied the "right" to use force to prevent its destruction. It is too late to expect the Israelis to give up without a struggle what they have earned and won. As soon as the *casus belli* becomes the existence of Israel, there is no right and no wrong; there is only force to determine whether Israel is going to live or die. The relationship of Israel to the Arab world can be discussed more or less rationally; whether there should be an Israel cannot.

From the second Arab-Israeli war in 1956, it is possible to learn what conditions were necessary to bring on another conflict.

These conditions have, in the main, been five: (1) a continuing campaign of Arab terrorism against Israel accompanied by Israeli military retaliation; (2) a significant imbalance in the level of arms available to both sides; (3) blockade of the Straits

II

of Tiran to prevent shipping from the Israeli port of Eilat; (4) Arab military pacts and troop movements encircling Israel; and (5) a marked shift in the policies of the Communist and the Western powers vis-à-vis Israel and the Arab states. No one of these conditions may be determining, but when all come together, the danger of conflict clearly approaches the boiling point.

As early as 1951, it was clear that a cycle of Arab raids and Israeli reprisals had started. By 1955, both Egypt and Israel were officially committed to one or the other phase of the cycle. The question that concerns us here is not which side was guilty or innocent in individual incidents; the determination was generally too much even for the United Nations Truce Supervision Organization, set up in 1948–1949 to supervise the execution of the armistice agreements, which forbade not only a further resort to force but even the threat of force.* We can view this problem only as a symptom of approaching war.

* Article I, paragraph 2, of the armistice agreements reads: "No aggressive action by the armed forces—land, sea, or air—of either Party should be undertaken, planned or threatened against the people or the armed forces of the other; . . ." Article II, paragraph 2, states: "No element of the land, sea, or air military or para-military forces of

15

Until 1955, no Arab government accepted responsibility for the attacks on Israeli life and property by small groups of Arab "infiltrators." Israeli policy, on the other hand, made retaliatory or punitive actions a government decision and a military operation. This policy was based on the belief that these raids were a form of irregular warfare and that the Arab governments were responsible for their recurrence. Where, as in Lebanon, the government discouraged border incidents, they were few, and where, as in Egypt, Jordan, or Syria, the government then encouraged or tolerated them, they were increasingly menacing. In any event, something changed in 1955. In August, it became known that Egypt was behind a campaign of sabotage and terrorism by groups known as *fedayeen*.* As more and more *fedayeen* incidents piled up, Israeli reprisals intensified, until small-scale battles were being waged.

In September 1955, the first Soviet-Egyptian arms deal was consummated, though it was at first publicly attributed to Czechoslovakia. Until then, both Israel and the Arab states had been dependent on Western arms. But these were in relatively short supply owing to a Tripartite Declaration by Britain, France, and the United States on May 25, 1950, barring an arms race in the area. Suddenly, Egypt's new source of supply completely upset the existing balance. Egypt received tanks,

---

either Party, including non-regular forces, shall commit any warlike or hostile act against the military or para-military forces of the other Party, or against civilians in territory under the control of that Party; or shall advance beyond or pass over for any purpose whatsoever the Armistice Demarcation Line set forth in Article VI of this Agreement; and elsewhere shall not violate the international frontier." The United States in particular has always recognized the rule of international law that each state is responsible for raids from its territory.

* Lt. Gen. E. L. M. Burns, the Canadian head of the United Nations Truce Supervisory Organization, by no means uncritical of Israeli policy, wrote: "I felt that what Egyptians were doing in sending these men, whom they dignified with the name of *fedayeen* or commandos, into another country with the mission to attack men, women, and children indiscriminately, was a war crime. It was essentially of the same character, though less in degree, as the offenses for which the Nazi leaders had been tried in Nürnberg, to cite the most recent examples" (*Between Arab and Israeli* [Ivan Obolensky, 1963], p. 88).

artillery, fighter and bomber aircraft, and other weapons in such numbers that, materially, Israel was far outclassed.* In 1956 as in 1967, Egypt lost the war not because it did not have the equipment but because it did not properly use what it had. Though the Tripartite Declaration had recognized that both Israel and the Arab states needed to maintain "a certain level of armed forces" to assure their self-defense, the United States and Great Britain refused to balance the Soviet arms shipments to Egypt with sales to Israel. Only France agreed to provide Israel with new arms, especially planes. A shipment of two hundred French trucks arrived two days before the outbreak in 1956 and, according to Major General Moshe Dayan, then Israeli Chief of Staff, "saved the situation." [1]

Eilat, the Gulf of Aqaba, and the Straits of Tiran, of which we heard so much in the days before the third Arab-Israeli war, were also prime factors in setting off the second. The Israelis never reconciled themselves to the Egyptian blockade of Eilat. They were prepared to deal with the illegal Suez block-ade diplomatically, but Eilat was always something else. For-mer Prime Minister David Ben Gurion made the freedom of passage from Eilat to Asia and Africa one of his main planks in the 1955 electoral campaign in Israel. Soon afterward, in September of that year, Egypt broadened the Eilat blockade to apply not only to Israeli ships but to ships of any other na-tion bound for Eilat, and even forced the Israeli commercial airplanes en route to South Africa to stop flying over the Straits of Tiran. From the fall of 1955, Ben Gurion made known publicly and privately that Israel could not tolerate the blockade of Eilat indefinitely. In November 1955, in a statement of policy of his new government, he warned: "This one-sided war will have to stop, for it cannot remain one-sided forever." As

* An authoritative source says that in 1955–1956 Egypt received about 150 MIG-15 and MIG-17 jet fighters, 40 IL-28 tactical jet bombers, several hundred tanks, and several submarines and destroyers. Major General Moshe Dayan estimates that the Soviet arms deal gave Egypt an approximately four-to-one advantage in tanks and planes (*Diary of the Sinai Campaign* [Schocken, 1967], p. 4).

we now know, the two war aims which the Israeli government set for itself in 1956 were to break the blockade of Eilat and to eliminate the *fedayeen* bases in the Gaza strip and the Sinai desert.[2]

T. E. Lawrence once said that "Arab unity is a madman's notion." If the Israelis could always count on this being true, they would have much less to worry about. Whenever the Arab countries show signs of uniting, the Israelis begin to worry because almost the only thing the Arabs can unite in favor of is against Israel. As someone has said, if Arab nationalists did not have Israel, they would have to invent it. When rivals, such as Syria and Egypt, and enemies, such as Jordan and Egypt, sign military pacts, they can mean only one thing—a two- or three-front war against Israel. An Egyptian-Syrian Mutual Defense Pact was signed on October 20, 1955, a similar Egyptian-Saudi Arabian military agreement came seven days later, and Jordan allied itself with Egypt the following October.

Finally, the outcome of the war of 1956 was as much determined by shifts in the policies of the Communist and Western powers as by anything else. The Soviet-Egyptian arms deal the year before was undoubtedly the decisive move which emboldened Egypt to take steps more reckless than ever before and to drive Israel into a state of desperation. At the same time, for reasons of their own, Britain and France decided to settle accounts with Nasser's Egypt. In July 1956, when the United States clumsily withdrew its offer to assist Egypt to construct the Aswan High Dam and Nasser struck back by nationalizing the Suez Canal Company, the Anglo-French reaction was less tolerant than the American. For the British, it was an opportunity to get back into the Canal Zone, which they had just evacuated, and to reassert themselves in their old imperial domain. The French were interested in punishing Nasser for helping the Algerian rebels as well as in getting back control of the Canal. The Israelis considered the Anglo-French resentments a windfall, enabling them to overcome Egypt's advantage in Soviet arms. Dayan says that it is doubtful whether Israel would have moved against Egypt on October 29, 1956, if it had not known that the British and French were planning an operation of their own, which they carried out two days later.[3] The Russians had their hands full because of their intervention in Hungary, which Soviet armed forces entered on November 1. The United States, having done more than its share to set all these moves going, surprised everyone by making common cause with the Soviets and by devoting itself to getting Britain, France, and Israel out of Egypt rather than getting the Soviets out of Hungary.

For the Israelis, the "primary aim" of the campaign, according to Dayan, was the capture of the Egyptian post of Sharm el-Sheikh, commanding the Straits of Tiran and, therefore, the route to the Israeli port of Eilat. This was the last and hardest battle, which the Israelis won on November 5. Dayan goes so far as to observe that the failure to take Sharm el-Sheikh would have meant, despite the other victories, loss of the entire campaign.[4] How much this position meant to them was also shown by how tenaciously they held on to it. When the British and French were forced by United States and Soviet pressure to give up their drive to Suez, the Israelis did not follow suit. Ben Gurion refused to get out of Sinai without guarantees that the blockade of Eilat and the terrorist raids from the Gaza strip would come to an end. It took four months, during which the Israelis held out alone, for these demands to be met. Neither Egypt nor the Soviet Union was able to force the Israelis out of Sharm el-Sheikh.

The power which had most to do with the Israeli evacuation was the United States. On February 11, 1957, Secretary of State John Foster Dulles presented to then Israeli Ambassador Abba Eban an *aide-mémoire* which was not wholly satisfactory from the Israeli point of view. It left the disposition of the so-called Gaza strip wholly to the United Nations and simply assumed that Egypt would not in the future interfere with Israel's "free and innocent passage" through the Straits of

Tiran if Israeli forces withdrew unconditionally from Sharm el-Sheikh. On the second point, the *aide-mémoire* declared in principle:

> With respect to the Gulf of Aqaba and access thereto—the United States believes that the Gulf comprehends international waters and that no nation has the right to prevent free and innocent passage in the Gulf and through the Straits giving access thereto.

But it went on:

> In the absence of some overriding decision to the contrary, as by the International Court of Justice, the United States, on behalf of vessels of United States registry, is prepared to exercise the right of free and innocent passage and to join with others to secure general recognition of this right.
>
> It is of course clear that the enjoyment of a right of free and innocent passage by Israel would depend upon its prior withdrawal in accordance with the United Nations Resolutions. The United States has no reason to assume that any littoral state would under these circumstances obstruct the right of free and innocent passage.

On February 20, 1957, President Dwight D. Eisenhower repeated publicly that "the Gulf [of Aqaba] constitutes international waters and that no nation has the right to prevent free and innocent passage in the Gulf." He then used somewhat stronger language than the Secretary of State had permitted himself in order to emphasize that the United States was prepared to do something to keep the Gulf open:

> We should not assume that, if Israel withdraws, Egypt will prevent Israeli shipping from using the Suez Canal or the Gulf of Aqaba. *If, unhappily, Egypt does hereafter violate the Armistice Agreement or other international obligations, then this should be dealt with firmly by the society of nations* [my italics, T.D.].

But what the United States was not willing to assume, Israel was not unwilling to assume. The United Nations had never been able to safeguard Israel's interests in the Suez Canal, and there was no reason to believe that it could do any better in the Gulf of Aqaba. Egypt was not likely to be any more kindly disposed toward Israel after the 1956–1957 defeat than it had been before, and a future renewal of the blockade could not be ruled out. As a result, Ambassador Eban and Secretary of State Dulles engaged in a lengthy, painful, and tortuous diplomatic negotiation to arrive at an understanding more satisfactory to both sides. Eban pointed out that, if the United States had the right to protect its ships through the Straits of Tiran, Israel could not be denied the same right. A meeting of minds was finally reached on February 28, 1957. It was set forth in a speech which was prepared in conjunction with United States officials for delivery at the United Nations by Israeli Foreign Minister Golda Meir. On March 1, Mrs. Meir's statement made the following points:

1. That interference, by armed force, with Israeli passage in the Gulf of Aqaba and through the Straits of Tiran would be regarded by Israel "as an attack entitling it to exercise its inherent right of self-defence under Article 51 of the United Nations Charter* and to take all such measures as are necessary to ensure the free and innocent passage of its ships in the Gulf and in the Straits."

2. That the Gaza area would be taken over *exclusively* by the United Nations Emergency Force for the purpose of providing, among other things, "efficient and effective police protection"; Israel reserved its freedom of action if conditions in

---

* The reference to Article 51 had been suggested by Secretary of State Dulles. Article 51 read: "Nothing in the present Charter shall impair the inherent right of individual or collective self-defense if an armed attack occurs against a Member of the United Nations, until the Security Council has taken the measures necessary to maintain international peace and security. Measures taken by Members in the exercise of this right of self-defense shall be immediately reported to the Security Council and shall not in any way affect the authority and responsibility of the Security Council under the present Charter to take at any time such action as it deems necessary in order to maintain or restore international peace and security."

the Gaza strip returned to "the conditions of deterioration which existed previously"; and Gaza would be administered by the United Nations "for a transitory period from the take-over until there is a peace settlement, to be sought as rapidly as possible, or a definitive agreement on the future of the Gaza strip."

It had been agreed that Ambassador Henry Cabot Lodge would support the Israeli position at the United Nations. Though the State Department knew what Mrs. Meir was going to say, the Israelis were unable, despite repeated efforts, to find out what Mr. Lodge was going to say. When he spoke on March 1, immediately after Mrs. Meir, the Israelis were unpleasantly surprised. As for the problem of the Gulf of Aqaba, he merely repeated what Secretary of State Dulles had stated on February 11. But the Israelis were most disturbed by his failure to live up to the Dulles-Eban understanding on the Gaza strip. On this point, Lodge merely noted that, juridically, the future of the Gaza strip would have to be worked out within the framework of the 1949 Egyptian-Israeli armistice agreement, as if that agreement had not already failed to prevent the war. On the same day, Secretary of State Dulles told representatives of the nine Arab states that the Israeli withdrawals from Sharm el-Sheikh and the Gaza strip involved "no promises or concessions whatsoever to Israel by the United States," and that the Israeli withdrawals were to be "full and unconditional." [5] This declaration and Lodge's speech proved so disappointing and disillusioning to the Israelis that Eban went back to Dulles to protest against what the Israelis considered to be an incomprehensible letdown.* Out of more turbulent meetings came a

---

* Arnold Beichman suggests that Lodge may have played a more or less independent role as the head of a "virtually autonomous" United States Mission to the United Nations (USUN) within the State Department. Beichman does not touch on this incident, and it is still unclear whether Lodge somehow upset Dulles's understanding with Eban, whether Dulles used Lodge to get out from under the understanding, or whether there was much understanding at all (Arnold Beichman, "The 'Other State Department,'" Interplay, August–September 1967, pp. 28–29).

diplomatic device which deviously tried to undo the damage that had been caused by Lodge's speech. On March 2, President Eisenhower sent Prime Minister Ben Gurion a letter which insiders could read one way and outsiders another. It expressed gratification that the Israelis had decided to withdraw from Egyptian territory and assured Ben Gurion that "Israel will have no cause to regret" this decision. It alluded to Mrs. Meir's speech the day before in terms that were supposed to mean more than they said: "Hopes and expectations [for a better future] were voiced by your Foreign Minister and others. I believe that it is reasonable to entertain such hopes and expectations and I want you to know that the United States, as a friend of all countries of the area and as a loyal member of the United Nations, will seek that such hopes prove not to be vain." [6]

But the United States-Israeli understanding, such as it was, did not amount to very much or hold up very long. Ben Gurion and Eban had made what they thought was some kind of "moral" or diplomatic deal with Eisenhower and Dulles, but no one had made a deal with Nasser. As soon as the Israelis withdrew their forces from the Gaza strip, Egyptian and not United Nations administrators moved in, and Nasser even appointed a Governor of Gaza on March 18. Foreign Minister Meir again hurried to Washington and conferred with Secretary Dulles that same day. She failed to get him to go beyond paying more lip service to Lodge's statement of March 1 and Eisenhower's letter of March 2.[7] The latter had assured the Israelis that, if they withdrew from the Gaza strip, they would have "no cause to regret" and the United States would make an effort to see to it that their hopes would "prove not to be vain." In a matter of days, the Israelis had good cause to regret, and their hopes had proved to be quite vain. The Israelis never succeeded in getting Dulles to put anything very clear or binding on paper, and they paid dearly for trying to read too much into his oracular diplomatic formulas.

The next move was up to Ben Gurion. The Gaza strip had

been given up to the Egyptians without a struggle, but the future of Sharm el-Sheikh was still open. Ben Gurion chose this moment to tell an American correspondent in Tel Aviv: "I don't want any of our young people to die. Nor do I want one Egyptian boy to die because of Nasser's mad schemes. But if Nasser tries to block our historic and legal passage into the Gulf of Aqaba, we will meet him not at a peace table, but elsewhere with our armies." [8]

The issue was not settled until United Nations Secretary General Dag Hammarskjöld went to Cairo at the end of March to get Nasser to agree on a new arrangement. Hammarskjöld was not willing or able to do anything about Nasser's administrative "coup" in the Gaza strip. But he decided to go ahead at Sharm el-Sheikh because, in effect, the Egyptians did not tell him not to. On this slender basis, Hammarskjöld, who believed in taking risks for peace, decided to station a small United Nations detachment at Sharm el-Sheikh. [9]

Thus, the United Nations Emergency Force (UNEF) took over at Sharm el-Sheikh, and the Straits of Tiran were thereby opened to Israeli shipping. The Egyptians, not UNEF, rushed into and administered the Gaza strip immediately after the Israeli evacuation. And ten years later, the Egyptians reoccupied Sharm el-Sheikh, without any clear understanding what the United Nations or the United States were bound to do about it. The strange fate of this 1957 "understanding" haunted the Israelis in 1967 and gave them reason to wonder what an American "assurance" might be worth in the end.

In other respects, too, the second Arab-Israeli war ended indeterminately. By staying out, Egypt's allies, Syria and Jordan, left open the question of what might have happened if they had stepped in. By getting in, Israel's adventitious allies, Britain and France, left open the question of what might have happened if they had stayed out. Nasser was able to emerge from the conflict unscathed because the Anglo-French retreat left him in full possession of the Suez Canal, and he could claim that Israel would not have defeated him alone. He seemed for a time to have both the Soviet Union and the United States on his side, at least for the purpose of bringing the war to a close before he had suffered an irretrievable defeat. In these ways the second Arab-Israeli war prepared the way for the third by giving the Arabs reason to believe, if they believed their own propaganda, that they could overwhelm Israel if they fought together and if Israel had to fight alone.

The Israelis were also deeply disturbed by the fact that they seemed to have given way to the pressure of the United States and the Soviet Union. A letter of November 5, 1956, by Soviet Premier Nikolai Bulganin to Israeli Prime Minister Ben Gurion had left a particularly disturbing scar on the Israeli consciousness. Bulganin had warned the Israeli government "to come to its senses before it is too late and to halt its military operations against Egypt" or it would "place in jeopardy the very existence of Israel as a State." The Israelis had defied this advice and especially the United States-USSR pressure to make them retire from Egyptian territory before gaining some compensating concessions. But the international complications had undoubtedly weighed heavily, if not decisively, on the Israeli government's deliberations in 1956–1957, and the Israelis had never reconciled themselves to the outcome. That experience had left Israel with a "never again" complex and a collective memory of having permitted itself to be taken in by false threats and empty promises. Ten years later the Arab leaders acted or at least talked as if Israel's relations with the Western powers were more or less the same as they had been during the "Sinai war," as the Israelis liked to call it, or the "Suez crisis," as it was known in the West. But the Israelis felt that they had burned their fingers the first time and were rather determined not to let history repeat itself. They were far more willing and able to go it alone in 1967 than they had been in 1956–1957, for one reason because they did not consider the earlier policy an unqualified success.

I have perhaps tried the patience of the reader eager to get to 1967 by going over this apparently old ground. I have done so because I think that what happened in 1956 is most pertinent, even indispensable, for an understanding of 1967. The similarity of all the problems of 1956 and 1967 was, as we shall see, striking. When American newspaper readers and others learned that President Nasser had decided to get rid of UNEF and renew the blockade of Eilat, the nature and significance of these actions may not have been too clear. But the Israelis had been all through this before and had thought that they would never have to go through it again. It had meant war in 1956, and if Nasser wanted to do it again in 1967, it could only mean that he wanted to have another war.

From 1955 to 1967, the one new, disturbing element in the Arab world was the Soviet Union. All the other elements had been present before that time and had receded as the Soviets had advanced.

Before World War II, the Soviet Union did very little to exert a direct influence in the Arab countries. Traditionally, Russia was primarily interested in Turkey and Iran, its Moslem but non-Arab

III

neighbors. In 1940, Stalin's Russia tried to establish a sphere of influence southward from Batum and Baku toward the Persian Gulf, a line of march which would have brought it next to two Arab countries, Iraq and Saudi Arabia. But this effort was made in collusion with Nazi Germany, not through the Arab countries themselves.* At the end of the war, Soviet ambitions in the Arab world were revealed by an unsuccessful attempt to obtain a mandate in Libya, which would have put Soviet forces in a most strategic position between Algeria and Tunisia on the west and Egypt and the Sudan on the east.

* On November 26, 1940, the German Ambassador in Moscow, Count Friedrich Werner von der Schulenberg, wired Berlin on Soviet conditions for a Soviet-German treaty: "In accordance with the foregoing, the draft of the protocol concerning the delimitation of the spheres of influence as outlined by the Reich Foreign Minister [Ribbentrop] would have to be amended so as to stipulate the focal point of the aspirations of the Soviet Union south of Batum and Baku in the general direction of the Persian Gulf." A year earlier, on November 23, 1939, Hitler told his Chiefs of Staff that "Russia strives to strengthen her influence on the Balkan peninsula and aims towards the Persian Gulf. But those are also aims of our own foreign policy." This Nazi-Soviet conflict of interest in the Middle East was one, but by no means the most important, of the divergences which brought about the Nazi attack on the USSR in June 1941.

Soviet military occupation of northern Iran enabled the Tudeh (Masses) Party, headed by well-known Iranian Communists, to set up Azerbaijan and Kurdish "autonomous regimes" in 1945, but they came to an end after Soviet troops were withdrawn the following year. After the war, however, the most notable aspect of Soviet policy in the Arab-Israeli area was, as we have seen, the backing of the United Nations' partition plan in Palestine in 1947–1949, one consequence of which was support for some kind of Jewish state. In 1950, Prime Minister Ben Gurion proposed to the Soviet Ambassador that his country should try to initiate peace talks between Egypt and Israel. Moscow never replied.[1] In 1950, too, Israel voted in favor of the United Nations resolution which approved resistance to the Communist threat in Korea, and undoubtedly the Soviets were not amused. On the other hand, Israel voted in 1950 for the admission of Communist China to the United Nations, much to the United States' displeasure. In later votes on the issue, Israel usually abstained.

The first grave break between Israel and the Soviet Union took place in 1953. It came soon after the Stalin regime, in its last stages of psychopathology, had accused a group of Soviet doctors, most of them Jews, of plotting to kill a number of Soviet military leaders. This "Doctors' Plot" was linked, in *Pravda* of January 13, 1953, with a "Zionist espionage organization" and thereby given international connotations. Czechoslovakia had already staged the so-called Slansky trial, with strong anti-Semitic and anti-Zionist overtones, and a Czechoslovak communication of February 5, 1953, referred to "the effrontery and arrogance of the Israel Zionist agents in Czechoslovakia" and "the American warmongers and their Israeli and other stooges." On February 9, 1953, a small bomb exploded in the garden of the Soviet legation in Tel Aviv. The Soviet government immediately charged Israel with responsibility for the deed and broke off diplomatic relations. They were renewed the following July, four months after Stalin's death and after Israel had given assurances that it would not join any aggressive alliance against the Soviet Union. But the shift in Soviet policy soon proved to be more than a Stalinist aberration.

In Stalin's last years, Soviet policy was less pro-Arab than anti-Israel. Ever since he had burned his fingers with Chiang Kai-shek in the 1920s, Stalin had not taken kindly to "bourgeois nationalists," in which category the leaders of the Egyptian revolution were first pigeonholed. The Soviets did not greet with enthusiasm the overthrow of the Farouk regime in 1952 by the military junta headed by General Mohammed Naguib and Colonel Gamal Abdel Nasser, and they were still outwardly reserved when Nasser ousted the more conservative Naguib in 1954.

But Stalin's successors were increasingly more flexible in this sphere, as in others, and their own inclinations happened to coincide with changes in Syria and Iraq as well as in Egypt. In 1954, the Syrian military dictatorship of Colonel Adib Shishakli was overthrown. The rising Syrian power was represented by the newly formed Arab Socialist Renaissance party, better known as the Ba'ath party from one word of its Arabic name (*Hizb al-Ba'ath al-'Arabi al-Ishtiraki*). No one, least of all its own leaders, has ever been able to explain very clearly what the Ba'ath meant by "socialism," but it was certainly second to none in its advocacy of Arab unity and nationalism. By 1957, the Ba'ath had gained the ascendancy over the Syrian military, and the Syrian Communists were considered the strongest single political force in the country. In 1958, the traditionalist regime of Nuri es-Said was overthrown in Iraq. The new military junta, headed by General Abdel Karim Kassim, also adopted a program based on Arab nationalism, Arab unity, and anti-Westernism. Like Egypt and Syria, Iraq turned to the Soviet Union for arms and economic aid. By the end of the decade, the Soviet investment and vested interest in these three countries had become a major factor in Middle Eastern diplomacy and strategy.

By turning the white man's burden red, the Soviets did not make it any lighter to bear. They were dealing with extremely insecure regimes and unstable societies. The propaganda of the new Egypt, the new Syria, and the new Iraq was almost identical in the rhetoric of Arab unity, but that was as far as they were united. The Ba'athists, Kassim, and Nasser wanted unity on their own terms—that is to say, an Egyptian- or a Syrian- or an Iraqi-dominated unity. They made and unmade deals with their local Communist parties, which were hard put to know whether the Nassers and the Kassims were an open door or a barrier to ultimate Communism. The merger of Egypt and Syria in 1958, out of which came the United Arab Republic, has been attributed to Nasser's fear that the Syrian Communists were getting too strong. Both Egyptian and Syrian Communists were brutally repressed after the merger, and its breakup in 1961 was no cause for them to lament.* Nasser managed to stay in power, but Kassim was overthrown in 1963, and Syria made a "right" turn in 1961 and then, with the Ba'athist coup, a "left" turn in 1963. After 1961, Nasser went to the "left" in both domestic and foreign policy—in the first through large-scale nationalization and in the second by declaring war on the Arab "reactionaries" in control of Saudi Arabia, Jordan, and other areas. To follow all the twists and turns, ups and downs of the various Arab regimes in the past ten years would be dizzying. It is enough to say, for our purposes, that the wild new Arabian horses have not been easy or inexpensive for the Soviets to ride. They have been able to stay on them largely by outbidding the West, from paying for the Aswan High Dam to providing a steady stream of cheap arms, rather than by exhibiting any particular wisdom or cunning.

It is a mistake, then, to imagine that these Arab states have simply lent themselves to Soviet purposes. The Soviets have curried favor with the Arabs mainly by giving them the arms to do what they wanted to do. Soviet arms have always talked

* Despite the breakup in 1961, Egypt continued to be known officially as the United Arab Republic. The two terms—Egypt and UAR—have come to be used interchangeably, but I have usually preferred the former as shorter and historically less confusing.

far more loudly and persuasively in this region than Communist propaganda. It was no accident, as the Soviets like to say, that their first historic breakthrough in Egypt took the form of an arms deal. A pro-Arab policy of this kind could not fail to prepare the way for a third Arab-Israeli war. It was not necessary for the Soviets to proclaim this war as their own aim; it was merely necessary for them to arm those Arab states which were proclaiming it as *their* war aim.

On April 17, 1963, Egypt, Syria, and Iraq signed an agreement in principle to federate as a single state, with its capital in Cairo. The agreement, among other things, pledged the projected United Arab Republic to a crusade for "liberating the Arab Nation from the peril of Zionism." It was the first time, Prime Minister Ben Gurion noted in a parliamentary address in May, that the destruction of Israel had been set forth in a constitutional document providing for the unification of the three Arab states. The agreement proved not to be worth the paper it was written on because the Ba'athists in Syria and Iraq refused to accept Nasserite domination in the name of unity. Nevertheless, in one way or another, Arab unity efforts and anti-Israel war aims continued to feed each other.

In January 1964, Nasser convened the first Arab "summit conference" to deal with Syria's demand for action against Israel. The Syrians wanted to divert the headwaters of the Jordan to prevent Israel from carrying out its share of the Jordan river project, worked out by Eric Johnston on the initiative of the Eisenhower administration. The Syrians knew that Israel considered such a diversionary measure as much a *casus belli* as a blockade of Eilat, but they demanded united Arab backing even at the risk of immediate war with Israel. At the "summit conference," Nasser took the position that the Arab states were not prepared to fight Israel immediately and had to prepare for the day by setting up a United Arab Command and a fighting organization of Palestine Arab refugees. A unified Arab command was nominally set up, commanded by an Egyptian, General Abdel Hakim Amer, and the Palestine

Liberation Organization (PLO), headed by Ahmed Shukairy, the former Saudi Arabian representative to the United Nations, was authorized at the second Arab summit conference in September of that year. The PLO was based in the Gaza strip and depended largely on Egyptian backing. In 1965, another organization of even more extremist tendencies, El Fatah (Conquest), started to operate out of Syria. It began to drag Jordan, which was not eager to provoke Israel on behalf of Syria and Egypt, into the melee by striking most often across the much longer, less easily defended Israel-Jordan frontier. One of its spokesmen has boasted that it was responsible for "almost daily operations" and that it deliberately provoked Israeli reprisals in order to "materialize the enemy before the [Arab] masses." [2]

Thus, the old cycle of raids and reprisals started again. This problem has always been most difficult for the Israelis to deal with. The Israelis could not ignore the terrorist tactics; yet they did not wish to emulate the Arabs and engage in transparently camouflaged terrorism of their own; instead, their reprisal policy was aimed at getting across the message that the Egyptian and Syrian governments were making undeclared and unofficial war on Israel through the PLO and El Fatah. Yet the Arab governments could refuse to accept responsibility for the terrorism, which their controlled press and radio acclaimed and encouraged, whereas Israel was unable, for reasons of policy, to disavow its reprisals. This disparity opened Israel to repeated censure in the United Nations, which took the position that Israel should rely on the United Nations' Truce Supervision observers and Mixed Armistice Commissions for protection against the terrorists. In August 1963, the Israelis decided to give the United Nations a chance to make good. When two Israeli farmers were ambushed and killed near the Syrian border, Israel went to the Security Council for redress or at least condemnation of the deed. On the basis of reports from the United Nations' Truce Supervision Organization's Chief of Staff, Britain and the United States introduced a resolution

condemning the ambush and implying that Syria had been remiss in permitting it to occur. On September 3, the resolution
obtained eight votes, one short of passage. The Soviet Union
cast the decisive veto. After another armed Syrian-Israeli incident in November 1964, Britain and the United States introduced a resolution in the Security Council calling for restraint
and cooperation by both sides. On December 21, it again obtained eight votes but once more ran into a Soviet veto—on
the ground that even this evenhanded appeal was unfair to Syria.

By 1965, then, the outlines of a third Arab-Israeli war were
clearly taking shape. If it did not break out that year, the primary cause was Arab disagreement as to how and when it
should be waged. Syria, under militant Ba'athist leadership,
was the most impatient. But the Syrians knew they were too
small and weak to take on Israel alone, and their strategy,
therefore, consisted in goading Egypt to attack Israel. Jordan
was most reluctant to get drawn into an open conflict, for one
reason because the Egyptians and Syrians had been vowing for
years to get rid of King Hussein's regime as well as Israel. The
middle ground seemed occupied by Nasser's Egypt. At a Palestine National Conference in Cairo in May 1965, the Syrians
complained bitterly that Egypt had not come to their aid when
Israel had blown up some El Fatah bases. Nasser took the following line against his Arab critics:

> They say "Drive out UNEF." Suppose that we do, is it not
> essential that we have a plan? If Israeli aggression takes place
> against Syria, shall I attack Israel? Then Israel is the one which
> determines the battle for me. It hits a tractor or two to force
> me to move. Is this a wise way? We have to determine the
> battle.[3]

This was the ambidextrous, double-edged Nasserite policy of
"neither peace nor war" that divided or confused both Arabs
and Israelis. In principle he seemed to agree with the Arab extremists, with whom his differences, on the surface, were
limited to timing and tactics. Nevertheless, timing and tactics

were most important to them, and on these he drew back from an immediate confrontation. Meanwhile, his relations with Israel appeared to be relatively tranquil, while the Syrian-Israeli border was exploding with violence. One school of Israeli thought argued that Nasser was merely biding his time; he was as dangerous and untrustworthy as any other Arab extremist. Another Israeli school considered that his actions were more important than his words; it believed that it might be possible eventually to come to terms with him.

While the Soviets were encouraging the Arab extremists, they also tried to reassure the Israelis. In 1964 and 1965, Soviet diplomats sought out Israeli diplomats in order to get across the following message: The Soviets and Arabs did not really have much in common. But the Arabs, as the Soviets had discovered a decade earlier, were determined to eliminate Western interests and influence in the Middle East. On this basis the Soviets and Arabs could make common cause. But the Israelis did not have to worry and should not get excited. The Soviets intended to be a moderating influence in the Arab-Israeli conflict; Nasser was merely the best means for getting the West out of the entire region.

In 1966, however, events in Syria made the balancing acts of both Nasser and his Soviet backers more difficult. On February 23, the inevitable army coup ousted the more moderate wing of the Ba'athist party and put little-known Ba'athist extremists in power. The new government, headed by President Nureddin el-Attassi and Prime Minister Yusif Zuayin, issued a statement calling on all Arab revolutionary organizations "to face Zionism and imperialism and to liberate usurped parts of Palestine." By "usurped," Syrian nationalists meant that Palestine actually belonged to Syria, not to any other Arab nation in particular or to an Arab state in general.* The new cabinet,

* This view was openly expressed in the United Nations by the Syrian Ambassador, Dr. George J. Tomeh, on October 17, 1966, as a reason why Syria could not commit any aggression against Israel: "We as Syrians consider Palestine to be, and to have been, historically, geo-

for the first time in Syrian history, included a Communist, Samih Ateyyeh, as Minister of Communications.[4] In a speech to a Ba'ath party congress on March 10, Dr. el-Attassi designated "the liberation of Palestine" as the keystone of the revolution. He indicated that the new Syrian regime was not satisfied with waiting for the right time to attack Israel:

> We believe that postponement of the liberation battle will increase the enemy's chances of survival. Through its call for the liberation war, the revolution believes that the chances of [Arab] unity will increase. Unity will be forged in the flames of the liberation war, which will be a decisive factor in providing the psychological, political and military atmosphere.

The new Syrian regime also introduced a Chinese Communist inflection in its war propaganda. On May 23, Dr. el-Attassi scoffed at waging a conventional war against Israel and urged what he called a "people's war of liberation," Chinese-Communist style. In a speech to army units on Syria's southwestern frontier with Israel, he declared:

> We want a full-scale, popular war of liberation, not only to destroy the Zionist base in Palestine but also to destroy oil monopolies and imperialist and reactionary interests. We want a policy of scorched earth, and it is only through this policy that we can hope to build a new life for the Arab masses.

In addition to Israel, he attacked the "reactionary" Arab states, Jordan, Saudi Arabia, and Kuwait. He told the soldiers:

> You have grown tired of piling up arms. I realize how eager you are that we should start the battle. The time has come to use these arms for the purpose for which they were created.[5]

It seemed to take a few weeks for the Soviets to evaluate

---

graphically, and from every point of view, a part of Syria. It was only colonial rule and imperialist intrigues that divided Syria into so many States. When we speak of Palestine we feel we are speaking about part of our own country" (United Nations, Security Council, Provisional Verbatim Record, October 17, 1966, p. 61). This claim, of course, put Syria as much in conflict with Jordan as with Israel.

the significance of the February 1966 coup in Syria. By May of that year, the decision had obviously gone in favor of a new, more intransigently pro-Arab and anti-Israeli policy. On May 7, after a long silence, *Izvestia* hit out against Israel, which it accused of causing "armed provocations" against Syria with the aim of overthrowing the new regime. A writer in *Izvestia* brought the United States into the plot by conveniently tying up "the expansion of the anti-Syrian campaign" with a visit to Israel by Raymond A. Hare, Assistant Secretary of State for Near Eastern and South Asian Affairs. On May 15, Premier Kosygin arrived in Cairo for a meeting with President Nasser. The latter took the occasion to threaten, if necessary, to wage an armed struggle against "reactionary-imperialist alliances," and Kosygin promptly responded with a Soviet pledge of support for Egypt's "struggle against imperialism." And on May 27, the Soviet press agency, Tass, publicly issued a statement, which was formally delivered to the Israeli government, accusing Israel of "provocations" against Syria and stressing for the first time how close Syria was to the Soviet Union: "The Soviet Union cannot and will not remain indifferent to the attempts to violate peace in a region located in direct proximity to the borders of the Soviet Union." [6]

This threat was sufficiently ominous to persuade Israeli Foreign Minister Eban that it was necessary for the United States to make a countermove. The Soviets, he believed, were trying to demonstrate that they could dominate the area and that the United States was incapable of making a stand in favor of Israel such as the Soviets had made in behalf of Syria. Israeli diplomats thereupon attempted to get the United States to make some fitting reply to the Soviet challenge. They were advised that the United States wished to avoid a "polarization" of power in the Middle East and that it was best to let well enough alone. The Israelis thought that such passivity would further encourage Arab extremists to think that they could count on the Soviet Union but that Israel could not count on the United States.

The year 1966 was, indeed, the worst since 1956 for Arab

terrorist raids and Israeli military reprisals. The United Nations Security Council spent a major part of its time that year on Syria-Israel and Jordan-Israel border incidents. One wrangle was especially revealing. Radio Damascus broadcast "Communiqué No. 53 of the General Staff of the El Assefa [military branch of El Fatah]," which read: "A force from Group 105 penetrated on October 8 into occupied Jerusalem and bombed two buildings. Two demolition charges exploded at 2345 hours and two others at 2400 hours." When Foreign Minister Eban, who was in New York at the time, complained on October 9 to Secretary General U Thant, Syrian Prime Minister Zuayin decided to hold a press conference in Damascus. On October 10, he served notice that Syria would never take measures to curb the new *fedayeen*. "We are not," he said, "sentinels over Israel's security and are not the leash that restrains the revolution of the displaced and persecuted Arab Palestinian people." And he promised that Syria would "never retreat from the popular liberation war to recover Palestine." * Israel thereupon decided to take the cases to the Security Council.

The situation was almost an exact replica of the one seven months later on the eve of the third Arab-Israeli war. The most remarkable similarities were provided by the Soviet Union. On October 12, Israel received a Soviet note which charged: "According to information in our possession, concentration of Israeli troops can again be discerned along the Syrian frontier,

---

* This version appeared in *Mideast Mirror,* October 15, 1966, p. 3. Eban cited a somewhat different and fuller version of Zuayin's remarks: "We are not guardians of Israel's safety. We are not resigned to holding back the revolution of the Palestine people. Under no circumstances shall we do so. We shall set the entire area afire, and any Israeli movement will result in a final grave for Israel." Eban also cited a public statement on these incidents by the Syrian Chief of Staff, General Sweidani, on October 11: "These activities which are now being carried out are legal activities, and it is not our duty to stop them but to encourage and strengthen them. We are constantly ready to act inside Jordan and inside Israel in order to defend our people and its honor. We will mobilize volunteers and we will give them arms" (United Nations, Security Council, Provisional Verbatim Record, October 14, 1966, p. 13).

and preparations are being made for an air attack on the areas bordering the Syrian frontier, so that in its wake Israeli troops may penetrate deep into Syria." Two days later, the Soviet representative, Nikolai T. Fedorenko, made a speech at the United Nations in which he went into even greater detail:

> Since the time when the Syrian people started to consolidate its independence and ensure its social progress, military tension has begun to build up on the borders of Syria, and we know that, of late, Israel has been concentrating large military forces on the Syrian border. In areas adjacent to Syria, military maneuvers are being staged. A large number of landing troops, equipped with artillery and mine-sweepers, have been thrown in. There has been a partial mobilization of reserves in Israel. In addition, there is information showing that an air attack is being prepared in Israel against neighboring Syrian territory in preparation for the intrusion of Israel forces deep in Syrian territory.[7]

The scare was so great that Secretary General U Thant asked Lieutenant General Odd Bull, Chief of Staff of the United Nations Truce Supervision Organization, to investigate. His report failed to bear out any of Fedorenko's charges of Israeli plans and preparations to invade Syria. A mildly worded resolution was submitted by Argentina, Japan, Netherlands, New Zealand, Uganda, and Nigeria which, among other things, called on Syria to take stronger measures to prevent further border incidents. It received ten votes in the Council. But it was killed by a Soviet veto, the first in two years and the first ever cast by the Soviets against a resolution proposed by African countries.

All through 1966, both the Soviet Union and Egypt drew closer to the Arab extremists, represented most uncompromisingly by the new Syrian regime. In April, Prime Minister Zuayin and a large Syrian delegation made a pilgrimage to Moscow and came back reporting a Soviet contribution of about $150 million to finance a Euphrates River dam and power station.* On July 8, Egypt and Syria signed a trade pact, the

* This project demonstrates how "unpolitical" and "without strings"

first agreement of this sort between them since the 1961 break. Late in July, an Iraqi delegation went to Moscow and returned boasting of a pledge of Soviet arms. And on November 4, Egypt and Syria signed a mutual defense agreement providing for a joint military command.

Soviet aid programs can be. The Soviets first promised to help Syria build this dam in 1957, but the Syrian-Egyptian merger the following year dulled the Soviets' enthusiasm and led to a withdrawal of the offer to finance the dam on the ground that it was not technically feasible. In 1959, West Germany took over the project, but it withdrew after the breakup of the Syrian-Egyptian merger in 1961. The West Germans signed another agreement in January 1963, but it was called off after the Ba'athists seized power two months later. The Left-Ba'athist coup of February 1966 brought back the Soviets, who suddenly discovered that the project was technically feasible after all.

As late as November 24, 1966, almost three weeks after he had signed the Egypt-Syria military pact, President Gamal Abdel Nasser still said publicly that "the way back to Palestine is hard and long." [1] Only six months later, he seemed to think that it had become much easier and shorter.

Why? The answer holds the key to the third Arab-Israeli war.

IV

The trouble, as usual, started on the Syria-Israel frontier. Here is a record of the violence that flared up in the first eleven days of January 1967, as recorded in an Arab factual source:

January 1: An Israeli spokesman in Tel Aviv said that three Israeli tractors near Haon village on the southeastern shore of the Sea of Galilee came under fire from a Syrian post. The fire was returned.

January 2: A military spokesman in Damascus claimed that Syrian armed forces had destroyed three Israeli outposts to the north of the Sea of Galilee.

January 4: An Israeli spokesman said that two armed Syrians had fired several shots at Israeli farmers southeast of Ein Gev on the eastern shore of Galilee. Nobody was hurt in this exchange.

January 6: A Syrian army spokesman said that Syrian arms fire had destroyed an Israeli tractor north of the Sea of Galilee. At least one Israeli was killed or wounded, as he was seen being removed from the tractor.

A later statement issued by the same spokesman said that Syrian armed forces had destroyed two Israeli outposts in a

clash between both sides. The clash began, he said, when
Israeli outposts shelled Arab farmers.

January 8: Syria claimed that its forces had demolished a number of Israeli military targets including an ammunition dump,
after Israeli troops had opened fire on its hillside positions.
A spokesman in Tel Aviv alleged that Syria had started the
firing, which continued for over three hours.

January 9: Firing broke out all along the frontier and lasted
for about two hours. Syria admitted losing one machine gun
and claimed to have destroyed one Israeli tank. The Israeli
countercharge said two Syrian tanks were destroyed and another hit after Syrian positions had opened fire on a tractor.

January 10: An Israeli spokesman said that tanks and heavy
mortars were used in a Syrian attack. He listed seven separate incidents of firing into Israel from the Syrian side of the
border.

January 11: According to the Syrian spokesman, heavy tanks,
weapons, tanks, and aircraft were used. The spokesman said:
"Enemy gun batteries and tanks were silenced for good, an
anti-tank gun was destroyed and a fuel dump burned out."
Israeli aircraft appeared but were forced back to base by
Syrian jets, the spokesman said.[2]

There is, of course, no point in trying to assess the blame for
these incidents. What is clear from both Syrian and Israeli versions is that a small-scale border war broke out early in 1967.
There could be no doubt, by this time, that these attacks and
counterattacks were deliberate, organized, and increasingly
costly. On January 14, an explosion took place in a pump-
house, damaging a wall in Dishon, a village in northern Israel.
A few hours later, an antipersonnel mine went off at a football
game in Dishon. A player set it off; one spectator was killed and
two were wounded. Israeli army sources reported that both the
explosives and the mine were East European in origin, of the
type used by the Syrian army.[3]

January was another month of futile Israeli-Syrian exchanges
at the United Nations. To the Israeli demand that Syria should

take steps to prevent these incursions, the Syrian head of state, Dr. Nureddin el-Attassi, replied with the utmost candor. On February 8, he declared publicly that "we shall not act as protectors of Israel against Palestine commandos defending their homeland." On February 22, he said: "It is the duty of all of us now, to move from defensive positions to offensive positions and enter the battle to liberate the usurped land. There is absolutely no scope for hesitation from now on and everyone must face the test and enter the battle to the end." On March 8, he made a speech which was reported by an Arab news source as follows: "Dr. Attassi called on Palestine Arabs to follow the example of the Algerians in their fight against the French and model their methods on the North Vietnamese fighting the Americans. Palestine will not be returned to its people except by 'an all-out war of liberation,' he said. He praised the bravery of Palestine Arab commandos inside occupied Palestine (Israel). 'Commando action in the occupied land will not cease,' he said. The Syrian army, he said, 'is ready to fight the decisive battle with Israel.' " [4]

For the Syrian government, then, the war against Israel had already started. It was being waged in the manner that Syria considered most advantageous. The old *fedayeen* tactics had been renamed the "people's war of liberation" and had been given new dimensions as well as new significance. The new *fedayeen* were trained and equipped by the Syrian army, which was itself being trained and equipped by the Soviet Union. Though these actions started as "commando" raids, the main Syrian military forces were inevitably drawn into the fighting by Israeli retaliatory measures. Battles with tanks, antitank guns, and planes early in January could hardly be dismissed any longer as minor border "incidents." The official Syrian radio broadcast the El Fatah communiqués as war bulletins.

Nevertheless, the Syrians were still far out. From their point of view, Egypt and especially Jordan were holding back. Nasser had always taken the position that the United Arab Command could not act unless the forces of one Arab country could pass through and fight in the territory of another. This was precisely what King Hussein of Jordan feared the most because the Egyptians and Syrians had been vowing for years to overthrow his "reactionary" regime. In January 1967, renewed pressure was brought on Hussein to permit other Arab military forces to move into Jordan. When he refused, Nasser assailed him mercilessly on February 22 as an American puppet, and Hussein retaliated by withdrawing his ambassador from Cairo. When the Arab Joint Defense Council met in Cairo on March 11, Jordan as well as Tunisia and Saudi Arabia refused to attend. As long as Hussein was actually more afraid of Egypt and of Syria than of Israel, the united Arab front which Nasser demanded as a precondition for an all-out war against Israel could not be realized. As late as March 1966, Nasser had taken the position that an attack on Israel from the south was not militarily possible; the Arab attack had to come from Syria and Jordan.*

To fight fire with fire, Hussein's government began to twit Nasser about the United Nations Emergency Force (UNEF), which the Arab militants had always regarded as an Egyptian alibi to refrain from attacking Israel. Prime Minister Wasfi Tell of Jordan even accused Nasser of having in 1957 entered into a "gentlemen's agreement" with Ben Gurion to set up a buffer between Israel and Egypt. An American correspondent reported:

> The whole question of UNEF has been brought up by Jordan in Arab defense councils, where Jordan has been under heavy pressure to admit foreign troops to defend the country against Israeli attacks.

* In an interview in the publication al-Hawadis (Beirut, Lebanon) of March 26, 1966, Nasser said: "We could annihilate Israel in twelve days were the Arabs to form a united front. Any attack on Israel from the south is not possible from a military point of view. Israel can be attacked only from the territory of Jordan and Syria. But conditions in Jordan and Syria have to be in order so that we in Egypt can be sure we will not be stabbed in the back as in 1948" (quoted in Near East Report, April 5, 1966, p. 26).

Jordan responded by insisting that other Arab states also go on a war footing for the battle with Israel, and specifically asked Egypt to get rid of UNEF so that the Egyptian army—the biggest in the Arab world—can take part in the battle.

The Egyptian response has been that the UN force was symbolic (it numbers about 3000 men) and would have no effect whatsoever if it tried to stop Egyptian army movements.[5]

Hussein and his advisers undoubtedly considered this riposte a clever way of embarrassing the Egyptians. In the circumstances of early 1967, however, it rather played into the hands of the Syrians, his most intransigent Arab enemies, who were telling Nasser exactly the same thing, though from undoubtedly different motives. Thus, from the Arab "left" and "right," pressure was building up for Nasser to "go on a war footing for the battle with Israel."

If internal Arab pressure was one factor in Nasser's decision, the other was external pressure on his policy.

Ever since 1955, Egypt had become increasingly dependent on Soviet military and economic largesse. The Soviet bloc in Eastern Europe had provided Nasser with at least $1.5 billion in economic aid, and probably more than that in military assistance. In 1965, according to Nasser himself, the Soviets had saved Egypt from "inevitable famine" by diverting 300,000 tons of wheat to Alexandria. By the beginning of 1967, Nasser was desperately in need of food again. He could not get it from the United States, which for a year had been holding up an Egyptian request for $150 million of surplus food in disapproval of Nasser's intervention in the Yemeni war, the magnitude of his military preparations, and a series of insulting anti-American speeches. In January 1967, the Soviets again agreed to tide him over with 250,000 tons of wheat in the next three months. On February 22, Nasser made another inflammatory oratorical attack on the United States in which he threatened not to pay Egypt's debts, which amounted to over $1 billion, of which short-term debts to Western banks accounted for about $250 million. In February, too, Egypt failed for the third successive month to make any payment to the International Monetary Fund, to which it owed some $105 million lent in the previous four years.

At this very time, the Soviets saw fit to contribute a major war scare to the sufficiently tense situation on the Syria-Israel frontier. The Soviet press, of course, wholly blamed Israel for the incidents. But it went further and, as in the previous October, discovered a virtual Israeli mobilization to invade Syria. A report in *Izvestia,* the Soviet government organ, of February 3, 1967, on Israel's "war psychosis," ran: "The country's armed forces are being alerted. All leave has been cancelled and more reservists have been called up. Large armed forces have been concentrated on the northern border. The incidents on the Syrian-Israel frontier, which began on the eve of the New Year, continue unabated." Thus for the second time in less than four months, the Soviets were responsible for spreading an unverified rumor, no doubt in the guise of intelligence reports, that could only serve to incite the Syrians and neighboring Arabs to stage a countermobilization and prepare for imminent war.

In these circumstances, the Soviet factor could not have failed to weigh heavily in Nasser's calculations. On March 29, Soviet Foreign Minister Gromyko suddenly arrived in Cairo for a three-day visit. Very little is known about it except that it was arranged hurriedly. Whatever it signified, it came on the eve of the final crisis before the third Arab-Israeli war.

On April 7, the biggest Arab-Israeli battle since 1956 was fought over Syria. It precipitated all the events which led to the larger war almost exactly two months later.

The escalation of the fighting that day was typical; only the magnitude of the forces and the losses suffered were not. According to both Israeli and Syrian versions, Syrian guns emplaced in the hills overlooking the Israeli frontier settlements opened fire on

an Israeli tractor plowing in the "demilitarized zone" that morning.[1] Soon tanks and mortars went into action. By the end of the day, Israel reported shooting down six MIG-21s of the Syrian air force with no losses of its own; Syria claimed that five Israeli Mirage jets and four Syrian MIGs had been shot down. Unfortunately for the Syrians, three of their planes crashed in Jordan, as a result of which these losses could be confirmed. The Jordanians were so unkind that they issued a report that the Syrian planes had been armed with dummy wooden rockets. The Damascus radio struck back: "The days of the treasonable regime in Jordan are numbered." [2]

For the Syrians, the April 7 battle was no setback. It was a welcome occasion for heating up the "popular liberation war" against Israel. On April 8, the Syrian Minister of Information, Mahmoud al-Zu'bi, declared that the clash "will be followed by more severe battles until Palestine is liberated and the Zionist presence ended." The fighting, he said, "is not the first battle nor will it be the last." He told reporters that there could be no permanent calm in the Arab areas adjacent to Israel "as long as there is Zionist occupation of Palestine." The battle, he boasted, proved Syria's superiority in land fighting, if not in the air, "since Israeli military outposts were destroyed and serious damage caused to four settlements." [3] On April 17, the Syrian head of state, Dr. el-Attassi, celebrated the same battle as having been "very useful to us." Syria, he said, "cannot but support Arab commandos" and "is prepared to wage the battle with all its resources, whatever the cost or sacrifices." He inveighed against Jordan, Lebanon, Saudi Arabia, Tunisia, and Morocco because they were not revolutionary enough.[4]

For Nasser, April 7 was a dividing line. It forced him to face as never before the problem of implementing the Egypt-Syria mutual defense pact of the previous November. Syria, after all, claimed to have been attacked by Israel, and whether its losses were four or six planes (the latter figure was generally accepted), they were evidence of the seriousness of the struggle. This meant that Nasser was obliged to come to the defense of Syria, wherever that might lead. The Jordanians, enjoying his dilemma, could not resist needling him. The leading Jordanian newspaper of April 8 demanded: "What has Cairo done in face of this flagrant air aggression on Damascus?" [5] On April 10, Cairo sent its air commander, General Mohammed Sidky Mahmoud, to Damascus to confer for twelve days. On April 17, Egypt's Prime Minister, Mohammed Sidky Soliman, came to Damascus for five days, the highest-ranking Egyptian official to visit Syria since the 1961 break. A communiqué on April 22 pledged both sides "to carry out joint plans under the joint defense agreement between them," and to consider the "battle for the liberation of Palestine" the main cause around which the Arab masses should rally.[6] On May 2, President Nasser felt it necessary to explain why Egyptian planes had not come to the rescue of the Syrians as a result of the April 7 clash. He attributed the failure to act to the limited range of Egypt's fighter planes, a restriction which he said had been pointed out to the Syrians, who had assured him that they had enough fighters of their own.[7]

As for the Soviets, the one-sided defeat of their MIGs by French Mirages, which was generally credited, gave them a direct stake in the outcome of the April 7 battle. Every move that Syria and Egypt might subsequently make had to be paid for largely by the Soviets, and without Soviet matériel, the two Arab states could not contemplate making war. The Soviets had invested so heavily in Syria and Egypt, as well as in Iraq, that they could not stay out of this runaway crisis even if they had wanted to do so. And far from wanting to stay out, they clearly tried to get more and more deeply embroiled in it.

On April 21, the Soviet government sent the Israeli government another "warning" note, filled with dark but unspecified threats of retribution:

> On various occasions, the Soviet Government has expressed its attitude to developments in the Middle East and has delivered a suitable warning. The Soviet Government sees no necessity to repeat it now.
>
> The world has again expected aggression by Israel, which has shown a tendency to embark upon ventures constituting a grave danger to peace. This particular instance can only create the impression that the military action of April 7th constitutes a part of these reprisals taken against the Syrian people by Imperialist forces who were disappointed by the brave struggle against the oil monopolies. As regards the Israeli attack of April 7th, the Soviet Government sees the necessity to repeat its warning to Israel that her risk-laden policies implemented for the past few years against her neighbours are pregnant with dangers, and she must bear full responsibility for them.
>
> The Soviet Government expects the Israeli Government to weigh the existing situation carefully and hopes that she will avoid being used by those circles whose political impatience makes them willing to turn their country into a puppet of foreign enemy forces, thus endangering the essential interests of their state.

The next round of "commando" violence showed how far the Arab and Soviet leaders intended to go. On May 5, Israeli territory was shelled from Lebanon, and on May 8, a military vehicle was blown up five miles inside Israeli territory. These exploits by El Fatah demonstrated such technical proficiency that the Israeli government decided to issue a stern warning.

This appraisal was fully backed up by the United Nations truce observers, whose reports led Secretary General Thant to declare on May 11:

> I must say, that in the last few days, the El Fatah type of incidents have increased, unfortunately. Those incidents have occurred in the vicinity of the Lebanese and Syrian lines and are very deplorable, especially because, by their very nature, they seem to indicate that the individuals who committed them have had more specialized training than has usually been evidenced in El Fatah incidents in the past. That type of activity is insidious, is contrary to the letter and spirit of the Armistice Agreements and menaces the peace of the area. All governments concerned have an obligation under the General Armistice Agreements, as well as under the Charter of the United Nations and in the interest of peace, to take every measure within their means to put an end to such activities.[8]

Apparently the full import of the crisis that gathered in May caught the Israeli government by surprise. In an interview in *U. S. News & World Report* of April 17, Prime Minister Levi Eshkol had been asked whether he expected a full-scale war with Egypt, Syria, or Jordan. He incautiously replied that "I don't think there will be full-scale war in the next few years—although we are, of course, preparing for such a possibility, and I say that openly to the world." * But on May 12, Eshkol spoke

* There are other indications that the Israeli government did not anticipate the seriousness of the crisis. At a luncheon of the Foreign Press Association in Jerusalem on January 24, 1967, Foreign Minister Eban said that Jordan, Lebanon, and Egypt "do not wish to become directly involved in hostility with us" (*Weekly News Bulletin,* Government Press Office, January 24-30, 1967, p. 6). In an annual review in the Israeli parliament on February 14, 1967, Eban said that "Arab feuding and internal complications preoccupy the Arab leaders at this moment more than does planning of the fight against Israel" (Ibid., February 14-20, 1967, p. 2). These statements may very well have been true at the time; if so, they would indicate that the May 1967 crisis developed at a pace which in a sense caught everyone by surprise. But

with less confidence in the future. Of attempts to commit sabotage on Israeli soil, he said: "There will be no immunity for any State which aids and abets such acts." He noted that Syria seemed to have taken on itself to assume the leadership in the Arab struggle against Israel. But, he added, Syria's forces were not great, and "not without reason is she looking for protection among larger countries." Although this need not cause any alarm, he cautioned, "we shall go on manning our posts, ready for any possible deployment." [9] The following day, he again spoke on the same theme without appearing to think that a showdown was imminent:

> The firm and persistent stand we have taken on behalf of our rights has strengthened the awareness among our neighbors that they will not be able to prevail against us in open combat. They recoil today from any frontal clash with Israel, and they postpone the date of such a confrontation to the remote future. Among the Arab rulers and their saboteur-minions, there are some who nowadays attempt to manifest their hostility to Israel in deeds, diligently in search of ways of attrition, subversion, and aggression against human lives. We have furnished proof that we shall not permit our borders to be opened to attack. We have proved that to their attempts to pick easy and exposed targets, we were able to respond at a place, time, and by a method of our own choosing. Thus, the saboteurs and their employers found out that they would not accomplish their aims this way. We do not recognize the limitations they endeavor to impose upon our acts of response. The Arab States and the nations of the world ought to know that any border which is tranquil from their side will also be quiet from our side. If they try to sow unrest on our border—unrest will come to theirs.[10]

I have cited the relevant portions of these two statements by Eshkol at some length because they—and particularly the first one of May 12—were later used by Nasser to justify his decision to move troops to the Israeli border and to renew the

---

they hardly suggest that Israel was putting into effect a long-prepared plan.

blockade of Eilat on the Gulf of Aqaba. In a long and most revealing press conference in Cairo on May 28, Nasser said:

> In its threats in the past few years, Israel has gone beyond every limit. The most recent thing was the Israeli Prime Minister's threat to attack Syria and his war threats. Israel has been continuously threatening war. On May 12, this threat reached an extent that no one would accept. It was the duty of every Arab to respond to this threat. Therefore, I said that if Israel wanted to threaten war—which it actually did—then Israel is welcome.[11]

Soviet Premier Kosygin also referred in his United Nations speech of June 19 to Prime Minister Eshkol's alleged threats:

> The Premier of Israel made it clear that the armed attack on Syria in April was not the last step, and that Israel was itself going to choose the method and time for new actions of this kind.

The reader may judge for himself whether Eshkol was guilty of threatening to attack Syria or of threatening war in Nasser's or Kosygin's sense. Ironically, the Israeli Prime Minister had opened himself to some criticism for refusing to believe that a full-scale war was so imminent. If we recall the kind of threats against Israel made for months and even years by the highest Arab leaders, this purported Israeli threat against Syria hardly seems to be sufficient cause for setting off a third Arab-Israel war. In any event, one of the alleged motivations for the Egyptian actions was the Eshkol statement of May 12. In any event, to make sure that the Egyptians did not misinterpret Israeli policy, the Israeli representative at the United Nations, Gideon Rafael, was instructed on May 15 to use Secretary General U Thant as the intermediary to assure the Egyptian government that Israel had no intention of initiating any military action, and Mr. Thant passed on this message to the Egyptians.

The other motivation directly implicated the Soviet Union. An Egyptian parliamentary delegation went to Moscow for the May Day celebration and stayed until May 14. In his speech of resignation on June 9, later withdrawn, Nasser claimed that Egypt and Syria had been persuaded that Israel planned to invade Syria. But, as if he felt these Arab sources might not be sufficiently convincing, he added:

> Even our friends in the Soviet Union told the parliamentary delegation which was visiting Moscow early last month that there was a calculated intention [to invade Syria].*

In a later speech on July 23, Nasser went into somewhat more detail:

> The information we had about the invasion of Syria came from different sources. We had information from our Syrian brothers to the effect that Israel had mobilized eighteen brigades. We investigated this information and confirmed that Israel was mobilizing no less than thirteen brigades on Syrian borders. Our parliamentary delegation which was headed by Anwar el-Sadat and which was visiting Moscow at the time was informed by our Soviet friends that the invasion of Syria was about to take place.

An official Soviet version was given by Premier Aleksei N. Kosygin to the United Nations on June 19:

> In those days, the Soviet Government, and I believe others too, began receiving information to the effect that the Israeli Government had timed for the end of May a swift strike at Syria in order to crush it and then carry the fighting over into the territory of the United Arab Republic [Egypt].

These statements raise a fascinating question about the Soviets' role in stirring up this conflict. In October 1966, as we have seen, Soviet Ambassador Fedorenko had rehearsed this very bit of intelligence. Fedorenko had solemnly assured the

---

* This is from the Reuters translation in *The New York Times,* June 10, 1967. There is a slightly different version of the same passage in a monitored radio broadcast: "Add to this fact [of Syrian and Egyptian information] that our friends in the Soviet Union warned the parliamentary delegation which was on a visit to Moscow at the beginning of last month that there was a premeditated plan against Syria."

United Nations that Israel had been "concentrating large military forces on the Syrian border," that it had been staging military maneuvers in areas adjacent to Syria, that it had partially mobilized reserves, and that it was preparing "for the intrusion of Israeli forces deep into Syrian territory." The same charges had appeared in the Soviet press in February 1967. In an area as small as the Syrian-Israeli border, such activities could not have been concealed from the United Nations truce observers, who reported no such things taking place. Now, three months later, the Soviets were assuring their Egyptian friends of another Israeli plan to invade Syria.

But Israel was not the main Soviet concern. The Soviet press was chiefly interested in giving the alleged Israeli designs an American inspiration. On May 16, *Pravda* linked an unsuccessful coup in Syria with the rising Arab-Israeli tension: "Certain American imperialist circles would have been highly pleased if the abortive May uprising in Damascus and Aleppo had ended differently. After its failure, the same people are interested in aggravating tension on the Syrian border in order to create new difficulties for the country." On May 18, *Izvestia* discovered that an "impression" had been created of "a secret agreement between the American, British and Israeli authorities." On May 20, *Izvestia* suggested that the Middle East crisis was a "means for Washington to divert attention from the new criminal escalation of aggression in Vietnam." And on May 22, *Pravda* published a front-page analysis by a major Soviet commentator, Viktor Mayevsky, who presented the full Soviet line in these terms: "The U.S.A. is unceremoniously pushing Israel towards an armed invasion of Syrian territory. At the same time, plans are made for introducing into Syria the troops of certain neighboring countries that are under the control of the imperialists." Mayevsky advised: "One should not, of course, look at the events in the Middle East in isolation. They are closely connected with the new crimes by U.S. aggressors in Vietnam—the encroachment into the demilitarized zone and the stepping up of the barbarous bombing of Hanoi, and with

the preparation of new provocations against Cuba." Thus
Soviet policy as reflected in the Soviet press was devoted, before Nasser announced the closure of the Gulf of Aqaba to
Israel on May 22, to pushing the United States into the fore-
front of the Middle East crisis by making Washington responsible for Israel's actions.

Ironically, the Chinese Communists soon gave the Soviets
the same treatment that the Soviets gave to the United States.
The Chinese Communist press charged that "Israel's armed
aggression against the Arab people was in essence a frantic attack jointly plotted by the United States and the Soviet Union."
The nature of this plot seemed perfectly clear in Peking: "The
Soviet revisionist clique on the one hand 'guaranteed' that Israel would not attack and on the other, working hand in glove
with the United States, instigated Israel to launch a surprise
attack on the Arab countries and catch them unawares." [12] Another Chinese Communist writer accused the Soviets of giving
aid to Arab and other Asian, African, and Latin American
countries merely "to strike dirty deals with the United
States." [13] Indeed, the Chinese Communist press was so bent
on blaming the United States and the Soviet Union that it had
almost no indignation left for Israel.*

Inasmuch as Nasser subsequently attributed so much importance to the Soviets' military intelligence in this period, it
would be interesting to learn what the Soviets had to go by,
except their own political line, to have charged that the United
States was really instigating the Israeli invasion of Syria and
even the introduction of troops of "certain neighboring countries," obviously Arabic, into Syria. Apart from other considerations, the whole Soviet scenario for the coming crisis was
based on a fundamental misconception; Israel always considered Syria and Jordan to be secondary in military importance,

* Still another variation on this theme was played by the East German
Communists. A statement by the East German Council of Ministers
charged: "This aggression on the part of Israel was long prepared together with the U.S.A. and the West German Federal Republic" (*Neues
Deutschland,* June 8, 1967).

and its strategic planning had long assumed that Egypt had to come first in any military showdown; it was hardly likely, therefore, that Israel should have intended to take on the Arab world by starting out with an invasion of Syria. Moreover, the Israeli command did not need to concentrate large forces on the Syrian frontier in order to strike a quick blow against Syria. The Israeli forces in the Haifa area were near enough to cover the distance in a matter of hours—or minutes in the case of the Air Force—without giving their plans away by massing near the frontier.

This peculiar Soviet effort to inflame the Arabs had a peculiar background. According to Prime Minister Eshkol, Soviet Ambassador Dmitri Chuvakhin had accused Israel before the incident of April 7 of mobilizing its reserves and of concentrating thirteen to fifteen brigades on the Syrian border. Eshkol has related that he jumped up and exclaimed: "How do you know that?" Chuvakhin is said to have replied: "You may not know it but you are the agents of a nation which wants to overthrow the Syrian regime"—meaning, of course, the United States.[14] After the battle of April 7, Soviet Deputy Foreign Minister Yakob Malik had called in the Israeli ambassador in Moscow, Katriel Katz, to accuse Israel of "aggression" and to threaten reprisals. On May 12, the Director General of the Israeli Foreign Ministry, Arye Levavi, had invited Ambassador Chuvakhin, who had again accused Israel of concentrating forces on the Syrian border, to visit the area to see for himself. Chuvakhin had refused the offer with the curt reply that his government's information was good enough for him. Again, on May 19, Eban tried to convince Chuvakhin. "I can state to you," Eban said, "that there are no concentrations on the Syrian frontier, and the Egyptians should know this." On another occasion (May 29), Eban informed the United Nations that "the Soviet ambassador complained to my Prime Minister of heavy troop concentrations in the north of Israel. But when invited to join the Prime Minister that very moment in a visit to any part of Israel which he liked, the distinguished envoy brusquely refused."

But the damage had already been done. Nasser has said that he received information on May 13 that "Israel was concentrating on the Syrian border huge armed forces of about eleven to thirteen armed brigades," south and north of Lake Tiberias.[15] For this reason, he claimed, the first Egyptian troops were sent to the Sinai border with Israel on the night of May 14. Inasmuch as an Israeli armored brigade numbered 3500 men and an Israeli infantry brigade 4500 men, eleven to thirteen brigades would have amounted to 45,000–55,000 men—a relatively large force to hide in a relatively small area.

There is also reason to believe that a serious domestic threat to the existing Syrian regime may have had something to do with the sudden Syrian alarm over the alleged external danger from Israel. On May 6, a general strike had broken out in Damascus in protest against the arrest of a religious leader who had made a speech denouncing an antireligious article in the Syrian army organ. The strike spread the following day to most other Syrian cities, especially to Aleppo, where several thousand arrests were reported. The Syrian authorities announced that they had uncovered a plot "prepared by the intelligence services of the United States, Saudi Arabia, Israel and Jordan"—a curious conglomeration.[16] On May 8, according to a correspondent in Cairo of the Paris newspaper *Le Monde*, two Syrian emissaries arrived in the Egyptian capital in a state of excitement bordering on panic. They brought word, allegedly attributed to Lebanese intelligence, that Israel had concentrated important forces on the Syrian frontier. The Egyptians, the report went on, sent their own investigators, who, two days later, came back with the same story.[17]

That Syria had been plunged into a grave domestic crisis in the first two weeks of May 1967, there can be no doubt; the rest of the story requires confirmation. It would not be the first time that a weak, unpopular regime decided to resort to a

foreign-war scare to bolster its shaking power. The Syrian protest strike showed that almost the entire middle class of shopkeepers and artisans had gone over to active opposition. The
strike was also an expression of the seething discontent among
the orthodox Sunni Moslem majority against the main leaders
of the regime, who belonged to the minority Alaouite sect. Such
a regime was peculiarly vulnerable to Soviet blandishments and
to the temptation to substitute foreign support and adventures
for domestic popularity and security. Five days later, Secretary
General Thant reported:

> There have been in the past few days persistent reports about
> troop movements and concentrations, particularly on the Israel
> side of the Syrian border. These have caused anxiety and at
> times excitement. The Government of Israel very recently has
> assured me that there are no unusual Israel troop concentra-
> tions or movements along the Syrian line, that there will be
> none and that no military action will be initiated by the armed
> forces of Israel unless action is first taken by the other side.
> *Reports from UNTSO Observers have confirmed the absence
> of troop concentrations and significant troop movements on both
> sides of the line* [my italics, T.D.].[18]

Israeli mobilizations, troop concentrations, and troop movements happen to be notoriously hard to conceal. A glance at
the Syria-Israel border shows how short it is, barely fifty miles
altogether. That United Nations truce observers should not have
been able to see what the Soviets were telling the Egyptians
and no doubt the Syrians about Israeli troops poised to invade
Syria is one of the more curious mysteries of the prewar
build-up.

W e have now come to the final or what may be called the Sharm el-Sheikh phase of the build-up.

As Secretary General Thant later told the story, the Commander of UNEF, Major General Indar Jit Rikhye, received a message from the Chief of Staff of the Egyptian Armed Forces, General Muhammed Fawzi, at 10 p.m. (Gaza time) on May 16. It requested the immediate withdrawal of all United Nations troops

VI

from two places, El Sabha, a strategic point in Sinai at the northern end of the Egypt-Israel border, and Sharm el-Sheikh, the camp overlooking the entrance into the Gulf of Aqaba. General Rikhye replied that he did not have the authority to order the withdrawal and was told that there might be clashes between Egyptian and United Nations troops that very night. While Secretary General Thant requested a clarification of the Egyptian request, Egyptian forces began on May 18 to take matters into their own hands. The observation posts at El Sabha and other points were occupied by Egyptian troops, and two Egyptian artillery shells burst between two United Nations posts, one of them El Sabha. At noon (New York time) on May 18, the Secretary General received the official Egyptian request to withdraw all United Nations forces "as soon as possible" from Egyptian territory and the Gaza strip. Mr. Thant expressed the intention of appealing to President Nasser for a reconsideration but was told not to do so or he would be sternly rebuffed. Two governments, undoubtedly India and Yugoslavia, which provided about half the troops for UNEF, took the position that they would comply with Egypt's request and withdraw their troops whatever the United Nations decided to do. On the night

of May 18, Secretary General Thant ordered the total withdrawal of UNEF as requested by Egypt.[1] While U Thant was on
his way to Egypt on May 22, Nasser, without waiting to see
him, officially announced the closure of the Straits of Tiran to
Israel and the consequent blockade of the port of Eilat.

Most of the controversy raised by these actions has concentrated on two questions. Was the Secretary General essentially
right or sufficiently adroit in withdrawing UNEF so quickly?
Was Egypt legally justified in closing the Straits of Tiran to
Israel and blockading Eilat? For the time being, only the second
concerns us.

If nothing else were at stake but the blockade of Eilat, it
would still have been a serious blow to Israel, for Eilat in 1967
was not what it had been in 1956. Israel had put a decade of
stupendous effort into building up the port, its only outlet to
the south. A pipeline had been built to carry the oil of Iran
from Eilat to Haifa. A large proportion of the mineral exports
from the Dead Sea and the growing copper production of
Timna went out from Eilat. The ambitious development plans
for the Negev largely depended on using the port of Eilat. Israel
might well have fought for Eilat, but the point is that, after May
18, Eilat was merely a symptom that Israel had to fight for
itself.

On May 18, Syria's Foreign Minister, Dr. Ibrahim Makhous,
gave the following interpretation of UNEF's withdrawal to the
Syrian news agency: "The withdrawal of the UN forces in this
manner, which means 'make way, our forces are on their way
to the battle,' proves that there is nothing that can stand in the
way of the Arab revolution and that reaction's attempt to raise
doubts regarding the presence of these forces had boomer-
anged." [2]

On May 20, Syria's Defense Minister, General Hafiz al-
Assad, told a Syrian newspaper that the Syrian air force had
violated Israeli territory "dozens of times" in the past year.
"The army, which has long been preparing itself for the battle
and has its finger on the trigger, demands in one voice that the

battle be expedited," he said. "At present we are awaiting the signal from the political leadership. As a military man I feel that the time has come to wage the liberation battle. In my opinion it is necessary to adopt at least the minimum measures required to deal a disciplinary blow to Israel, which should restore its senses and bring it to its knees, humiliated and terrified to live in an atmosphere of awe and fear which will prevent it from contemplating another aggression." [3]

On May 22, President Nasser delivered a radio address announcing the closing of the Gulf of Aqaba. In it he revealed for the first time what he had had in mind. First, he seemed preoccupied with explaining away the Egyptian defeat in 1956. He blamed it on the Anglo-French invasion which, he claimed, had prevented Egypt from fighting Israel. Then he boasted of his new Soviet planes: "At that time we had a few Ilyushin bombers. We had just acquired them to arm ourselves. Today we have many Ilyushins and others. There is a great difference between yesterday and today, between 1956 and 1967." And so the time had come to demonstrate what Egypt, if it did not have to worry about Britain and France, could do to Israel. "Today we have a chance to prove the fact. We have, indeed, a chance to make the world see matters in their true perspective. We are now face to face with Israel." Referring to Israeli Prime Minister Eshkol's statement of May 12, he took up the alleged challenge: "The Jews threatened war. We tell them: You are welcome, we are ready for war." [4] On that same day, Israeli Prime Minister Eshkol called for mutual withdrawal of Egyptian and Israeli troops from the border.

The Egyptians have generally defended the closure of the Straits of Tiran to Israel on the ground that it is only about nine miles wide and, therefore, clearly within Egyptian territorial waters. If this were all to the issue, the Egyptians would have an airtight case. In international law, however, the problem is far more complicated. An authoritative treatise on international law has stated the conditions of "free and innocent passage" in the following terms: "Gulfs and bays surrounded by the land of one and the same littoral State whose entrance is so wide that it cannot be commanded by coast batteries, and further, *as a rule, all gulfs and bays enclosed by the land of more than one littoral State, however narrow their entrance may be, are non-territorial"* (my italics, T.D.).[5] Far more important than the width of the Straits of Tiran, therefore, was the number of states that bordered on the Gulf of Aqaba. The number of such states was indisputably four: Egypt, Saudi Arabia, Jordan, and Israel. In fact, Egypt once recognized that it had no right to close the Straits of Tiran. When the first Egyptian guns were installed at the entrance of the Straits at the end of 1949, the United States embassy in Cairo asked the Egyptian government about the possible significance of the move. The Egyptian reply of January 28, 1950, gave assurances that Egypt "in no way conceived in a spirit of obstructing in any way innocent passage" through the Straits and promised that the passage would "remain free, as in the past in conformity with international practice and recognized principles of the law of nations." Nevertheless, Egyptian authorities soon confiscated cargoes en route to the Israeli port of Eilat.

Significantly, the Soviet Union never took a position on the Egyptian right to close the Straits of Tiran to Israel. The reason for this unusual diffidence was probably the potential effect of the Egyptian claim on the Soviets' own maritime interests. The entrance to the Black Sea through the Dardanelles and the Bosporus is at least as much in Turkish territorial waters as the Straits of Tiran is in Egyptian territorial waters. For this, if for no other reason, the Soviets preferred to base themselves on alleged Israeli plans to invade Syria rather than on the merits of the Egyptian case dealing with the Straits of Tiran, which was, after all, the immediate *casus belli* of the third Arab-Israeli war.

U Thant reached Cairo on May 23 and stayed two days. As he has reported his conversations with the Egyptian President and Foreign Minister, the most important point made to him was a statement of their "general aim" in closing the Straits of Tiran to Israel. It had been done, they said, "for a return to the conditions prevailing prior to 1956." [6] As we shall see, this was not the only aim or purpose given by Nasser to explain why he had decided to take over Sharm el-Sheikh; it may be considered the minimum aim which could be stated to someone like the Secretary General.*

The first official Soviet and American reactions came on May 23. The Soviet statement did not refer to Sharm el-Sheikh and the renewed blockade of Eilat at all. It merely reiterated the charge that Israeli statesmen had threatened to attack Syria, and, therefore, the Arab states had acted to repel the expected "aggression." It broadened the scope and implications of the crisis by contending that Israel's actions had been directly and indirectly encouraged by "certain imperialist circles which seek to bring back colonial oppression to Arab lands." In effect, it avoided all the concrete issues by giving general backing to the Arabs and making a general indictment of Israel.† President

---

* In his speech on July 23, 1967, Nasser referred to a curious incident that took place during Thant's visit: "He [U Thant] asked us for a respite for the Gulf of Aqaba and we agreed. He said he wanted some time to give everybody a breathing space. The first point was that no Israeli ships were to go through the Gulf and at the same time we were not to carry out inspection." It should be added that U Thant had suggested something of the sort for a period of two weeks to gain time for the Security Council to deliberate and act. His actual suggestion was that the Israelis should agree not to send any of their flagships through the Straits of Tiran into the Gulf of Aqaba, and that the Secretary General would ask all other maritime powers not to send oil or strategic materials, which he left undefined, to Eilat, in return for which Egypt would not search any ships going through the Straits. Nasser agreed; Eban refused. On his return to New York, U Thant recognized that the idea was untenable because it would have given United Nations sanction to a form of the Egyptian blockade, and it was dropped.

† Text in Appendix 19. Yet the Soviet statement may have gone too far and may give the Soviets future trouble even if the apparent commitment was general. It also said: "But let no one have any doubts about the fact that should anyone try to unleash aggression in the Near East, he would be met not only with the united strength of Arab coun-

Johnson's statement of May 23 made two main points. The United States, he said, was "dismayed at the hurried withdrawal" of UNEF, an implied criticism of the Secretary General's decision. The other recommitted the United States, at least formally, to the 1957 understanding opening the Straits of Tiran to Israel:

> The United States considers the gulf [of Aqaba] to be an international waterway and feels that a blockade of Israeli shipping is illegal and potentially disastrous to the cause of peace. The right of free, innocent passage of the international waterway is a vital interest of the international community.[7]

However, all this was not really pertinent to what Nasser thought he was doing. On May 26, he made a speech to the Central Council of the International Confederation of Arab Trade Unions. In it he said many things that would not have been fitting in conversations with the United Nations Secretary General. Most of this speech was devoted to explaining why he had waited so long to seek a showdown with Israel. Nasser explained:

> We awaited the proper day when we would be fully prepared and confident that we would adopt strong measures if we were to enter the battle with Israel. I say nothing aimlessly. One day two years ago, I stood up to say that we have no plan to liberate Palestine and that revolutionary action is our only course to liberate Palestine. I spoke at the Arab summit conferences. The summit conferences were meant to prepare the Arab states to defend themselves. Recently we have felt strong enough that if we were to enter a battle with Israel, with God's help we could triumph. On this basis, we decided to take actual steps.

---

tries, but also with strong opposition to aggression from the Soviet Union and all peaceloving states." And it concluded: "With due account taken of the situation, the Soviet Union is doing and will continue to do everything in its power to prevent a violation of peace and security in the Near East and safeguard the legitimate rights of the peoples." But none of this was spelled out concretely.

Then he went on to explain why he had waited so long to get rid of UNEF:

A great deal has been said in the past about the UN Emergency Force. Many people blamed us for UNEF's presence. We were not strong enough. Should we have listened to them or built and trained our army instead while UNEF still existed? I said once that we could tell UNEF to leave within half an hour. Once we were fully prepared we could ask UNEF to leave. And this is what has actually happened.

After this came the explanation for Sharm el-Sheikh:

The same thing happened with regard to Sharm el-Sheikh. We were also attacked on this score by some Arabs. Taking over Sharm el-Sheikh meant confrontation with Israel. *Taking such action also meant that we were ready to enter war with Israel. It was not a separate operation.* Therefore, we had to take this fact into consideration when moving to Sharm el-Sheikh. The present operation was mounted on this basis [my italics, T.D.].

And if it came to war, what was the final aim? Nasser answered:

The battle will be a general one and our basic objective will be to destroy Israel. I probably could not have said such things five or even three years ago. If I had said such things and had been unable to carry them out my words would have been empty and valueless. Today, some eleven years after 1956, I say such things because I am confident. I know what we have here in Egypt and what Syria has. I also know that other states —Iraq, for instance—has sent its troops to Syria; Algeria will send troops; Kuwait will also send troops. They will send armored infantry units. This is Arab power.[8]

On May 26, too, Nasser's journalistic spokesman, Muhammad Hassanein Heikal, published in his newspaper, *al-Ahram,* an article entitled "An Armed Clash With Israel Is Inevitable. Why?" which best expressed the Egyptian mind and mood after the closing of the Gulf of Aqaba. Heikal's "first observation" was:

> I believe that an armed clash between the UAR and the Israeli enemy is inevitable. This armed clash could occur at any moment, at any place along the line of confrontation between the Egyptian forces and the enemy Israeli forces—on land, air or sea along the area extending from the northern part of Gaza to the southern part of the Gulf of Aqaba at Sharm el-Sheikh.

His "second observation" dealt with the Egyptian strategy of the "second blow":

> As of now, we must expect the enemy to deal us the first blow in the battle. But as we wait for the first blow, we should try to minimize its effect as much as possible. The second blow will then follow. But we will deal this blow to the enemy in retaliation and deterrence. It will be the most effective blow we can possibly deal.

This point was so important that Heikal elaborated on it:

> The next move is for Israel to make. Israel has to reply now. It has to deal a blow. We have to be ready for it, as I said, to minimize its effect as much as possible. Then it will be our turn to deal the second blow, which we will deliver with the utmost possible effectiveness.
>
> In short, Egypt so far has exercised its power and achieved the objectives of this stage without resorting to arms. But Israel has no alternative but to use arms if it wants to exercise force. This means that the logic of the fearful confrontation now taking place between Egypt, which is fortified by the might of the masses of the Arab nation, and Israel, which is fortified by the illusion of American might, dictates that Egypt, after all it has now succeeded in achieving, should wait, even though it has to wait for a blow. This is necessitated also by the soundness of the course of battle, particularly from the international point of view. Let Israel begin! Let our second blow then be ready! Let it be a knockout! [9]

At a press conference in Cairo on May 28, Nasser reiterated for a non-Arab audience what the problem was not:

The problem all of us are experiencing now and are concerned about—all of us, statesmen, journalists, and the multitudes of peoples—is neither the problem of the Tiran Straits
nor the withdrawal of the UN Emergency Force (UNEF). All
those are side issues of a bigger and more serious problem—
the problem of the aggression which has taken place and continues to take place on the Arab homeland of Palestine and the
continuous threat posed by that aggression against all Arab
countries. This is the original problem.

For the nature of this threat, Nasser again referred to Prime
Minister Eshkol's statement of May 12:

Israel has been continuously threatening war. On May 12
this threat reached an extent that no one would accept. It was
the duty of every Arab to respond to this threat. Therefore I
said that if Israel wanted to threaten war—which it actually did
—then Israel is welcome.

Once more Nasser explained that his actions the week before
had "restored the situation to what it was in 1956." They were,
he made clear, a challenge to Israel to capitulate or fight:

We have taken these measures to restore things to what they
were before. Now we are waiting to see what Israel will do next.
Should Israel provoke us or any other Arab country, such as
Syria, we are all prepared to face it. If Israel chooses war, then,
as I have said, it is welcome to it. . . .

Toward the end of the conference, Nasser gave a peculiar
definition of Israeli "aggression":

As I have said, Israel's existence in itself is an aggression.[10]

Finally, on May 29, the same question of what the crisis was
all about came up in a speech which Nasser made to members
of the National Assembly who visited him:

The issue now at hand is not the Gulf of Aqaba, the Straits
of Tiran or the withdrawal of UNEF, but the rights of the Palestinian people. It is the aggression which took place in Palestine
in 1948 with the collaboration of Britain and the United States.

He went on:

> The issue today is far more serious than they say. They want
> to confine the issue to the Straits of Tiran, UNEF, and the right
> of passage. We say: We demand the full rights of the Palestin-
> ian people. We say this out of our belief that Arab rights cannot
> be squandered, because the Arabs throughout the world are de-
> manding these Arab rights.[11]

In effect, Nasser had set up a situation in which, from his
point of view, he could not lose. If the Israelis decided to
capitulate to the new blockade of the Gulf of Aqaba, it would
set them back to the pre-1956 situation. They would be put in
the position of acknowledging that they had fought the second
Arab-Israeli war of 1956 in vain. They would surrender a
decade of effort and treasure poured into the port of Eilat and
the economic interests dependent on it. They would be forced
to admit such military inferiority to the Arab states that they
could only look forward to a future of waiting helplessly for
the Arabs to make further demands. Nasser's minimum aim,
therefore, amounted to winning the prize of a war without firing
a shot.

But Nasser did not really expect the Israelis to capitulate.
He recognized, as he stated openly on May 26, that his move at
Sharm el-Sheikh was "not a separate operation" but was more
likely to bring about "a general war with Israel." Throughout
May, the Egyptian and Syrian leaders gave every indication of
deliberately trying to provoke Israel into a general war. As
Nasser put it on May 28, "Now we are waiting to see what
Israel will do next," and "if Israel chooses war, then, as I have
said, it is welcome to it." And if Israel chose war, he was
confident that the Arabs would accomplish their maximum aim
—to set Israel back to the pre-1948 situation, that is, before
there was a state of Israel.

Thus far we have been considering statements made by
Nasser before June 5. In his important speech of July 23, he
retrospectively went over the same ground again, and the defeat

had obviously made it impossible for him to be as indiscreet and boastful as he had been on the eve of expected victory. Nevertheless, in the end, his story was essentially the same.

After claiming that he had received information from Syrian, Egyptian, and Soviet sources of an imminent Israeli attack on Syria, Nasser gave a curiously contradictory account of his reaction. He explained that the question arose "whether we should be the first to deal a blow in the armed battle." He blamed pressure from the United States and the Soviet Union, and what he called "a diplomatic trick, a political deception" on the part of the United States, for giving him the impression that "the explosion would not occur soon." This portion of Nasser's speech implied that Egypt might have struck the first blow if there had not been United States-USSR pressure and that the outbreak of the war on June 5 had come as something of a surprise to him.

But then Nasser went on in a rather different vein. When he first concentrated the Egyptian armed forces against Israel on May 14–16, he said, he had estimated the likelihood of war at twenty per cent. On May 22, he had held a meeting at his home of the Higher Executive Committee of the Arab Socialist Union, the political arm of his regime, at which the closure of the Gulf of Aqaba had been discussed. At this meeting, before the official notice of closure, he had estimated the possibility of war at fifty per cent. At another meeting of the Higher Executive Committee, for which he did not give the date, he had raised the likelihood of war to eighty per cent. Nevertheless, he insisted, the Egyptian policy had still been "defensive" and contemplated "attack only if aggression was launched against Syria" on the ground that an Egyptian attack would have risked bringing the United States into the war.

Therefore, Nasser concluded, Egypt had deliberately decided to let Israel strike the first blow. By the beginning of June, as a result of "political changes in Israel," by which he meant the inclusion of General Moshe Dayan in the Israeli government as Minister of Defense on June 1, the probability of war for Nasser became one hundred per cent. On the following day, June 2, Nasser related, he had told a meeting attended by all the senior officers of the armed forces that they "must expect the enemy to strike a blow within 48 to 72 hours, and no later." He also claimed that he had told the same meeting to expect this attack on Monday, June 5, with the first blow struck at the Egyptian air force.

From all this, Nasser proceeded to disavow the idea, previously planted by him, that he had been tricked and deceived by diplomatic maneuvers. Instead, he now insisted that "we did not underestimate the situation" and "it was quite clear by any political calculation that Israel was bound to take military action, especially after Iraqi forces moved and Jordan joined the joint defense agreements." In the end, then, his speech of July 23 again admitted that Arab moves had driven Israel into the war and that, at least after June 1, the Arabs had been fully aware of the fatality of the collision. If Nasser can be trusted, they merely miscalculated the effect, not the event. "After what has happened," Nasser declared, "we must faithfully and honorably admit that the military battle did not go as we had expected and hoped." [12]

In view of the outcome of the war, it may be hard for some to imagine that Nasser deliberately set up a situation in which he considered the Israelis practically forced to attack. It may be difficult to believe that he could have so fantastically miscalculated the balance of power on both sides.* But if politicians and generals did not make mistakes, there would never be any losers in wars. The evidence is overwhelming that Israel acted exactly as Nasser expected it to act. The only question is why he expected it.

* He was not the only one. *The Economist* (London) of June 3, 1967, opined that Nasser's "gamble looks like coming off," thought that it was difficult "to see what action Israel can take on its own that would be conclusive enough to reverse the Arabs' chief gains," considered that "the Israelis are not any longer arguing from a position of obvious strength," set forth "the blunt fact" that "the Israelis have been out-manoeuvred," and advised them to make "concessions."

Part of the answer lies in what the Arabs, especially the Egyptians, thought they had learned from the wars of 1948 and 1956. In the first, a number of Arab states had started out fighting together, but the Egyptians had borne the brunt of the final phase and considered themselves betrayed by the others. The lesson seemed to be that Egypt had to reform itself and depend on its own resources. In the second, Egypt had fought alone, despite pacts with Syria and Saudi Arabia which it had never put into effect. The lesson seemed to be that Arab unity was necessary to defeat Israel. Beyond this, the Egyptians also convinced themselves that they could have handled Israel alone if they had not been forced to use their best forces against Britain and France. Thus Arab unity plus an isolated Israel came to be the foolproof formula for victory in the third war.

Of the several prewar studies made of Arab-Israeli military capabilities, one is especially noteworthy because it comes from an Arab source. Some of the author's conclusions undoubtedly help us to get an insight into the thinking that led to Egypt's prewar policy. After examining the advantages and disadvantages offered by Israel's geographical position, the author observes: "Above all, the advantages accruing from Israel's compactness apply only when she is fighting on a single front at any one time—which she managed to do even in 1948 when engaging four Arab armies. The geographic fact that the Arabs surround Israel on three sides would be turned into a crushing military advantage once Arab military operations against Israel are conducted according to a single, coordinated plan." Then the study makes a very significant connection between Israel's manpower problem and the length of the war. The 250,000 men and women whom Israel could probably mobilize, it notes, would immobilize the entire economy, for which approximately half that number is needed, if the war went on for even a few days. His verdict is that "any war with Israel that lasts for over a week and which calls for more than 100,000 Israelis being mobilized would, by that fact and apart from the military outcome, do very extensive if not permanent damage to the economic life of Israel." In the air, this writer thought that Egypt had all the advantage. He was especially impressed by the heavy TU-16 bombers and medium IL-28 bombers which the Soviets had given Egypt. "Israel suffers from lack of territory which means that an Egyptian bomber based in Sinai would be over Israel within minutes of taking-off," he pointed out. "The opposite case does not apply to Egypt and Israeli bombers since these planes would have to cross the whole of Sinai and/or the Delta area before being within striking distance of Egypt's industrial centers." After making a survey of each of six Arab states which might possibly be involved in such a war, Egypt, Iraq, Syria, Jordan, Lebanon, and Saudi Arabia, the study came to this final conclusion: "The only chance that the Arabs have of beating Israel in the field is through a properly unified and coordinated military action in which narrow nationalistic interests must give way to a sincere feeling of unity." [13]

The emphasis in this analysis was, then, on Arab unity, Israeli isolation, and the inability of Israel to fight a "long" war (more than a week!). If the first two conditions could be achieved, the outlook for the Arabs seemed most promising. For the Israelis, the same factors operated; Arab unification and their own isolation meant the approach of war, and to save themselves they had to fight at all costs the shortest possible war (less than a week!).

According to a well-informed French correspondent, not unsympathetic to the Egyptian cause, pressure from Egyptian officers was at least partially responsible for the change that took place in Nasser's attitude in May 1967. This pressure, it is said, soon became "very strong" and helped to change Nasser's mind about the advisability of waiting many more months or even years before "unleashing a war against Israel." [14]

The first fatal step was taken on May 14. On that day, the Israelis detected the movement of Egyptian military reinforcements into the Sinai desert. The news was brought to Prime

Minister Eshkol by Israeli Chief of Staff Major General Yitzhak Rabin during the military parade in Jerusalem celebrating Israel's Independence Day. As Eshkol told the story, he invited Rabin to come to his home after the military parade to give him a full report. But Eshkol had heard about Egyptian troop movements before, involving as much as a brigade or even a division, and this one did not yet seem to be too different from the others. The Israeli reaction was not alarmist.[15]

On this same day, by chance, a leading Israeli newspaper, *Ma'ariv,* published an interview with General Rabin. The interview reflected the Israeli military viewpoint just before the arrival of the news about the latest Egyptian troop movement. Rabin was asked about the recent intensification of Arab "terrorist activities." He replied that he did not think it could be regarded as "extreme or qualitative." He thought that these activities were still more or less similar to those in the past, though he warned that an increase could lead to a "qualitative significance," which, he explained, "could compel us to adopt a different approach from the methods we would adopt if the activities were more restricted and confined."

Rabin went on to discuss Egypt's intentions in some detail. Despite Egypt's past opposition to terrorist operations, he advised against "making misleading assumptions regarding Egypt's long-term plans." He did not attribute too much importance to the visit to Syria by the Egyptian Prime Minister after the Syria-Israel air battle of April 7. He pointed to an article by Muhammad Hassanein Heikal, known to be an intimate friend of President Nasser and his authoritative journalistic mouthpiece, who had written that full-scale action was incumbent on Egypt only if the confrontation between Syria and Israel should take on a broad character, implying that the incident of April 7 did not fall into this category. Rabin also cited Nasser's speech of May 2 as indicating that some bitterness in the relations of Syria and Egypt still remained from their rupture in 1961.

Another interesting feature of the interview, in view of subsequent events, was a reference to the United Nations Emergency Force in the Gaza strip. General Rabin was asked how important UNEF was "as a factor contributing to the stability of the region." He did not value it too highly: "The Emergency Force can carry out its function as long as Egypt is not interested in worsening the situation along its border with Israel. I do not believe that the UN is capable of fulfilling this function with its own forces alone." [16]

This interview suggested that the Israeli military leaders were not prepared to jump to the conclusion that a serious crisis loomed on May 14. Their initial reaction was based on the assumptions that Nasser recognized that it was still too dangerous for the Egyptian armed forces to take on Israel and that he had given other objectives a higher priority. Both Prime Minister Eshkol and General Rabin later admitted that the change in Nasser's policy after May 14 came to them as a surprise. "It was then assumed," General Rabin related, "and we had every reason to believe, that no war was imminent; that the Arabs would not, in the near future, wish to play with destiny and get involved in a war which could only cause them a disaster." [17]

The Israeli command, therefore, at first watched the Egyptian military build-up in Sinai after May 14 without alarm. As General Rabin later explained, it sized up Egyptian intentions at that stage as primarily "deterrent," that is, "to deter Israel from attacking Syria—and thus gain political profit." The first Egyptian reinforcements were not considered strong enough to launch a large-scale assault against Israel. Nasser's move reminded them of a similar maneuver in February 1960. After Israel had carried out a retaliatory raid on the Syrian village of Tawafik, in reprisal for attacks on the Israeli settlements of Haon and Tel Katzir, Egypt had feared that Israeli forces might go farther and had moved part of its army into Sinai to discourage them. After a month, Nasser had withdrawn the reinforcements, and the incident had blown over.[18] The Israeli command viewed the Egyptian troop movements from May 14 to May 21, 1967, as possibly modeled on the 1960 precedent, and if they had stopped there, no blood would have been spilled.

On May 15 the Cairo radio officially announced the Egyptian troop movement into the Sinai area. On the same day, according to Prime Minister Eshkol, "the great powers" assured the Israeli authorities that the Egyptian "show" was "not serious." Only on May 16 was a joint meeting of the Israeli ministerial committee on matters of security and the parliamentary commission on foreign affairs and security called together. The first mobilization of Israeli reserves was also ordered on May 16. But even after the Egyptian troop movement was known to have passed the 30,000 mark, according to Prime Minister Eshkol, the Israeli mobilization continued "without great panic." [19]

The first Israeli military turning point came on May 19. It took the form of an expansion of the military mobilization, brought about by a realization that the Egyptian threat in the Sinai was greater than had been expected. The chief factor in the new Israeli evaluation was apparently news of the transfer of Egyptian forces from Yemen to the Sinai area. The Israeli leaders held two meetings on May 19 and were particularly concerned about a report that Egyptian planes had penetrated Israeli air space from Jordan. They ordered a tightening of antiaircraft defense and for the first time came to regard the situation as "very serious." [20] By May 22, Prime Minister Eshkol estimated, the Egyptian forces in Sinai had increased from less than two divisions before May 14 to close to four divisions—including a substantial increase of armored units, artillery, and aircraft—or from a total of 35,000 men to 80,000. These were, he said, "grave developments." [21]

What the Egyptians had in mind in this period was later revealed by Muhammad Hassanein Heikal in a series of postmortem articles that appeared in October 1967. Heikal admitted that the enlarged Egyptian forces had taken up "offensive positions" in the Sinai. He justified this disposition on the ground that the Egyptians wanted to force the Israelis to shift their alleged troop concentrations from the Syrian to the Egyptian front. Once they had achieved this objective, he argued, the Egyptian forces should have fallen back to "defensive positions." Unfortunately, however, they did not do so. He suggested the reason by observing: "Some of us were dazzled by the spectacle of the force we moved into Sinai between May 15 and May 20." [22]

If we may trust both Israeli and Egyptian sources, then, the build-up on both sides before May 22 was neither premeditated nor foreseen. The Egyptians charged that the Israelis had decided to attack Syria. The Israelis charged that the Egyptians had decided to attack them. Neither charge may have been originally justified in fact. But it may well be that the Egyptians were led by their own charges to take military actions which then impressed them so much that they went beyond their original intentions or calculations. These actions set in motion Israeli countermoves that set the stage for an explosion. The charges may have been unfounded, but they produced actions that seemed to give them substance. The third Arab-Israeli war may well have resulted from an experiment in controlled escalation that went out of control. It appears to have been brinkmanship that went over the brink.

The Israeli command began to press for action only after Nasser announced the closure of the Gulf of Aqaba to Israel on May 22. Egyptian prisoners later informed the Israelis that a group of officers had been told on May 20 by Field Marshal Abdel Hakim Amer, the Deputy Commander of the Egyptian Armed Forces, that the entrance to the Gulf of Aqaba would not be closed.[23] If so, the decision to close it was made somewhat hastily on May 21 and announced the following day to the surprise not only of some Egyptian officers but to the Soviet and other Arab leaders as well.

If, as Muhammad Hassanein Heikal put it, the Egyptians were "dazzled by the spectacle of the force we moved into Sinai between May 15 and May 20," the shift into the second phase took place because the same force could easily slip from being regarded as a deterrent to being used as a basis for offensive demands on Israel. Once the Israeli military leaders decided that Nasser's military moves were no longer deterrent in character, the General Staff constituted the main pressure group on the government to make war. Prime Minister Eshkol has related that the military told him "every half-hour or every hour of delay is dangerous."

At this time, however, the Israeli cabinet, with one exception, held out against precipitating a military showdown. The political leaders were mainly swayed by the international ramifications of the problem. The United States was urging a respite of forty-eight hours, and the United Nations was planning to send its Secretary General to Cairo. On the morning of May 23, the cabinet's committee on matters of security met with representatives of the opposition parties. The decision, as Eshkol put it later, went in favor of giving the United States a chance to reopen the Straits. Eshkol then paid a visit to the Israeli General Staff to explain the government's decision to wait two or if necessary more days.[24]

On May 22, then, the nature of the Arab-Israeli crisis changed abruptly. Until then, Nasser had claimed that, by threatening Syria, Israel had obliged him to send massive reinforcements into Sinai. The Israelis denied that they had threatened Syria with invasion, but they were inclined to accept Nasser's reasoning for his own moves. They were not alarmed as long as there was in implicit understanding between them that he wanted to relieve the alleged pressure on Syria by putting similar pressure on Israel.

By May 22, however, he had accomplished this aim, whether or not the Israelis had actually concentrated large forces on the Syrian border as he had been led to believe or merely wanted others to believe. If Nasser had been satisfied with this achievement, the crisis should have abated at this point. Instead, by closing the Gulf of Aqaba to Israel, the Egyptian role went over from what was ostensibly the defensive to what was ostentatiously the offensive. The May 1967 crisis began because Israel had supposedly threatened Syria; it shifted into a new and more dangerous phase as soon as Nasser began to threaten Israel.

The Israeli reaction on May 22–23 hardly bore out the contention that Israel had been planning to invade Syria about a week earlier and thus set off a war that could only have brought in Egypt on the side of Syria. If the Israelis had wished to go through with their Syrian invasion, they could easily have done so before the Egyptians had moved troops into position on the Egypt-Israel border. If the Israeli government had wished to provoke Egypt into a war, it could easily have taken its military leaders' advice and attacked Egypt immediately after the closure of the Gulf of Aqaba. On the other hand, Nasser sent the bulk of his armed forces to the Israeli border, disposed them offensively, and then settled down to a war of nerves. There is reason to suppose that neither side was as eager for war as the other suspected.

By the third week of May, then, both sides were fully mobilized. Nasser had sent the bulk of his forces to the Sinai border with Israel, an effort so arduous and costly that it would have been well-nigh ruinous to both morale and equipment if he did not use them. The Israelis could not maintain a full-scale mobilization without straining themselves to the breaking point, war or no war. Both the Arabs and the Israelis circulated "intelligence information" that one planned to attack the other by the end of May. From this point on, the slightest incident could have triggered the war because each side knew the other was ready to go into full battle, and the Israelis, from the point of view of both geography and manpower, were in the worst position of all to wait to see whether it was just another incident or the opening shot of the expected war.

Nevertheless, while the Arabs could do something about their own unity, they could not by themselves do much about isolating Israel, the second key condition for victory in their war planning. To make sure that the lesson which they thought they had learned from 1956 would be carried out, they had to count on the Soviet Union. The Arabs were too sure of themselves to demand Soviet assistance in the form of Soviet armed forces in the coming war. It was enough that the Soviets had provided them with what seemed overwhelming superiority in military equipment for their numerically superior manpower. But the Soviets had to perform one more indispensable service for them—to give them a guarantee against any Western intervention on the side of Israel, as had happened in 1956.

This additional assistance to the Arab cause the Soviets were able and willing to contribute. The first indication of what the Arabs expected from the Soviets in this respect came in a press conference on May 21 in Cairo held by the uninhibited Shukeiry of the PLO. The question and answer went as follows:

> Q. Do you think that the Soviet Union will intervene to stop the fighting or do you think it might take either side?
> A. I think it will not take part in the fighting in terms of supporting the Arab forces, but in terms of supporting the Arab position like trying by all means to avoid any U.S. military intervention. This by itself is a great service to the cause of peace. I believe the efforts of the Soviet Union will be directed in one direction—that is, the localization of the war in the Middle East and to prevent the United States from any military involvement.[25]

Four days later, President Nasser decided to make sure. On May 25, he sent his War Minister, Shamseddin Badran, to Moscow. Badran returned on May 28, and the following day Nasser told publicly what he had accomplished.

> Badran relayed to me a message from Premier Kosygin saying that the Soviet Union stands with us in this battle and will not allow any country to intervene, so that the state of affairs prevailing before 1956 may be restored.*

* This version appeared in *The New York Times,* May 30, 1967. The version in the monitored radio broadcasts is: "When I met with Shamseddin Badran yesterday he handed me a message from the Soviet Pre-

Just how far the Soviets were willing to go may also be surmised from statements by anonymous Soviet officials for the benefit of Western public opinion. One version of the Middle East crisis was allegedly given by "a high Soviet official" to an anonymous correspondent in Moscow for the Paris weekly *Le Nouvel Observateur*. The sequence of events, as related by this Soviet official, went as follows:

Soviet intelligence evaluated as very serious reports of an Israeli plan to stage a deep raid in Syria on May 15 and eventually to push as far as Damascus to overthrow the Syrian government. Nasser, with full Soviet approval, massed his troops on the Sinai border to discourage Israel from launching such an attack on Syria. But Nasser informed the Soviets of the blockade of the Gulf of Aqaba only after he had decided on it, and they warned him that he was taking the risk of unleashing "unpredictable reactions." When U Thant quickly agreed to withdraw the United Nations forces at Sharm el-Sheikh, Nasser's confidence in being able to handle the situation seemed justified. "From that date," this account alleged, "we warned Nasser, however, that we would commit ourselves only to neutralizing the United States, that is, we would respond by an escalation equal to any escalation on the part of Washington—and that our support would not go beyond this." [26]

After the Arab defeat, Soviet officials talked to Eric Rouleau of *Le Monde* (Paris) in a similar vein. "Not without bitterness," as he put it, they said:

> Nasser never consulted or even informed us of the measures which he intended to take. We have told him: You have not thought it best to treat us like friends. You wanted to act alone, without asking our advice. We could have given you friendly and useful counsel. You cannot easily reproach us today for having let you down.

Soviet spokesmen also told Rouleau:

----

mier Kosygin saying that the USSR supports us in this battle and will not allow any power to intervene until matters were restored to what they were in 1956."

We think that Nasser went too far. Of course, he should have reacted to the threats which Israel made against the Syrian regime. But he should have proceeded in a more prudent and especially a more moderate fashion. He should not, in any case, have made threats to exterminate the state of Israel.

When Rouleau asked why the Soviets had advised Nasser not to attack, he received the following answer:

We knew that the situation would have been even more catastrophic if Egypt were guilty of an aggression. A large part of world opinion was already conditioned against Nasser. If he had launched his army against Israel, the whole world would have been against him. He would have perhaps scored in the beginning some military success, but the international reaction, particularly in the United States, would have been terrible. In any case, Egypt's military defeat cannot be solely attributed to the fact that the Israelis took the initiative. Indeed, we advised Nasser not to plunge into an adventure, but we did not tell him that his airmen should leave their planes and drink coffee during an alert. Prudence should have been coupled with vigilance.[27]

Another "high official" of the Soviet Foreign Ministry discussed the third Arab-Israeli war with a veteran journalist, Alexander Werth, who has more often than not given the Soviets the benefit of a doubt. Werth was told:

There are rights and wrongs on both sides. The Israelis did attack Syria in April. On the other hand, Nasser did not play his hand too well. We were *not* consulted about the withdrawal of the UN troops from Sinai and *not* informed of the closing of the Gulf of Aqaba by the Egyptians. When the Israelis hit out on June 5, they were guilty of a gross act of aggression. But the attack was not entirely unprovoked. It is *not* true that Nasser, who has the makings of a real statesman, threatened to destroy, like Hitler, "every man, woman and child in Israel," but the head of the Palestine Arabs, a real son of a bitch, *did* say it.

The Soviet official also said that, if the Israelis had captured the Syrian capital, Soviet armed forces would have intervened one way or another. Werth added that he encountered "great contempt" for the Egyptians as soldiers; they had been caught "idiotically unprepared" and had wasted a billion dollars' worth of Soviet equipment.[28]

What seems to emerge most clearly from these statements is the Soviets' anxiety to establish two things: their willingness to accept responsibility for the ostensibly pro-Syrian, pre-May 22 phase of Egyptian policy, and their unwillingness to accept any responsibility for the Sharm el-Sheikh, post-May 22 phase of Egyptian policy. This distinction implicitly recognized that Nasser moved from what the Soviets considered to be a defensive, acceptable position to one that was offensive and provocative. Inasmuch as the Soviets had prodded him with their "intelligence" reports to take action in behalf of Syria, they had, in effect, started something that he had finished without asking them for permission. Nevertheless, this is not all they did to encourage him. Once he announced the closure of the Straits of Tiran and seemed to get away with it as far as the United Nations was concerned, they went one step further and gave him an assurance that they would "neutralize" the United States by matching any United States "escalation" with one of their own. Without this commitment, it is doubtful whether Nasser would have dared to go as far as he did. The Soviets may not have encouraged him to close the Straits of Tiran, but they did little to discourage him from taking advantage of it. They were less interested in how his actions looked to the Israelis than how they might have looked internationally. And, in the end, it was the Israeli reaction that counted, not that of world opinion.*

* Another view of Soviet intentions seems to have been favored in the State Department. It stressed that the Soviets wanted to lure the United States into intervening in the Middle East, after which the Soviets themselves would have stayed out, despite their broad assurances of help to the Arabs. This view also preferred to emphasize that the United States deterred the Soviets from getting in rather than that the Soviets undertook to deter the United States. It is hard to believe that the Soviets could have hoped to reap any benefit from open intervention by the United States not matched by intervention of their own. The

Soviets were clearly on record with a minimum commitment to help the Arabs to the extent that the United States would help Israel, and their failure to do so could only have been devastating to their credibility as an ally or even as a "Big Brother" of other nations in Egypt's position. The United States and the Soviet Union may have deterred each other from intervening militarily, but the former was no more anxious for a direct confrontation between them than the latter. The Arabs tried to drag the Soviets in—but only after the Arab airfields were knocked out and defeat loomed.

None of the great, not-so-great, and no-longer-so-great powers distinguished itself in this war crisis.

For the United States, the third Arab-Israeli war was the final stage of bankruptcy of a Middle Eastern policy that went back to the Baghdad Pact of 1955. This association of Britain, Turkey, Iraq, Iran, and Pakistan, which the United States did not join but with which it maintained an intimate liaison, was undoubtedly the most dubious and rickety of John Foster Dulles's diplomatic brain children. Each of its members was less interested in any of the others than in pleasing the United States in order to get on the high priority list for American arms. The only Arab member was Iraq, which was then challenging Egypt for leadership in the Arab world. As a result, Egypt under Nasser took umbrage and considered the pact a threat to its own pretensions and ambitions. For once, Egypt and Israel agreed on something— neither had any use for the pact. When Britain tried to get Jordan into it, the opposition was so great that two Jordanian governments fell in one week and King Hussein had to get rid of Sir John B. Glubb (better known as Glubb Pasha, Chief of the Jordanian General Staff),* terminate the Anglo-Jordanian

---

* Sir John's own story of how he broke the news to his wife of his abrupt dismissal, after twenty-six years' loyal service, deserves some kind of immortality. He records the following dialogue:

"Hullo!" she said. "How nice! You're back earlier than usual. Were things slack today at the office?"

"My dear," I said, "the King has dismissed me. We leave Jordan at seven o'clock tomorrow morning—and we shall never come back."

"We'll have some tea now," she said. "Then I'll put the children to bed early, and we'll pack all night."

"Thank you, my dear," I said, and she walked past me out of the room (*A Soldier with the Arabs,* op. cit., p. 424).

treaty, and cancel British rights to bases in Jordan. When the Iraqi strong man, Nuri es-Said, was assassinated in 1958, Iraq was quickly knocked out of the pact, which had to be reorganized the following year as the Central Treaty Organization (CENTO) without any Arab membership at all. As John C. Campbell dryly noted, CENTO remained "a rather artificial combination of three Middle Eastern states which have few natural ties with each other," [1] a condition which surely made this alliance one of the most unnatural on record. In addition, it might be added, it contained the one Western power that had been the most long-standing bête noire of Arab nationalism. Of the three remaining CENTO states, over $4 billion of United States aid did not prevent Pakistan from turning to the Soviet Union in 1965, and a somewhat less astronomical handout did not prevent Iran from accepting $286 million of economic aid from the USSR in 1966 and signing a $100 million military aid agreement with the USSR in January 1967.

As ironies of history go, one of the most delectable is the fact that John Foster Dulles found some of his most successful, if unauthorized, disciples—in Moscow. Once the Soviets decided to compete actively with the United States for influence in the so-called underdeveloped or developing countries, they did not have to exhibit any marked originality; it largely sufficed for them to take over and adapt for their own uses the instrumentalities of foreign policy which Dulles did not invent but which he elevated in importance to a degree that only the United States could afford—economic aid and military assistance. The United States could hardly complain if the Soviet Union, using the former's own methods, outbid it in selected countries. The Soviet footholds in Egypt, Syria, and Iraq were not for the most part gained by using the local Communist parties but by making direct state-to-state economic and military deals with whichever amenable government happened to be in power. In making these deals, however, the Soviets did have one advantage. The United States could not or would not adopt a hard, gross anti-Israeli line to please the Arabs; all it could do was try to maintain friendly relations with both sides. The closer the Soviets got to the Arabs, the more virulently anti-Israel they became. According to Soviet spokesmen in the United Nations, the Arabs could do no wrong and the Israelis no right; there has never been a Soviet word of protest against the *fedayeen,* the Palestine Liberation Organization, or El Fatah raids on Israeli territory; there has never been anything for the Soviets but Israeli "aggression" and "provocation."

The United States had given over one billion dollars to Egypt and over one-half billion dollars to Jordan in aid in the past two decades. Jordan, in addition, had been fully armed by the United States. Egypt had been a lost cause for years and hopelessly lost since 1966. But the case of Jordan demonstrated far more flagrantly the failure of United States policy in this region. Jordan had been armed supposedly to make it capable of resisting the inroads of its Arab antagonists, Egypt and Syria. It cannot be said that this calculation was altogether wrongheaded. But in the pay-off, the arms given to Jordan might just as well have been added to the Soviet arms given to Egypt and Syria. The policy failed when it was needed the most.

In the days immediately before the outbreak of the third Arab-Israeli war, therefore, the United States was caught with almost no leverage on the Arab side. For years the United States had tried not to get too close to Israel in order not to estrange itself from the Arab states; now it was virtually estranged from the Arab states without getting close enough to Israel to make a difference.

About 11 p.m. on May 22, after Nasser's announcement of the closure of the Straits of Tiran to Israel, Under Secretary for Political Affairs Eugene V. Rostow met with Israeli Minister Ephraim Evron at the State Department. (The Israeli Ambassador, Avraham Harman, happened to be out of Washington on an engagement.) Rostow told Evron that the United States hoped there would be no shooting over the incident and asked him to remain in closest consultation for the next few days. Rostow had previously delivered the same message to the Egyptian ambassador in Washington. About the same time, the Israeli government was asked more precisely by the United States ambassador in Tel Aviv, Walworth Barbour, to wait forty-eight hours before taking any action.

On May 23, the Israeli government rejected the plea of its military command for immediate action and decided to send Foreign Minister Eban to Paris, London, and Washington. His conversation with President Charles de Gaulle confirmed the Israeli suspicion that there had been a basic change in French policy and that no help could be expected from that quarter. The discussion with Prime Minister Harold Wilson was encouraging but inconclusive because both recognized that Britain could not act alone and that the final decision had to be made in Washington. But before Eban could get to Washington, the very nature of the problem had changed in the view of Prime Minister Eshkol and his chief advisers. As the Egyptian military build-up continued, Eshkol has related, he changed his mind on May 24 about Sharm el-Sheikh being "the heart of the matter." Eban had been sent to Washington to find out what the United States could do about the closure of the Gulf of Aqaba, and the Israeli government had relegated this question to second place before he could get there. The main question had now become the offensive build-up of the Egyptian army on the Israeli borders, and to make it even more pressing, it was now the turn of the Israeli government to claim that it had information of an imminent attack—by Egypt.[2]

While Eban was still en route, Eshkol sent him a message to this effect. It greeted him as he stepped off the plane in Washington on May 25 and was met by Ambassador Harman and Minister Evron. The message was so alarming that Eban asked Secretary of State Dean Rusk to advance the time of their first meeting, which had been set for 5:30 p.m. that day, by two hours. When Eban conveyed Eshkol's message to Rusk, he was told that the information at the disposal of the United States did not bear out this grim prospect. According to the

best United States estimate, Rusk said, Egypt was not prepared to strike a quick blow.

That same evening, May 25, the top Israeli diplomats, including Eban and Harman, and the leading United States
officials, including Rostow and Lucius Battle, continued to
wrestle with the problem at a "working dinner." The Israelis
urged speed and pressed for a "time table." The Americans
were not prepared as yet to suggest much more than "going
to the UN." As one participant later put it, this represented
a "cold shower" to the Israelis, who had no confidence that
anything could be achieved in the Security Council in view of
the Soviet veto. Indeed, nothing had been done, the Israelis
pointed out, even when the Security Council had voted unanimously, as in the case of opening the Suez Canal to Israeli
shipping. That night the two sides seemed sufficiently far apart
for the Israelis to regard the situation pessimistically.

Nevertheless, as a safeguard against a possible mishap,
Under Secretary Rostow called in the Egyptian ambassador
about 10:30 p.m. on May 25 and, on behalf of President
Johnson, asked him to request the Egyptian government not
to resort to force.* The same appeal was made to the Israelis
in similar terms. On the following day, President Johnson sent
a message to Premier Kosygin suggesting Soviet cooperation
to restrain the Egyptians.

In preparation for Eban's visit, a joint memorandum had
been drawn up by the Secretary of State and by Secretary of
Defense Robert S. McNamara. They advised President Johnson that the United States was faced with two basic policy

---

* On July 23, 1967, Nasser gave the following version of this meeting:
"The Counsellor of the American President summoned our ambassador at a late hour in the night in Washington and told him that Israel
had information that we would mount an attack, adding that this
would expose us to a dangerous situation. He asked us to retain self-
control and said that the Americans were doing the same thing with
Israel to have it maintain self-control. There was the message which
we received from U.S. President Johnson in which he spoke about the
United Nations and appealed to us to have self-control" (Appendix
14).

choices in making good its commitment to Israel to keep open the Straits of Tiran. They were (1) to permit Israel to deal with the problem alone,* and (2) for the United States to assume responsibility for opening the Straits. Rusk and McNamara rejected the first and supported the second.

The policy outlined in the Rusk-McNamara memorandum envisaged three phases or stages:

1. To exhaust all possibilities of resolving the conflict peacefully in the United Nations.

2. To draft and circulate a declaration to be signed by as many maritime powers as possible in support of freedom of passage through the Straits of Tiran and in the Gulf of Aqaba.

3. If all else failed, to use warships to escort vessels through the Straits of Tiran.

The key meeting between President Johnson and Foreign Minister Eban, together with their main advisers and leading officials, took place on May 26. Eban made an eloquent statement of the Israeli position, which he defined as one of "surrender or fight." The President made clear his determination to live up to the commitments made by previous administrations, especially the assurance given by the Eisenhower administration in 1957 to uphold the right of Israel's "free and innocent" passage in the Gulf of Aqaba. But he also drew attention to the constitutional and congressional difficulties to be faced before the United States could take any action. In the end, Eban put the following question to the President: Would the United States make every possible effort to assure that the Straits of Tiran and the Gulf of Aqaba would be open to free and innocent passage? The President answered: Yes. In return, Eban was asked for two weeks to enable the United States to attempt to settle the dispute peacefully.†

---

* In official circles, this was sometimes referred to as the "unleashing Israel" alternative.

† Prime Minister Eshkol later stated: "We were at first asked to wait two days. Then we sent Abba Eban to the United States—and were asked to wait a further fortnight. They told us that forty to fifty maritime powers would sign a guarantee for free passage through the Tiran

The Israelis left the meeting with President Johnson feeling that he sincerely intended to take whatever action might be necessary to open the Straits of Tiran and the Gulf of Aqaba to Israeli shipping. But they had also been made acutely aware of the fact that he did not feel that he could act on his own and that much would depend on the international and domestic support he might be able to muster. Meanwhile, Mr. Johnson had taken the precaution of obtaining the backing of former President Eisenhower. The latter was called to give his opinion of what the United States had committed itself to in 1957, and he forthrightly answered that he considered it a "commitment of honor" for the United States to live up to his implicit assurance to former Israeli Prime Minister Ben Gurion that the Straits would be kept open. Eban returned home recommending that President Johnson should be given a chance to see what he could do to reopen the Straits of Tiran one way or another.

Before Eban could get home, the Soviets again injected themselves into the Egyptian-Israeli dilemma. The Soviet ambassadors in both Cairo and Tel Aviv were instructed to see President Nasser and Prime Minister Eshkol without delay, even if it meant waking them up in the middle of the night.

As we know from Nasser, Soviet Ambassador Dmitri Pozhdaev saw Nasser at 3:30 a.m. on May 27. In his first reference to this meeting, Nasser said that Pozhdaev "told me that the Soviet Government strongly requested we should not be the first to open fire." [3] Later, Nasser added that the Soviet ambassador "requested a meeting with me and conveyed to me a message from the Soviet Prime Minister asking us to have self-control and telling me about a message he had sent to the

Straits" (*The New York Times,* June 10, 1967). I have been informed that ten days to two weeks were mentioned by a high United States official on May 25; President Johnson mentioned two weeks on May 26; and a letter from Prime Minister Eshkol on May 28 confirmed the period of grace but gave no date as the starting point, the assumption being, from the Israeli side, that it dated from May 25 or 26.

Israeli Prime Minister telling him that any action on the part of Israel would expose the world to grave dangers." [4]

According to another Arab source, the Soviet ambassador also assured Nasser that Israel was neither willing nor able to attack.[5] Nasser later attributed the Egyptian decision to refrain from striking the first blow to United States and Soviet pressure.

Nasser left the impression that the Soviet ambassador's visit to him in the early morning hours of May 27 had persuaded him not to fire the first shot and, therefore, had given Israel the advantage of initiative and surprise. There is some reason, however, to doubt this version of events. On May 26, as we have seen, Muhammad Hassanein Heikal had published an article in which he had clearly expressed the Egyptian view that war was inevitable and that Israel had to strike the first blow. This article must have been written at least twenty-four hours before the Soviet ambassador's visit and, therefore, the Egyptian authorities may already have made up their minds to strike the second blow. Also, as we have seen, Nasser had estimated the chance of war at fifty per cent as early as May 22, when the Gulf of Aqaba was closed, and he had rated the probability at one hundred per cent on June 1, four days before the outbreak. Thus the decision to lure the Israelis into striking the first blow could have come before the Soviet ambassador's visit in the early morning hours of May 27, and the Israeli action may not have come as a surprise.

At about 2:30 a.m. on May 27, Soviet Ambassador Chuvakhin accompanied by his First Secretary Bykov woke up Prime Minister Eshkol. As Eshkol later told the story, Chuvakhin presented him with a "more or less polite" letter from Premier Kosygin. It warned of a "tremendous error if arms began talking" instead of "serious political thought." Then the two Soviet diplomats and the Israeli Prime Minister settled down to a two-hour discussion. Eshkol soon realized that they had come to get an answer to one question: Will you fire the first shot? Instead of answering the question, Eshkol talked "philosophy," which at that time of the night must have sorely tried the Soviet ambassador's patience. After Eshkol had side-stepped the same question for the fourth time, Bykov protested and brought forth an outburst from the Israeli Prime Minister. Eshkol accused the Soviets of ignoring the Arabs "first shots" and demanded, "Aren't mines which explode all the time a first shot? Isn't the shelling of Nachal-Oz [an Israeli village near the Gaza strip] a first shot? What does a first shot mean today?" [6]

The Israeli leaders deliberated from the evening of May 27 to 5 a.m. the next morning on the situation brought about by Foreign Minister Eban's report from Washington, Soviet Ambassador Chuvakhin's intervention, and the Israeli military's continued pressure for action. While the meeting was still in session, a message from President Johnson to Prime Minister Eshkol arrived. The message strongly urged restraint and re-iterated the President's request to Foreign Minister Eban for a waiting period. According to Eshkol, it also cited a warning by Premier Kosygin to President Johnson that the Soviet Union would help whichever side was attacked. Another message followed from Secretary of State Rusk warning the Israel government that one-sided Israeli action would be catastrophic and holding out the promise of United States action to reopen the Straits of Tiran. Eshkol says that he was then prepared to go to war but that the President's letter persuaded him to wait. "I did not want," Eshkol recalled, "to give him a pretext to say later: 'I told you so.' "

An informal poll at the meeting disclosed that the Israeli cabinet was evenly divided—nine for war and nine for waiting. Eshkol says that he could have exerted enough pressure to gain two more votes for a prowar majority of eleven to seven but that he was loath to take the country into war without a greater degree of political unity. One of those outside the government who apparently thought that the time for action had already passed was former Prime Minister David Ben Gurion, whom outsiders generally considered one of the most extreme of the Israeli "hawks." The decision to wait was made official at a second meeting on the afternoon of May 28. Eshkol conveyed the news to the Israeli military, who still tried to impress him with the danger. The Prime Minister also sent a reply to President Johnson agreeing to the request for a waiting period without specifying its duration.[7] The Americans assumed that it would be two weeks.

On May 28, then, the government of Israel was too divided to take military action. The division was not between those who favored war immediately and those who opposed it indefinitely. There were, roughly, three viewpoints—that Israel had "missed the boat" by waiting too long, that it was necessary to fight without further delay, and that it was necessary to exhaust all other possibilities before going to war. The third was not so much a "peace party" as a "not-yet-war" party. For this group, of whom Prime Minister Eshkol was the central figure, the main inhibition came from President Johnson's request to let the United States and the "maritime powers" open the Straits of Tiran for Israel. While Soviet and Arab propaganda was accusing the United States of inciting the Israelis, the latter were being held back by the fear of giving offense to the President of the United States. If Soviet pressure succeeded in restraining the Egyptians in the early morning hours of May 27, United States influence accomplished much the same thing on the Israeli side the following day. Indeed, both the Soviet Union and the United States were virtually working together on May 27–28 to prevent an outbreak of hostilities. But they were also working at cross-purposes politically, and, in the end, they negated more than they supported each other.

In retrospect, the last chance to prevent the third Arab-Israeli war passed on May 28. If, as the Israelis wavered, other forces had pulled back, the crisis might have reached its peak and gradually subsided. Instead, the worst was still to come.

For one thing, the Arab military pressure on the Israeli borders continued to increase. The Israeli command was especially disturbed by the movement of Egypt's strategic reserve, the Fourth Division, into the Bir Gafgafa and Mitla areas in Sinai on May 26 and the continued pull-out of Egyptian troops from

Yemen.[8] That the bulk of the Egyptian army should have been sent to the Israeli front to take up positions that, as Muhammad Hassanein Heikal admitted, were clearly offensive rather than defensive, drove the Israeli military to persist in demanding action to forestall an Egyptian attack. The Egyptians may meanwhile have decided not to strike the first blow, but the Israelis had no way of being sure what was in their minds. The contradiction between Egyptian strategic intentions and Egyptian tactical maneuvers provoked the Israelis and paralyzed the Egyptians.

In addition to moving his troops around too much, Nasser may also have talked too much. For a statesman who had previously spoken out publicly at intervals of weeks or even months, he now seemed to address his nation and the world every few days or even hours. He made long, uncompromising pronouncements on May 22, May 26, May 28, and May 29. In the last, he served notice to the Israelis that, if they permitted him to push them back to the *status quo ante* of 1956, he did not intend to stop before he had pushed them back to the *status quo ante* of 1948.

> Now, eleven years after 1956, we are restoring things to what they were in 1956. This is from the material aspect. In my opinion this material aspect is but a small part, whereas the spiritual aspect is the great side of the issue. The spiritual aspect involves the renaissance of the Arab nation, the revival of the Palestine question, and the restoration of confidence to every Arab and to every Palestinian. This is on the basis that if we were able to restore conditions to what they were in 1956, God will surely help and urge us to restore the situation to what it was in 1948.*

The Egyptian war aim of closing the Gulf of Aqaba, which meant in Nasser's language, "to restore conditions to what they were in 1956," was to the Israelis intolerable enough,

* This is the monitored radio broadcast version. The last sentence appeared in *The New York Times* of May 30, 1967, as follows: "Now that we have the situation as it was before 1956, Allah will certainly help us to restore the status quo of before 1948."

although it was the kind of problem that could conceivably have been resolved by some face-saving formula, assuming that both sides did not finally think it was worth a war. But the further Egyptian war aim of "restoring the situation to what it was in 1948," which meant before there was a state of Israel, could not possibly be compromised or adjudicated. It would have been hard in any case to convince the Israelis that they were not fighting for the state of Israel by resisting the strangulation of the port of Eilat. But, on May 29, Nasser himself chose to do his utmost to convince the Israelis that the defense of Eilat was the defense of Israel. The Arabs never made up their minds in 1967 whether their war aims were limited or unlimited. They wanted to have it both ways, for different purposes and different audiences. Whether clearly delimited war aims would have staved off the war may be doubtful, but it cannot be doubted that unlimited war aims could not be achieved without war.

Twenty-four hours later, the Israelis suffered another blow, all the more stunning because it was unexpected. On May 30, King Hussein of Jordan suddenly flew to Cairo and signed a Jordan-Egypt mutual defense pact.

The Israelis made two major, prewar miscalculations. One was their assumption that Nasser would not or could not risk a war before the 1970s. This assumption made them reluctant to commit themselves to war as long as they were not sure what Nasser's intentions were. But as Nasser's armed forces were moved into Sinai in numbers and dispositions incompatible with defensive requirements, the Israelis came to feel that they had been living in a fool's paradise. The second assumption— that Hussein would risk a war even less than Nasser, or perhaps would not risk one at all—also backfired. Later, Hussein sadly reflected that it would have been better if Nasser had consulted him and the other Arab leaders before closing the Gulf of Aqaba to Israel. As a result, Hussein said, "the [Israeli] aggression took us by surprise a year or a year and a half too early." [9] But this was the wisdom of hindsight. It might have been closer to the truth for Hussein to have said that Nasser's offensive military moves and political propaganda had taken him by surprise a year or a year and a half too early. Between May 22 and May 30, 1967, Hussein was sufficiently impressed by Nasser's extraordinary military build-up and militant rhetoric to jump to the conclusion that the Arabs' moment had come, as he put it on June 4, to "fight the fateful battle." The Israelis had always counted on Hussein to be most cautious and circumspect in his own interest, and, ironically, he now helped more than anything else to convince the Israelis that the time had come to fight *their* fateful battle. If Hussein thought by May 30 that he could not afford to stay out of Nasser's war, Israel's reaction was not too different.

Strategically, Israel had always lived with the nightmare of encirclement. A British study in 1965 had pointed out that "whereas Israel, fighting on narrow fronts, might be able to hold both the Egyptians and Syrians at once, even against superior odds, she would be extremely vulnerable to a simultaneous broad-fronted attack from Jordan, which would quickly cut her communications between north and south." [10] The Egypt-Jordan pact of May 30 seemed to convert the nightmare into a reality. Prime Minister Eshkol later related that, on learning that Hussein had gone to Cairo, he said: "Gentlemen, it [war] will come sooner or later." [11]

For a few days, Arab unity seemed more than a "madman's notion," and all of it turned against Israel. Iraqi and Kuwaiti troops arrived in Egypt on May 31. Jordan, which had ordered the Syrian ambassador out of the country on May 23 as a result of a border incident, resumed full diplomatic relations with Syria on June 1. Iraqi President and Commander in Chief of the Armed Forces, Lieutenant General Abderrahman Arif, told air force officers on June 1: "Brethren and sons, this is the day of the battle to avenge your martyred brethren who fell in 1948. It is the day to wash away the stigma. We shall, God willing, meet in Tel Aviv and Haifa." [12] On the same day, Ahmed Shukairy, the chieftain of the Palestine Liberation Organization, gave an interview in the Jordanian sector of Jerusalem. Asked whether the PLO or the Jordanian army would fire the first shot against Israel, he replied blithely:

> Why not? This is likely. It is most likely and possible that the Jordanian army will begin the battle and march to liberate the country—our country.

Asked what would happen to native-born Israelis if the Arab attack succeeded, he answered:

> Those who survive will remain in Palestine. I estimate that none of them will survive.

By this time, the Israeli government had to take account of another factor—Israeli public opinion. It had become increasingly uneasy as the Egyptian military build-up continued, as other Arab states became more deeply embroiled, and as Arab spokesmen from Nasser to Shukairy made more and more inflammatory statements. Inasmuch as Nasser subsidized Shukairy, it was not easy to know where one ended and the other began. The Arab calculation that Israel could not afford a lengthy period of full mobilization was not unfounded, psychologically as well as materially. The longer the mobilization lasted, the more it worked in favor of the Arabs. But this only meant that the Israelis could not afford to permit it to last very long. Geographically, demographically, and economically, the Israeli leeway was so limited that the Israelis could no more envisage a long mobilization than a long war, if they could help it. Nasser could force Israel to the wall in more than one way, and one was a protracted mobilization. For this reason, every day of mobilization itself brought war nearer, as it might not have done in a larger, more populous, and more affluent country. By the end of May, the tide of war had to go one way or the other; it could not remain still.

Israeli public opinion reacted by losing confidence in the Eshkol government's will to act. Eshkol has charged that this "psychosis and panic" were artificially stimulated by his political rivals and were totally devoid of foundation. He has pointed to his willingness to go to war on May 28, if the cabinet had not been so evenly divided and if it had not been necessary to give President Johnson "a few days" to see what he could do. For our purposes, it is enough that this popular mood existed. It expressed itself in an irresistible demand for the inclusion of the former Chief of Staff, Major General Moshe Dayan, who enjoyed a reputation as a "hawk," in the government. Despite his reluctance to give way, the Prime Minister surrendered his second post as Minister of Defense to General Dayan on June 1 in a reorganization of the Cabinet which was enlarged to include two other representatives of opposition parties without portfolio. According to Eshkol, Dayan had asked him as early as May 20 for permission to make a tour of inspection of the Israeli armed forces, and Eshkol had agreed. That Dayan had taken the initiative signified that his activity in this period did not in any way indicate which way government policy was moving. Eshkol vigorously denied that Dayan's appointment had been necessary or had made any difference in governmental policy. Nevertheless, it certainly made a big difference to Israeli public opinion, and it was interpreted by the outside world as a sign that Israeli patience was nearing the end. This was true, but not necessarily because Dayan had entered the government. What Eshkol averted by appointing Dayan was a government crisis, which everyone wished to avoid; whether the government's policy would have been different without Dayan is more doubtful.

After June 1, then, only a determined, dramatic effort on the part of the great powers, especially the United States and the Soviet Union, could have averted the war. The Israelis and the Arabs were already locked into a combat position from which they could not extricate themselves alone. The momentary pause on May 28 had given way to a feeling of greater desperation than ever on the part of the Israelis. By June 1, the question they asked themselves was whether they had not already waited too long. The Arabs decided not to strike the first blow only because they expected to gain more by striking the second blow. The antagonists had already made up their minds what each one would do; they merely wanted to know, in varying degrees, what the Soviet Union, the United Nations, and the United States intended to do.

The most striking thing about Soviet policy was the abrupt change of tactics that took place after Nasser's closure of the Gulf of Aqaba to Israel. The visit of Soviet Ambassador Pozhdaev to President Nasser at 3:30 a.m. on May 27 for the purpose of asking the Egyptian ruler not to fire the first shot will long provide one of the most intriguing and debatable episodes of this war.

The implication was that the Soviet Union considered the international ramifications of an Arab-Israeli war too explosive to risk setting it off with an Egyptian attack. By putting pressure on both the Egyptians and the Israelis to abstain from striking a first blow, the Soviets seemingly tried to stop in mid-course what they had started with their charge of an Israeli plan to invade Syria. If they failed, another assurance which they gave Egypt at the same time was largely responsible.

As we have seen, the Egyptian War Minister, Shamseddin Badran, went to Moscow on May 25 and returned on May 28 with a message from Premier Kosygin "that the Soviet Union stands with us in this battle and will not allow any country to intervene, so that the state of affairs prevailing before 1956 may be restored." The three high Soviet officials (if they were not the same one) cited by *Le Nouvel Observateur,* Eric Rouleau, and Alexander Werth agreed that the Soviets were not consulted on the closure of the Gulf of Aqaba to Israel. But, if we may trust Nasser (and his statement was not denied by any Soviet source), the Soviets quickly recovered from their surprise and decided to back him on the issue anyway, at least to the extent of "neutralizing" the United States. The Soviet official in *Le Nouvel Observateur*'s version quickly added that "our support would not go beyond this"—but this was enough. For the main concern of the Arabs was to unite against an isolated Israel. As Nasser saw the balance of forces before the war, the Arabs did not need more than this Soviet assurance of Israeli isolation to stand firm on two things: the closure of the Gulf of Aqaba to Israel and the strategy of the second blow.

If neither Egypt nor Israel had struck the first blow, there would have been no war. But neither would there have been any reopening of the Gulf of Aqaba. The Soviets were committed to what Nasser euphemistically called "restoring things to what they were in 1956"—and this was not possible to achieve without war. It was impossible because it was equivalent to the prize of war and because Nasser himself had said that the Arabs could not have turned the clock back to 1956 and stopped. Thus it may be true that the war broke out despite efforts by the Soviets to stop it; it also broke out because the Soviets made themselves guarantors of the conditions that brought about the war; and, at the last moment, they were willing to do something about the consequences, not the conditions.

How ruinously negative Soviet policy was came out most crudely at the United Nations.

On the evening of May 23, Canada and Denmark requested an immediate meeting of the Security Council to deal with the Middle Eastern crisis. After the closure of the Gulf of Aqaba, the full dimensions of the emergency were clearly visible. Indeed, four days earlier, on May 19, Secretary General U Thant had already advised the Council that "the current situation in the Near East is more disturbing, indeed, I say more menacing, than at any time since the fall of 1956." [13] The Canadian-Danish request was supported by United States Ambassador Arthur J. Goldberg, who offered to join with the Soviet Union, Britain, and France "in a common effort to restore and maintain peace in the Middle East." [14]

But the Soviet Union was already running interference for the Arab states, and Egypt in particular, to prevent any "intervention" by outside powers in the consummation of the Arab

plan. Therefore, Soviet Ambassador Fedorenko barred the way
on May 24 to the Security Council's even taking up the subject.
The reason he gave shows to what extreme lengths the Soviet
leaders were willing to go to give the Arabs a free hand.
"Having heard the statements of representatives of the Western
powers," Fedorenko said loftily, "we are even more convinced
that certain forces are *artificially heating up the climate* for
reasons that have nothing to do with a true concern for peace
and security in the Near East" (my italics, T.D.). He brusquely
rejected the proposal that the Soviet Union should take part in
consultations.[15] The Soviet press did not even deign to mention
the Security Council session of May 24. Then came Premier
Kosygin's note of May 26, delivered in the early morning hours
of May 27, warning that it would be a "tremendous error if
arms began talking" instead of "serious political thought." This
note suggested that the Kremlin was taking the situation somewhat more seriously than it permitted its spokesmen in the
United Nations to let on. In the United Nations, Ambassador
Goldberg tried to spell out a key phrase in Secretary General
Thant's report of May 27. Thant had urged "all the parties concerned to exercise special restraint, to forgo belligerence and to
avoid all other actions which could increase tension, to allow
the Council to deal with the underlying causes of the present
crisis and to seek solutions." In his statement on May 29, Mr.
Goldberg paid special attention to the words, "forgo belligerence." He said: "We believe, from the context of the situation,
that with respect to the particularly sensitive area of Aqaba,
forgoing belligerence must mean forgoing any blockade of the
Gulf of Aqaba during the breathing spell requested by the Secretary General, and permitting free and innocent passage of all
nations and all flags through the Straits of Tiran to continue as
it has during the last ten years." [16] It was a good try, but the
Egyptian spokesman, Ambassador Mohammed Awad el-Kony,
made short work of it by explaining in brutally frank terms why
Egypt had been justified in closing the Gulf of Aqaba to Israel:

The continued violations and the numerous premeditated acts of aggression in all dimensions against the Arabs, which culminated in the cowardly attack on Sinai in 1956, clearly means that *a state of overt war has been existing.* Hence my Government has the legitimate right, in accordance with international law, to impose restrictions on navigation in the Straits of Tiran with respect to shipping to the enemy [my italics, T.D.].[17]

This candid rationale for Egypt's actions meant, if it meant anything, that *overt* war had already broken out in the Middle East and, indeed, had been going on ever since 1956. But if Ambassador el-Kony was right—and he was merely repeating assertions that had been made for years in Cairo and Damascus —anything the Israelis did after May 29 was also justified. If the Egyptians and the Israelis were already in a state of "overt war" on that date, it is hard to see how the Israelis could be charged with an "aggression" that started the war a week later. The logic used by the Egyptians for closing the Gulf of Aqaba to Israel contained a built-in justification for any military action that the Israelis might take in retaliation. Yet the Egyptian case against Israel seemed to be based on the flagrant contradiction that Egypt could close the Gulf of Aqaba because it was in a state of war with Israel, but Israel could not strike back because it was not in a state of war with Egypt. One never ceases to wonder at the human predilection for having one's cake and eating it too.

As late as May 29, however, Ambassador Fedorenko still accused Ambassador Goldberg of attempting "to dramatize the situation," as if anything could have been more dramatic than the Egyptian declaration, made only a few hours earlier, that "a state of overt war" existed in the Middle East. Fedorenko, however, was not above dramatizing the situation in his own way. A "dangerous aggravation of tensions" existed in that part of the world, he declared, but there was only one "real culprit" —Israel. His solution was extraordinarily uncomplicated. All that was necessary was that the Western powers, who were allegedly using Israel to restore their former colonial rule, should "simply call to order" their Israeli "friends and allies."[18]

On May 31, Ambassador Fedorenko took a different tack. He defended the Arab cause mainly by attacking a mythical United States "naval blockade" of Cuba,* which he seemed to equate with the Egyptian blockade of Israel.[19] And on June 3, at the last meeting of the Security Council before the outbreak of hostilities, he contented himself for the most part with again complaining about Cuba and by attacking United States policy in Vietnam.[20] Thus Soviet strategy in the United Nations consisted of preventing serious discussion of the issue first by belittling its gravity and then by talking of other things.

When the United Nations might have done something about preventing the war, the Soviets did everything in their power to reduce the organization to impotence and bring it into disrepute. When the lightning Israeli victory proved that the Soviets had not done enough for the Arabs merely by forcing Israel to fight alone, they attempted to turn the United Nations into an anti-Israeli coalition to restore the *status quo ante* that the Arab states had previously repudiated but now, in defeat, regarded as the lesser evil.

After this, the three-point plan of the United States and Great Britain was effectively reduced to two points—the declaration of the "maritime powers" and, as a last resort, the naval escort through the Straits of Tiran.

The "Maritime Declaration" took some days to draft to the satisfaction of all parties concerned because its sponsors did not wish to make it too threatening in tone and yet wished to

* Fedorenko seems to have confused the refusal of the United States to trade with Cuba with a "naval blockade" of Cuba. Even Western powers, such as Britain and France, trade freely with Cuba. About one-quarter of Cuba's trade in 1967 was with non-Communist countries. The only semblance of a United States blockade was imposed during the "missile crisis" of October 1962 for about a week, and that was limited to offensive military equipment involving a nuclear threat.

hint that some action might be forthcoming if Egypt proved to be completely unyielding. As finally adopted, the brief statement contained this key paragraph:

> In regard to shipping through the waterways that serve ports on the Gulf of Aqaba, our Governments reaffirm the view that the Gulf is an international waterway into which and through which the vessels of all nations have a right of passage. Our Governments will assert this right on behalf of all shipping sailing under their flags, and our Governments are prepared to cooperate among themselves and to join with others in seeking general recognition of this right.

In Cairo, meanwhile, the United States embassy was having peculiar troubles of its own. For three months before the May crisis, the ambassadorial post in the Egyptian capital had been vacant. No United States official in all that time had talked to President Nasser. The new United States ambassador, Richard H. Nolte, a respected student of Islamic jurisprudence and culture but without diplomatic experience and with an excessive deference for Arab sensibilities, did not arrive at his post until May 21, on the eve of Nasser's closure of the Gulf of Aqaba to Israel. When Nolte was asked at the airport what he thought of the approaching crisis, he replied, according to one version, "What crisis?" and according to another, "There is no crisis in the Middle East. This thing will not amount to much." [21] This thing was too much for David G. Nes, who had been Deputy Chief of Mission in Cairo in the absence of an ambassador. Nes later took the extraordinary step for a career diplomat of making public his alarm and dismay at the way the Egyptian build-up had been handled. Nes revealed that he had been convinced as far back as January 1967 that Nasser had been planning a major confrontation with Israel and the West. Apparently unable to get through to his superiors in Washington, Nes wrote a letter in the first week of January to Senator J. William Fulbright, Chairman of the Senate Foreign Relations Committee, urging that a top professional diplomat or a well-known business executive close to President Johnson be appointed as ambassador in Cairo inasmuch as the incumbent, Lucius Battle, was scheduled to leave the post in March. When Mr. Nes protested to Mr. Nolte that his remarks at the airport had greatly underestimated the seriousness of the situation, the latter reportedly replied that Washington thought Mr. Nes was being an alarmist.* The imbroglio in the embassy was so embarrassing that the State Department sent its adviser on the Middle East, Charles W. Yost, to Cairo to calm the troubled diplomatic waters.

In Washington, Nes's charge that the State Department had neglected the area or was not aware of the forces at work in it was strongly rejected. Nes himself came under fire as a troublesome, unreliable official of long standing. If so, however, the Cairo embassy left something to be desired before Nolte's arrival, since it had been headed by Nes, and it was not much improved by Nolte's presence. In fact, the State Department had for some time encountered difficulty filling the post of Assistant Secretary for Near Eastern and South Asian Affairs —responsible for a peculiar hodgepodge of about twenty countries, extending from Greece to Pakistan—in Washington.

* Nes's story appeared in an interview with Thomas T. Fenton in the Baltimore *Sun,* June 13, 1967. A State Department spokesman, Carl Bartch, did not deny any of Nes's assertions but protested that "any inference that the United States regarded the situation in the Middle East as anything other than very grave is erroneous" (ibid., June 14, 1967). The "explanation" for Mr. Nolte's unguarded remarks at the airport seems to be that he thought he was speaking off-the-record, which hardly explains the substance of what he said.

Mr. Nolte later denied that the Cairo embassy had been warning the State Department for several months "that the Egyptians were building up to a deliberate confrontation with Israel and the West and that those alleged warnings were ignored in Washington." Even if there had been warnings, Mr. Nolte also said, the United States could not have dissuaded Nasser short of the use of force. According to Mr. Nolte, there had been only one "vital" difference between the embassy and Washington: the former believed that Nasser would not be "bluffed, winkled or traded out" of his blockade of the Straits of Tiran, whereas the latter thought there was some "give." Mr. Nolte insisted that the Egyptian challenge to Israel had not been clearly foreseen by any United States officials and had caught both them and the Israelis by surprise (interview, *The New York Times,* September 12, 1967).

Raymond A. Hare, a veteran of forty years' diplomatic service, had been appointed in July 1965, but he was due for retirement and accepted the post for one year only. Hare suddenly resigned from the service in October 1966 in the midst of one of the worst raid-reprisal blowups that month. Battle was appointed to replace him in January 1967 but was not confirmed until April of that year, about six weeks before the closure of the Gulf of Aqaba.

In any event, the negotiations for the maritime powers' declaration dragged on.* At the same time, but far more quietly, plans were being worked out for a collective maritime flotilla—soon dubbed the "Red Sea Regatta"—to provide a naval escort for ships through the Straits of Tiran if Egypt did not heed the declaration. The United States had the fifty-ship Sixth Fleet with its two aircraft carriers, *America* and *Saratoga,* and a third carrier, *Intrepid,* in the area, and the British had about half a dozen ships there, but two British aircraft carriers, *Victorious* and *Hermes,* were about a thousand miles away in the vicinity of Aden. In the Pentagon, where the military plans were taking shape, officials made no secret of their misgivings. They were haunted by the prospect of a "second Vietnam" in the Middle East, for which they were totally unprepared. Moreover, the administration was making no effort to prepare American public opinion for such a dire eventuality. Even at the White House and the State Department, those who supported Israel's right to freedom of passage through the Straits of Tiran in principle could hardly bring themselves to con-

* Charles W. Yost later admitted that the maritime powers' declaration had few potential signatories: "Equally unavailing were efforts made to forestall a unilateral Israeli response by organizing a group of maritime powers to issue a declaration reaffirming the right of free passage through the Strait and presumably, if passage continued to be denied, to take effective multilateral action to reopen it. Very few maritime powers showed any interest in participating in a confrontation with Nasser and the Arab world, nor did members of the U.S. Congress who were consulted manifest any enthusiasm for risking another conflict in addition to Viet Nam" (Charles W. Yost, "The Arab-Israeli War: How It Began," *Foreign Affairs,* January 1968, p. 316).

•

template what might be necessary to enforce it in practice.

Meanwhile, the United States hoped that diplomacy had not yet been exhausted. On May 31, Robert B. Anderson, former Secretary of the Treasury in the Eisenhower administration, met with President Nasser in Cairo. Anderson had been sent as President Johnson's personal envoy on a mission of inquiry that was one of the best-kept secrets of the period. According to Nasser, Anderson proposed that an Egyptian Vice President should be sent to the United States to explain the Arab viewpoint to President Johnson.* Nasser agreed, and on June 2 sent a message to Johnson offering to send Vice President Zakaria Mohieddin to Washington for that purpose. Nasser's offer was accepted on June 3, and the Mohieddin visit was scheduled for June 7.[22]

Despite his more belligerent utterances, Nasser was not altogether averse to having his way in the Gulf of Aqaba without firing a shot, thereby enabling him to claim in the Arab world that he had taken from the Israelis the equivalent of what the latter had had to gain by fighting a war. Nasser was not unwilling to permit the great powers to "prevent war," in his sense, as long as he did not permit the Israelis to get back into the Gulf of Aqaba. For this reason, as he agreed to send Mohieddin to Washington, on June 4 he told the so-called maritime powers what price they would have to pay for doing business with him: "We shall consider any declaration by them as a transgression of our sovereignty. It would be considered a preliminary to an act of war." [23]

Nevertheless, telegrams went out on the weekend of June 3–4 from the State Department in Washington to United States envoys abroad requesting definitive answers to the proposed Maritime Declaration by the close of business on June 5. The declaration was to be issued publicly during the week the hostilities actually began.[24]

* It is not altogether clear, however, whether the proposal first came from Anderson or from Nasser. The idea arose because President Johnson had previously offered to send Vice President Hubert H. Humphrey to Cairo.

The trouble with all this diplomatic byplay from the Israeli point of view was that it had become largely irrelevant. For Israel was faced with two problems, and Washington wished to concern itself with only one. The two were the blockade of the Gulf of Aqaba and the Egyptian military build-up on the Sinai border. By May 25, as we have seen, the build-up was so great, and the Israeli strain of countermobilization so intense, that the question of the Gulf of Aqaba had taken second place in the Israelis' calculation of the danger before them.

For the Israeli government, the problem was to decide whether it could afford to wait the full two weeks that President Johnson had asked for on May 26. After ten days, there was no visible sign that he was going to be able to carry the Congress and the American people with him in any action that might have required force to break through the Straits of Tiran or even that any major American ally would back him up fully. The more the Israelis thought about it, the less they could see what the President could accomplish. They were ready to grant that it was a fair assumption the Egyptians would not open fire on an American warship. But suppose Nasser decided to bide his time and outwait the Americans. Was it feasible to expect the Americans to escort every commercial ship through the Straits of Tiran to the port of Eilat? Were the Americans thinking of a one-shot test case or a permanent naval force? These were, at best, very troublesome questions. But no one outside Israel was talking or thinking of doing anything about the overwhelming military pressure that the Arab states had developed on the Israeli borders. As the Washington correspondent of the London *Times* had already observed: "At the State Department it was emphasized that the naval planning was concerned only with securing passage for international shipping through the Strait of Tiran to the Gulf of Aqaba. There was no question of intervention in a possible land war." [25]

As the Egyptian build-up increased and other Arab military units hastened toward the Israeli frontiers from near and far, the pressures on the Israeli government to make a life-or-death decision became irresistible. On June 2, the Israeli government received another threatening note from the Soviet Union. It sought to make the Israelis back down from their declared determination to open the Straits of Tiran by themselves if the maritime powers failed to do it. The note concluded ominously that "should the Israeli government decide to accept the responsibility for the outbreak of armed conflict, it will have to pay the consequences in full." Also on June 2, *Pravda* published lengthy documents issued by a Conference of Representatives of Communists of the Arab countries, held some time in May 1967, one of them a "Statement on the Situation in the Arab Countries." * It was mainly notable for its obeisance to the Soviet Union ("the cradle of the Great October Socialist Revolution, the loyal friend of the Arab people, the bulwark of peace throughout the world") and an attack on "the reactionary regimes" of Saudi Arabia and Jordan ("they have entered into open collusion with the imperialists," etc.)—the latter in open collusion with the "liberated Arab states" by the time the statement was published—but it offered little in the way of concrete advice in the current crisis.[26] For most of June 3, the Israeli authorities still wavered. That nothing had yet been decided was evident from a press conference that afternoon by Minister of Defense Moshe Dayan. "I would think just now," he said, "it's too late and too early—too late to react right away on the blockading of the Strait of Eilat [Tiran] and too early to draw any conclusions on the diplomatic way of handling the matter." But a few hours later, the Israeli military persuaded the government that it was not "too late."

The crucial meeting of the Israeli cabinet and its chief military advisers started on the evening of June 3. In sub-

* One of the more piquant aspects of the Communist movements in Syria, Lebanon, Egypt, and Iraq is that they were largely organized in the nineteen-twenties by Palestinian Jews (Michael W. Suleiman, "The Lebanese Communist Party," *Middle Eastern Studies* [London], January 1967, pp. 136–37 and p. 155, note 10).

stance, the civilian political leaders were told that every day worked in favor of the Arabs and that further delay might be fatal to Israel's very existence. It was impossible for the political leadership to withstand this degree of peril. On the following day, June 4, Iraq officially joined the Egypt-Syria-Jordan military pact. It was the last straw.

When the war broke out on June 5, the worst Israeli apprehensions of United States immobility seemed justified by the statement later that day by the State Department's press officer, Robert McCloskey, that "our position is neutral in thought, word, and deed." This remark was an inadvertence never intended to represent United States policy. How it came about may well become a classical diplomatic nightmare. Leading officials were called to the State Department in the early hours of June 5. A message soon came in to the effect that five Egyptian airfields had been knocked out. Some junior officials discussed the news without remorse for Nasser's apparent distress. About 3 a.m., a senior official jokingly admonished them to remember that "we are neutral in thought, word, and deed." The same official later briefed Mr. McCloskey for the State Department's press conference that afternoon without using these words, and they did not appear in Mr. McCloskey's opening statement. But a reporter asked him whether he would reaffirm the United States' neutrality in the war. Mr. McCloskey replied that he would be glad to do so and, remembering the words he had heard about 3 a.m., proceeded to repeat them.

The White House press secretary, George Christian, soon made known that McCloskey's *faux pas* had not been cleared with the White House. Secretary of State Rusk tried to "clarify" the matter by saying that the "use of this word neutral—which is a great concept of international law—is not an expression of indifference, and indeed indifference is not permitted to us"—as if this needed to be said and somehow took the edge off being neutral. It would appear that the White House and the State Department found it so hard to recover from this incredible blunder because they were then confronted with a most awkward question: If the United States was not "neutral," what was it?

In fact, the United States was not neutral in word or thought. President Johnson's public statement of May 23, let alone his private statements to Foreign Minister Eban, committed the United States politically to the Israeli position on the opening of the Straits of Tiran. Indeed, the United States had been committed to this position for at least ten years. Nor did the United States propose to be neutral in deed if nothing else succeeded in swaying the Egyptians. The only question was what the United States would do about it if it came to deeds.

As far as the Arabs were concerned, nothing American spokesmen said could convince them that the United States was not fighting Israel's war. For months, Nasser had been telling his own people and the Arab world that Israel was merely a creation and puppet of "Western imperialism." On May 26, 1967, Nasser said: "What is Israel? Israel today is the United States. The United States is the chief defender of Israel. As for Britain, I consider it America's lackey." On May 29, he declared: "We are not facing Israel, but those behind it. We are facing the West, which created Israel." If Nasser actually believed this, it led him to think that he was safe so long as he did not have to worry about the United States or the West, thanks to the Soviet Union's good offices, or that the Israelis could not move without United States permission.* In fact, the Israelis felt that they had to fight alone and that there was very little the United States would or possibly could do to help them. The last thing the Israelis as

* This point was made by the "high Soviet official" in *Le Nouvel Observateur,* op. cit.: "He [Nasser] has partially been the victim of his own propaganda to the effect that the government of Tel Aviv is only a simple pawn of Washington, and that he could not see that this pawn could give proof of a certain amount of autonomy." But the high Soviet official neglected to mention that the government of Moscow was guilty of exactly the same kind of simple-minded propaganda which might have helped Nasser to deceive himself.

well as the Pentagon wanted was to have the United States intervene à la Vietnam and make Israel into a "second Vietnam."

After his defeat, Nasser concocted a story that United States
and British planes had been responsible for his military de-
bacle, especially for the virtual destruction of his air force
on the first day of the war. This invention has been generally
interpreted as a desperate effort to drag the Soviet Union into
the conflict. But there may have been different motivations
for the story at different times. According to the intercepted
telephone conversation between Nasser and Hussein, Hussein
seems to have been responsible for telling Nasser that United
States aircraft were attacking Jordanian airfields. Later Nasser
revealed: "On the night of June 7, King Hussein had a telephone conversation with me during which he told me that 400
planes were attacking the Jordanian front and that the radar
networks in Jordan had registered this huge number of planes.
From where did these planes come?" Hussein himself protested
against what he thought was United States air intervention
to the United States ambassador in Amman, Finley Burns,
who quickly obtained a denial from Washington. In his speech
of June 9, in which he first publicly charged that United States
and British aircraft had helped Israel, Nasser admitted that
he had underestimated Israel's strength. In the next breath,
however, he sought to account for the "stronger [Israeli] blow
than we had expected" by maintaining that "it was much
stronger than its resources allowed" and that Israel had operated an air force "three times its normal strength." At this
time, for some reason, Nasser accused British aircraft of having
actually raided Syrian and Egyptian positions but was content
to blame United States aircraft for merely having "recon-
noitered" some Egyptian positions. In his speech of July 23,
Nasser reduced the entire United States intervention to "two
planes carrying the American insignia" which had been seen
flying over the Egyptian lines on June 7, after the Egyptian
air force had already been largely destroyed. But President
Johnson had assured him that very night the planes had been

sent in connection with the unfortunate Israeli attack on the United States electronics ship, *Liberty,* which had been stationed off the shore of Egypt.

The Syrian response to the war was apparently even less responsible. A seemingly firsthand account of the Syrian reaction to the outbreak appeared in the militantly "anti-imperialist" organ *Jeune Afrique* (Paris), normally sympathetic to the Syrian regime. According to this version, an editor of the official French press agency in Damascus telephoned the official in charge of the Syrian Foreign Ministry's press section and suggested that he look at the French agency's teletype machine in his office. That is how the Syrian government learned about the outbreak of hostilities on the morning of June 5, 1967. The press official telephoned the news to the Secretary General, who transmitted it to Foreign Minister Ibrahim Makhous, who happened to be at the airport seeing off the Foreign Minister of Libya. Makhous jumped with joy.

The same day, at noon, Foreign Minister Makhous called a meeting of the leading officials of his ministry. He is reported to have said: "We are a few hours from victory, and it is necessary to act quickly. Prepare a message for dispatch to our missions abroad and to the embassies in Damascus, in which you will subtly intimate that we were the ones who provoked the war, that we are going to carry off the victory, and that the UAR [Egypt] only went along with the current. . . ." Unfortunately, the Syrian army had only two elite brigades capable of operating offensively, and they were needed to defend the regime against its internal enemies.[27]

In the confusion of the first forty-eight hours of the battle, there is reason to think that the Egyptians and Jordanians could not bring themselves to believe that Israel alone could have struck them such devastating blows from the air, and the slightest indications of United States or British planes on their radar screens or over their lines caused them to jump to the conclusion that Israel was being helped by Western powers, as in 1956. Hussein, in particular, entered the war because he was so sure of an Egyptian victory, just as Mussolini could not stay out of World War II because he was convinced that Hitler's Germany was bound to win. On the morning of June 5, Israel sent messages to Hussein through General Odd Bull and the United States and British ambassadors in Amman assuring him that Israel had no intention of doing Jordan any harm if the latter would stay out of the war.* One Western ambassador was present when the Jordanian king decided to reject Israel's overture. Hussein told him that he had to enter the conflict because Nasser had just assured him the Egyptian army was quickly advancing on Tel Aviv and the Egyptian air force could give him the necessary air cover to protect his forces from Israeli retaliation.† Hussein's vaunted "moderation" was far more a function of his circumstances than of his inclinations. As in 1956, when his pact with Egypt had helped to touch off the second Arab-Israeli war, his role in 1967 was maleficent, as long as he thought that he was sure to be on the winning side.

Thus, the indications are that the Arab charge of United States and British air attacks reflected more than a reckless, unconscionable plot to drag the Soviet Union into the war.‡ Though it also served as an incitement and an alibi, it was in its origins the fantasy of men who did not know what had hit them.

* This message read: "We shall not initiate any action whatsoever against Jordan. However, should Jordan open hostilities, we shall react with all our might and he [King Hussein] will have to bear the full responsibility for all the consequences."

† Hussein told *Der Spiegel* (Hamburg), September 4, 1967, p. 98, that he had received reports that "a large part of the Israeli Air Force had been destroyed in attacks over Egyptian territory."

‡ King Hussein later withdrew these charges publicly. In New York on June 30, 1967, he told the Associated Press: "So far as I am concerned, no American planes took part [in the air attacks against the Arabs], or any British planes either." Diplomatic sources in Washington subsequently reported that President Nasser also repudiated the same charges at the conference of Arab leaders held in Khartoum early in September 1967 (*The New York Times,* September 16, 1967).

More than the usual quota of misunderstanding and nonsense has been uttered and written on the relationship between the third Arab-Israeli war and the Vietnam war. Some of it was set off by a statement, which appeared as an advertisement in *The New York Times* of June 7, 1967, calling on President Johnson "to act now with courage and conviction, with nerve and firmness of intent, to maintain free passage in those waters [of the Gulf of

VIII

Aqaba]—and so to safeguard the integrity, security, and survival of Israel and its people, and to uphold our own honor." The statement had been written before the outbreak of the war but was published two days later. There was nothing in it to which the Johnson administration had not already pledged itself, and it was little more than an expression of sympathy for Israel's cause. It said nothing about unilateral United States intervention and, in fact, had been outrun by events because it was still primarily concerned with free passage in the Gulf of Aqaba. Some who signed it (including myself) were critics of United States policy in Vietnam; some were not. But it moved one of President Johnson's consultants in the White House to suggest that the statement should have been signed "Doves for War"—a suggestion evidently made half in jest but reflecting a point of view that was meant to be taken seriously —and was. William F. Buckley, Jr., wrote a column on the same statement, which he also tied up with the Vietnam war and which so bemused him that he gave it credit for having put "most of the critics of our policy in Vietnam on the run." On the other hand, some of those critics refused to sign the statement on the ground that it would be inconsistent with their position on Vietnam.

117

The issue this raised far transcended the statement which occasioned it. The implication was that Vietnam "doves" had to be dovish everywhere or, conversely, Israeli "hawks" had to be hawkish everywhere. Indeed, one did not have to do very much thinking any more. One merely had to take a position on Vietnam, dovish or hawkish, and every problem in every country in every region of the world automatically fell into place. On principle, one had to be all hawk or all dove in United States foreign policy, and there was only one touchstone to determine which one it was—Vietnam.

I cannot imagine a more dangerous and pernicious doctrine. The difference between Vietnam and Israel was not evidence of contradiction on the part of critics of the Vietnam war; the disposition to equate them was rather evidence of obsession on the part of that war's proponents. The cost of the Vietnam war has been high enough, but if it is to become the one, determining factor in United States foreign policy halfway across the globe, in totally different circumstances, the result must be war everywhere or paralysis everywhere. There is no inherent reason why one cannot criticize the abuse of power in Vietnam and the abdication of power elsewhere. Indeed, this very conjuncture has become the real problem of United States foreign policy: our overinvestment and overindulgence of power in Vietnam has made it in short supply for use elsewhere. As the Vietnam war drags on, a "second Vietnam" has become the nightmare of United States policy-makers and military planners. Indeed, the nightmare of the "second Vietnam" was a peculiar reflection of the fact that the first one had become somewhat nightmarish.

In any case, even if the principle of "consistency" is accepted, the Vietnam hawks cannot have it both ways. After all, they happen to be in control of our government, and nothing could be more ironic than the fact that they had to be urged on by Vietnam doves to be hawkish in Israel. Some hawks were, no doubt, hawkish on both issues, but the outstanding phenomenon in Washington was the dovishness on Israel of the Vietnam hawks, especially in the hawk headquarters, the Pentagon. If consistency were all that mattered, one would imagine that it was more important for those in power than for those not in power to be consistent. Yet, curiously, the grim joke was "doves for war," not "hawks for peace."

Actually, United States intervention on the Vietnam model in the Arab-Israeli struggle was never a realistic alternative, if only because Israel would not have permitted itself to become another South Vietnam. The defense of South Vietnam has caused such havoc in South Vietnam that the example has frightened our potential allies at least as much as it has deterred any present enemies. The crisis in the Middle East should again have shown how limited the application of Vietnam tactics may be in the rest of the world; it reinforces one of the main criticisms of our Vietnam policy—that it has claimed to influence events elsewhere far more than it can ever do. Yet, President Eisenhower undeniably assumed an obligation to Israel when his administration persuaded Israel to withdraw from Sharm el-Sheikh in 1957 in return for an explicit United States assurance that Israel would "have no cause to regret" giving up this hard-won vantage point. Subsequently, according to Prime Minister Eshkol, United States officials told Israel it did not need United States arms because it could rely on the United States Sixth Fleet.* Fortunately for both Israel and

---

* This point was discussed by Eshkol a month before the outbreak of the war. Asked what help he would expect from the United States and possibly Britain and France, he replied: "Surely, we expect such help —but we would rely primarily on our own army. I wouldn't want American mothers crying about the blood of their sons being shed here. But I would surely expect such help, especially if I take into consideration all the solemn promises that have been made to Israel. We get these promises when we ask the United States for arms and are told: 'Don't spend your money. We are here. The Sixth Fleet is here.' My reply to this advice is that the Sixth Fleet might not be available fast enough for one reason or another, so Israel must be strong on its own. This is why we spend so much money on arms proportionately to our population" (U.S. News & World Report, April 17, 1967, p. 76). Curiously, the same magazine later distorted a reference to its own interview. In its issue of June 19, 1967, it stated: "Israeli Premier Levi

the United States, the Israelis never took these assurances too seriously and always counted on having to do their own fighting. Nevertheless, there was a problem of some kind of United States commitment. I have been one of those who have criticized the Johnson administration for distorting and exaggerating our past commitments to South Vietnam. But this does not mean that we do not have any real commitments anywhere; here again the worst thing that could have happened to our foreign policy was to shape it, commitments and all, completely in the image of our Vietnam policy. The problem of living up to our commitments to Israel was primarily one for the Johnson administration, not for the critics of its Vietnam policy. It was a measure of the difficulty of that problem that neither the administration nor its critics created it and neither would have found an easy solution for it. But some of the men around the President would have been better advised to resist the temptation to use the Israeli crisis to discredit their Vietnam critics. Since Vietnam, our far-flung commitments have become an extremely difficult and embarrassing question; a review of those commitments has been long overdue; it will never be faced if all that matters, everywhere, is what one thinks about our policy in Vietnam.

Eshkol said in an interview April 11, 1967, that the U.S. Sixth Fleet would support Israel. Arab newspapers around the world headlined his statement. Despite denials of U.S. officials, Arab leaders assumed this was a firm commitment." As may be seen from the wording of the interview itself, Eshkol said *that United States officials had implied* the Sixth Fleet would support Israel, and he had been most dubious. In his speech of July 23, 1967, Nasser also played fast and loose with this alleged commitment: "Simultaneously, the Israelis secured pledges from the United States that if the Arabs attempted to enter Israel, the Sixth Fleet would prevent them. This was published by the press. Furthermore, the Israeli Premier Levi Eshkol expressed his gratitude to the American President for having told him that the Sixth Fleet was there to help Israel. When Eshkol told him that he might be busy on his ranch in Texas, he reassured him that the Sixth Fleet will protect them if the Arabs penetrated the borders of Israel. All this was published by the press."

The real problem of United States-Israeli relations was not what the United States could have done once the war started, but what the United States should have done before the war and what it should have done afterward. United States military equipment made up a very minor part of Israeli arms in the recent war because the United States had pursued a policy of restricting arms sales to Israel. The Israeli air force was French, most of its tanks were British, and its small arms were produced mainly at home. It was the influx of Soviet arms on the Arab side and the increasing difficulty with which Israel could match it in the West that encouraged Nasser and contributed to this war. If quantity of arms had been the decisive factor, the Israelis would have been in grave trouble.* The problem arose again after June 1967 with the renewed influx of Soviet arms to Egypt and Syria. In view of the Arab propaganda about Jewish influence in the United States, one wonders whether any non-Jewish state in Israel's position, faced with enemies armed by the Soviet Union and enjoying the full support of Soviet propaganda and diplomacy, would have found it so difficult to *buy* arms in this country. This is the real problem of the past and future, not "doves for war."

One issue was, in my view, blown up by Israel and to a lesser extent by the United States and other countries far beyond what it merited. It concerned the removal of the United Nations Emergency Force (UNEF) from Sharm el-Sheikh and the Egypt-Israel border.

The main charges against Secretary General U Thant's order

* An Israeli story, related by Terence Prittie of the *Guardian* (England), may cast some light on the recent Israeli victory. It seems that the Polish *émigré* leader, General Sikorsky, met a rabbi during the dark days of World War II and asked him how it might be won. "By one of two ways," the rabbi answered, "by a miracle or by a natural way." The general asked: "What would be the natural way?" Answered the rabbi: "To win it by a miracle." The general: "And what, then, would be the miracle?" The rabbi: "To win it in a natural way" (*Israel: Miracle in the Desert* [New York: Praeger, 1967], p. 10).

on the night of May 18 for the withdrawal of UNEF in response to the official Egyptian request a few hours earlier were made by Israeli Foreign Minister Abba Eban at the UN General Assembly on June 19. He complained that U Thant's action had been "disastrously swift" and that the Secretary General should have made a greater effort to play for time. "What is the use of a fire brigade," Eban asked dramatically, "which vanishes from the scene as soon as the first smoke and flames appear?"

This controversy will undoubtedly provide international legal authorities with seminar material for years to come. Ordinary mortals may enter this arena only at their own peril. The problem, nevertheless, cannot be entirely avoided because it raises the question of how the war came about and because the answer may help to determine the future usefulness of the United Nations.

Some things seem reasonably clear. UNEF was set up in November 1956 "to secure and supervise the cessation of hostilities." At that time, it was clearly understood that the force was only to be "of a temporary nature." But how temporary? The answer to this seemed to depend on who was to decide when it had fulfilled its mission. Dag Hammarskjöld, then Secretary General, foresaw that there could be heated dispute on this point. He recognized that UNEF could come into Egypt only with Egypt's consent. But what was necessary to get it out? He resisted the idea that the Egyptians alone could decide when to get rid of UNEF. In lengthy negotiations with the Egyptians, especially one seven-hour session with President Nasser on November 17, he arrived at a rather tricky formula, namely, that the force would leave whenever it had "completed its task." In an *aide-mémoire* of November 20, Egypt promised that it would be guided by "good faith" in relation to UNEF. But who was to decide when the "task" was completed? According to Hammarskjöld, in a private memorandum which he wrote about eight-and-a-half months later, he understood "good faith" to mean—and he thought the Egyptians had tacitly agreed—that the Egyptians and the General Assembly would have to agree on the completion of the task.*

But this private memorandum of August 5, 1957, was never entered into the official records or even files of the United Nations. Egypt never agreed publicly and, on at least one occasion, disagreed publicly with Hammarskjöld's version, holding that it alone was entitled to decide the fate of UNEF on its territory. It is interesting that the Egyptian Foreign Minister also resorted to the "fire brigade" analogy by saying on November 27, 1956, that "no one here or elsewhere can reasonably or fairly say that a fire brigade, after putting out a fire, would be entitled or expected to claim the right of deciding not to leave the house." At this time, it should be remembered, the "task" of the "fire brigade" was still defined as solely to "secure and supervise" the cessation of hostilities.

Subsequently, in February 1957, UNEF was given the additional functions of serving as a buffer and deterring infiltration at the Egypt-Israel armistice line and at Sharm el-Sheikh. It is questionable whether the "good faith" commitment of November 20, 1956, applied to the additional functions three months later. Moreover, Hammarskjöld's understanding, whatever it was, implied that there was a task of a "temporary nature" that could be completed in a relatively short time, certainly months rather than years. The buffer and deterrent

* Text in Appendix 3. That Hammarskjöld knew he was skating on thin legal ice is shown by his self-revelation that "I was guided by the consideration that Egypt constitutionally had an undisputed right to request the withdrawal of the troops, even if initial consent had been given, but that, on the other hand, it should be possible on the basis of my own stand as finally tacitly accepted, to force them into an agreement in which they limited their freedom of action as to withdrawal by making a request for withdrawal dependent upon the completion of the task—a question which, in the UN, obviously would have to be submitted to interpretation by the General Assembly." That Hammarskjöld could really "force" anything on the Egyptians with a "tacit" agreement is more than doubtful. At most, his private memorandum suggests a "gentlemen's agreement"—but one of the gentlemen died prematurely and of the other it might be said that when men decide to go to war they cease being gentlemen.

functions, which were added later, could go on indefinitely and did, indeed, go on for over ten years, a length of time never envisioned in 1957.

So much for the legalities. Here again, they really made very little difference. Whatever Thant might have done to stall in New York, Nasser was making the real decisions in Egypt. UNEF consisted of only 3400 men from seven countries, of whom no more than 1800 were available for policing a line of 295 miles along the Egypt-Israel border and the Gaza strip. All of 32 men were stationed at Sharm el-Sheikh, the main neuralgic point. India and Yugoslavia, which contributed over half the total force, informed the Secretary General that they were withdrawing their men whatever he decided to do.* At most, UNEF was a purely symbolic presence. It had no authority to "enforce" the peace—in other words to fight, except as a last resort in self-defense. It was totally dependent on Egyptian good will for its logistical support. Israel had from the first refused to permit it to be stationed on the Israeli side of the border and, therefore, it could not be moved from the Egyptian side.

By the night of May 18, U Thant did not have to "withdraw" the force; he could merely recognize that it had already been, for all practical purposes, withdrawn. The Egyptian troops had simply shunted the UNEF units aside. As the Secretary General later reported: "Early on 18 May the UNEF sentries proceeding to man the normal observation post at El Sabha in Sinai were prevented from entering the post and from remaining in the area by United Arab Republic soldiers. The sentries were then forced to withdraw. They did not resist

* On May 17, the Egyptian Foreign Minister had called in the ambassadors of the seven nations which contributed units to UNEF and informed them that Egypt wanted UNEF out immediately. The Yugoslav and Indian ambassadors agreed on the spot. When Secretary General Thant met with representatives of the seven countries at 4 p.m. on May 17 (New York time), he was informed of the Yugoslav and Indian decisions; the other five said that they had not yet received instructions.

by use of force since they had no mandate to do so." Egyptian officers gave the Yugoslav detachment at Sharm el-Sheikh fifteen minutes to reply to a demand for an Egyptian takeover of the UNEF camp. As the Secretary General's report put it, "the effectiveness of UNEF in the light of the movement of United Arab Republic troops up to the line and into Sharm el-Sheikh, had already vanished before the request for withdrawal was received."

What, then, could stalling tactics at the UN by the Secretary General have achieved? They could possibly have put Egypt temporarily on the defensive in purely legalistic terms, assuming that the legalities were not on their side. They could not have prevented the Egyptian takeover of UNEF posts in the Sinai or at Sharm el-Sheikh. This takeover was accomplished by overwhelming superior forces on the spot, not by legalistic maneuvering in New York. Mr. Thant might have ordered resistance to the Egyptian diplomatic delegation at the United Nations, but he could not order resistance to the Egyptian troops, tanks, and guns in the desert. The reports from the field on May 18 were such that the truly pressing, realistic problem was how to prevent bloody incidents between the virtually defenseless UNEF and the onrushing Egyptian forces and even to forestall the unseemly disintegration of the UNEF units. It should also be remembered that Mr. Thant held out for two days after he received the first Egyptian notification on May 16, and that war did not break out immediately after the order for withdrawal on May 18. Eighteen days intervened between May 18 and June 5, and it would have mattered very little in that period with respect to the efforts to prevent the war whether UNEF had still occupied their observation posts or not. UNEF could not get out overnight anyway; the first units did not leave until May 29.

Foreign Minister Eban's analogy between UNEF and a "fire brigade" may have been effective oratorically, but it unwittingly betrayed what was wrong with his reasoning. In no sense was

UNEF comparable to a fire brigade; or it was, at most, a "symbolic" one. The "smoke and flames" which this "fire brigade" was supposed to fight were made up of overwhelmingly superior Egyptian armed forces. UNEF had the alternative of "vanishing" or fighting fire with fire, of resisting physically. In practice, UNEF was so outnumbered and outclassed that it mattered little whether it stayed or left, except perhaps to establish a legal point. The melancholy fact is that the basis for UNEF's operation throughout its existence was, as the Secretary General's report of June 27 put it, "essentially fragile." It was, in a sense, a "fire brigade" as long as there was no fire; it was a "fire brigade" merely to signal by its forced withdrawal that a fire was coming; but it was not a "fire brigade" which the international community had set up with the authority, the numbers, and the equipment to put out a real fire.* In fact, UNEF was not ever, in any meaningful sense, a "Force." Its name was misleading and promised far more forceful action than it could deliver.

Whose fault was that? Surely not that of UNEF or the Secretary General or the "United Nations." It is time to put a stop to the sanctimonious swindle the individual states which make up the United Nations have been perpetrating. The founders of the United Nations set it up in such a way that it has only the collective authority and force that its members, especially the great powers, and more particularly only two of

---

* Eban's harsh judgment of Thant's action was later qualified by Israeli Ambassador to the United Nations, Gideon Rafael, who gave an interview to the newspaper *Ma'ariv* of August 4, 1967, in which the following exchange took place:

QUESTION: Do you think that the Secretary General of the United Nations was mistaken in his handling of the UNEF problem and its withdrawal from Egyptian soil?

ANSWER: I have already said and I repeat: The Secretary General tried to control the situation and failed but he cannot be blamed for it. I oppose the tendency which tries to put the blame for what took place in the Middle East on the Secretary General. U Thant is not responsible for crisis in the Middle East. The ones to blame are Nasser and the Soviets who have incited him to do it.

them, the United States and the Soviet Union, permit it to have. The great-power veto in the Security Council prevents even a two-thirds majority in that body from getting anything through. The Security Council was immobilized by the Soviet Union between May 18 and June 5 despite the most urgent pleas by the Secretary General. But when his worst fears materialized, it was said that the United Nations or the Secretary General had "failed." That there was failure—tragic, ominous, and perhaps unnecessary failure—there can be no doubt. That the responsibility for the failure must be fixed on the individual states, there can also be no doubt. The United Nations does not live a life of its own; it does only what they permit or empower it to do; if it fails, they have directed and doomed it to fail. The worst of it is that the United Nations has become an alibi, a stratagem, a scapegoat, for deflecting attention from where the real evil hides—in the sovereign states. These states are not equally culpable in all cases, but where there may be guilt, it should at least be looked for in the right place—among them.

Finally, the campaign against U Thant was as tactically unsound as it was legally and realistically unjustified. Some writers even used the phrase, "U Thant's war." This and other grotesqueries only had the effect of letting off the real culprits too easily. It may be called "Nasser's war" or perhaps "Nasser's and Kosygin's war," but to call it "U Thant's war" makes it appear as if U Thant had the power to prevent, let alone to start it. To some extent, the campaign against U Thant was based on a misapprehension of what UNEF could do in the circumstances of May 18, but some of those in high places who took part in the campaign should have known better. Instead of putting the blame squarely where it belonged, on the Egyptian leaders who ordered their troops to take over UNEF's posts in the hot desert before U Thant even ordered the force's official withdrawal, and on those powers, including the Soviet Union, India, Yugoslavia, and others, which took Egypt's side in the United Nations, the anti-Thant camarilla pursued a vendetta of long standing, some of it based on his repugnance for the Vietnam war. It would be absurd to go to the opposite extreme and suggest that the Secretary General or the United Nations covered themselves with glory. They were reduced to impotence, and the cause of world community has suffered immeasurably. But they were as much victims of the real ringleaders and wirepullers of this war as the miserable *fellaheen* in uniform whose bodies rotted in the burning sands.

The United Nations is subject to periodic, built-in seizures of paralysis because it is primarily a place where the member-states pursue their individual self-interest. In order for the peacemaking or peacekeeping function to work reasonably well, one of two conditions is necessary: either the self-interest of the great powers must happen to coincide or the issue must happen to bypass their self-interest. The first condition has usually been the *sine qua non* of United Nations usefulness, but the second has become increasingly rare of fulfillment. The more obvious reason for the latter state of affairs is the growing competition between the United States and the Soviet Union for the support—or to deny the other the support—of the "underdeveloped" part of the world and particularly of the nations founded since World War II. The new nationalism of the new nations is sometimes about all that holds them together, and the only virtue they have to sell. As a result, no nationalism is as obsessive and single-minded as the latest one. The great powers which seek to use them must do so through playing on a species of primitive self-interest that is far more difficult to control than that of the old-style client states or the new variety of satellite states. The Soviet Union, for example, wooed Nasser's Egypt more by serving Egypt's nationalistic interests than by getting Egypt to serve its own. But Egypt is neither an old-fashioned client state nor a newfangled satellite. It represents rather a new-style "give-me" nationalism; Gamal Abdel Nasser has been one of the world's great practitioners of the new golden rule that it is better—for the great powers—to give than to receive. The United States has, of course, practiced handout diplomacy for the longest time and on the most lavish scale. It is, however, one of the less-publicized aspects of the "affluent society" which the Soviet Union has of late attempted to crash.

But there is another, related reason why the great powers have exacerbated the nationalistic ambitions of the newer and smaller states. For a number of years, students of war have concerned themselves with the problem of small or big, local or general, guerrilla or conventional, nuclear or nonnuclear conflicts. This preoccupation was partially dictated by the obviously catastrophic character of the big, general, conventional, nuclear war. In order to avoid destroying themselves as well as their enemies, the great powers began to take an inordinate interest in small, local, irregular, and nonnuclear conflicts. In theory, the latter seemed infinitely preferable because they could be "controlled," and a great deal of thought and ingenuity have been expended on the techniques and mechanisms for controlling them. But, increasingly, even this type of war has become too dangerous because of the reluctance of a great power to take a limited setback if it can give itself a second chance by escalating the struggle. This has typically happened to the United States in Vietnam. A new type of war, therefore, has been creeping up on us that is relatively small, local, nonnuclear but hopefully more controllable. It may be called the "war by proxy."

Wars by proxy are not new, and no one power has had a monopoly of them. The United States tried to wage a war by proxy in Cuba in April 1961 with a pitifully small Cuban exile force. Before 1966, when the United States began to take over the main fighting from the South Vietnamese, the Vietnam war was largely a war by proxy, especially in the United States view which then conceived of the real antagonists as being the Israeli war was pre-eminently the Soviet Union's version of a war by proxy. The great Soviet Union was above regarding United States and Communist China. But the third Arab-

Israel as worthy of its unfriendly attention. To justify the expenditure of three billion dollars or more of economic and military assistance to the Arab states, a more deserving foe was needed. For this reason, Soviet propaganda and diplomacy were so insistent that Israel was merely an instrument of the "imperialist powers" or that they were behind Israel, so that by striking at Israel, the Arab states backed by the Soviet Union were really striking at "world imperialism." In his speech to the General Assembly on June 19, Premier Kosygin went out of his way to emphasize that "the events that took place recently in the Middle East in connection with the armed conflict between Israel and the Arab states should be considered precisely in the context of the general international situation." Later he helpfully provided the context by charging that the United States and Great Britain were "promoting" Israeli "aggression"—one of the more polite formulas of Soviet displeasure.

The Soviets were playing for great stakes. They aimed at nothing less than the virtual elimination of Western interests and influence from the Middle East. They hoped to achieve the outflanking of the NATO alliance, the denial of Arab oil to the West, and the total dependence of the Arab world on Soviet-controlled aid and arms. But the war-by-proxy strategy implied that the Soviets ruled out using their own armed forces or risking a third world war. They preferred to work through those Arab states which, for their own ends, wanted to eliminate the Western powers and, to this extent, were working for the Soviets by working for themselves. The Soviets would have liked to see the entire Arab world dominated by Nasser's Egypt and the latter dependent on them. This would have been brought closer to accomplishment if Egypt could have obtained a major victory by closing the Straits of Tiran to Israel —not necessarily by war—or if the Arab-Israeli war had resulted in some form of stalemate or at least of protracted conflict that would have given the Soviets the possibility of acting as arbiters in the struggle or somehow dragging the United States into a "second Vietnam."

In a sense, then, Israel was tangential to the main Soviet objective, which rather required the hegemony of the pro-Soviet Arab powers, chiefly Egypt and Syria, over neighboring Arab countries. Inasmuch as Syria was relatively weak, the main Soviet reliance had to be on Egypt, which contained a population twice the size of those of Jordan, Syria, and Iraq combined. Egypt had first tried to dominate the Arab East without taking on Israel—or rather, before taking on Israel. But the long-drawn-out war in Yemen had demonstrated that Egypt was incapable of imposing its will even on a single recalcitrant Arab power. When Nasser decided to turn on Israel, he reversed the order of Egyptian priorities in an effort to recoup his losses elsewhere at one blow. A victory over Israel would undoubtedly have enabled him to claim a prize overshadowing his domestic and pan-Arabic setbacks.

Thus, Israel became the linchpin in both the larger Soviet and Egyptian plans. Yet Israel impinged on Arab interests directly, on Soviet interests indirectly. What happened to Israel was of far less immediate importance to the Soviets than to the Arabs. What happened to the Western powers in the Middle East was of far greater immediate importance to the Soviets than to the Arabs. These disparities may help to explain why Soviet policy in May 1967 was so ambivalent and even tortuous. For about two-thirds of the month, Soviet propaganda seemed to be bent on urging the Arabs to mobilize against Israel. But after Nasser's closure of the Straits of Tiran on May 22, without as far as we know obtaining the Soviets' approval in advance, a note of caution crept into the Soviet press, usually by way of cautioning everyone else to be cautious. Then, on May 27, came the peculiar 3:30 a.m. visit by the Soviet ambassador to President Nasser, advising him not to strike the first blow, a move made following a message suggesting some such admonition by President Johnson to Premier Kosygin. After blaming the United States for all the trouble, the Soviets seemed to be acting in conjunction with the United States to prevent it from getting any worse. When the Arabs, for whatever reason, decided to spread the story that they had been defeated by British and American rather than by Israeli planes, Soviet authorities told their hard-pressed Arab protégés that they knew better and that they did not relish the implication that Soviet planes were bound to bomb Israel as British and American planes had allegedly bombed Egypt and Jordan. It is quite clear that Soviet officials told Arab leaders in no uncertain terms that, in effect, they did not approve of alibis which risked setting off World War III.

The Soviets were willing to sacrifice Israel to Arab ambitions. But they were unwilling to assume full responsibility for the Arab forces which they had set in motion, as evidenced by their failure to approve or disapprove of the closure of the Straits of Tiran, and they were even more unwilling to give the United States any provocation or pretext for intervention, as evidenced by their advice to Nasser against firing the first shot. As Nasser understood this advice, and as he interpreted it publicly, it meant that he had to provoke Israel into firing the first shot. The only thing wrong with this stratagem was that it fatally miscalculated the relationship of forces of Israel and its Arab antagonists. The Soviets and Arabs counted men and machines, in which the Arabs enjoyed a seemingly decisive advantage, and not men and machines in combat preparedness and effectiveness, a rather different equation.

In the end, the Egyptian strategy failed for at least two reasons. One was that the closure of the Straits of Tiran to Israel, which initiated the war crisis, was presented in a form most calculated to bring on a shooting war. The Egyptians themselves admitted this by saying that the closure made war inevitable. As long as Nasser refused to budge on this point, he was aiming at a victory without war, and even he did not believe in this eventuality. If it was inevitable, as the Egyptians professed to believe, the question that will long haunt this war is why the Egyptians were not better prepared for it. The answer given by both Nasser and Heikal is relatively simple— the old, old story of miscalculation. For whatever reason, the Egyptians thought that it was in their interest to let Israel strike the first blow because they expected to be able to withstand it and then administer a crushing second blow of their own. As Muhammad Hassanein Heikal explained later, the Egyptian command did not believe that the Israeli air force was capable of repeating the kind of attack that the British had carried out from Cyprus in 1956.[1] The Egyptians were caught off guard on June 5, 1967, primarily because they had disastrously miscalculated the balance of forces and could not bring themselves to recognize that their margin of safety was so slim. They were defeated not because the Israelis had shockingly struck the first blow, since they had expected it, but because they were incapable of striking a second blow, which they had deliberately set up.

The Soviet miscalculation was all the more curious on the part of self-styled Marxists, one of whose key concepts has always been the "relationship of forces." In a strictly Marxist sense, the military relationship could have been based only on modes of production, technological progress, and social organization. That Israel should have been "Western" in these respects is something that a Marxist could hardly hold against it, for the "West," in Marxist terms, has represented the more advanced economic and political order. Arab anti-Westernism has signified the struggle of nationalism against imperialism; it has also signified the reluctance of backward societies to modernize themselves—a modernization which in many respects, crucial for Marxists, can only be a form of Westernization. The "West," in this sense, is not a geographical expression but rather a stage of economic, social, and political progress. Israel owed its victory in 1967 to its "Western orientation" in technology and education far more than in diplomacy or trade. Indeed, the Western powers did so poorly in 1956 and were at such a loss in 1967 that it is hard to see how Israel could have survived if it had been as dependent on them as Communist and Arab propaganda likes to maintain. It is understandable that traditional Arab nationalists should object to Israel as an "outpost of the West" in the Arab East. But "Marxists" might be expected to take a somewhat less simplistic view of Israel and the West, good and bad.

Instead of forcing the third Arab-Israeli war into the Procrustean bed of the "cold war" between the great powers, as if Egypt were merely a Soviet tool and Israel an American agent, it might be more useful to reflect on the limits of power of the great powers which this war demonstrated. In effect, as far as direct physical intervention was concerned, the two greatest powers canceled each other out. Both had great stakes in the Arab-Israeli conflict, but the nearer it came, the less they could do about it. The so-called bipolarity of the post-World War II world need not mean that one or the other, or both together, have the power of decision; it may, in some circumstances, mean that neither has the power of decision. In such cases, they may try to wage a war by proxy, but they cannot be sure that the "proxy" will not, at some stage, make decisions for them or without them.

If the two greatest powers could not decisively influence the outbreak and course of this war, Great Britain and France were even less capable of doing so. The last time Britain had attempted to play an independent role in the Middle East had been in 1956, and it had ended ignominiously. This time Prime Minister Harold Wilson recognized that Britain could do nothing without the United States and contented himself with verbal initiatives, not without the encouragement of Washington, hungry for allies to assume part of the responsibility. The three-phase plan—United Nations mediation, declaration of the maritime powers, and in the final extremity, a naval escort through the Straits of Tiran—was even dubbed "British," though it was at least as much American, and the final decision to implement it was clearly understood to rest in the White House. In the five sessions of the Security Council on

May 24 (morning and afternoon), 29, 30, and June 3, the British representative spoke only at the second and third. By the beginning of June, American and Israeli diplomats suspected that traditional pro-Arab influences had made themselves felt in London and that the Foreign Secretary, George Brown, had not been immune to them. The nearer the war came, the less the British leaders had to say, and without the United States, they could do even less.

The French case illustrated the plight of secondary powers in this crisis in another way. French public opinion was overwhelmingly pro-Israel, so much so that the minority were represented by a somewhat anomalous, *ad hoc,* and, of course, informal united front of the French Communist Party and President Charles de Gaulle. The former merely followed in the wake of Soviet foreign policy, as was its wont, but the latter was probably motivated by anti-American more than by pro-Soviet sentiments. Yet, as long as he was determined to demonstrate his independence from Washington, he was unable to demonstrate his independence from Moscow. Thus, on May 24, when Soviet Ambassador Fedorenko was pooh-poohing the seriousness of the Middle East situation in order to sidetrack the United Nations, he was abetted by the French spokesman, Roger Seydoux, who admitted that he had also tried to prevent the Security Council from meeting.[2] In Paris, General de Gaulle could think of nothing more original or positive than a warning to the Israelis not to fire the first shot and a call for a four-power conference of the United States, USSR, Britain, and France to come to some agreement among themselves. The Soviets rudely brushed off the latter proposal, leaving General de Gaulle with nothing more to contribute. When the Security Council debated the Secretary General's report of May 29, Ambassador Seydoux had nothing to say the first two days, May 29 and May 30, and finally spoke up on June 3 to advise the Council that the best it could do was to appeal to all parties in the dispute to refrain from resorting to force, by which time it was almost too late.[3] General de Gaulle tried to balance so precariously between the Arabs and Israelis, the Americans and the Russians, that even well-chosen words seemed on this occasion to fail him, and for once he appeared to be at a loss for either ideas or actions to uphold French prestige or dignity.

In any event, this war by proxy showed how difficult and treacherous the new genre is. The nationalistic interests of both Israel and Egypt made it impossible for any of the great powers to "control" them. The Egyptians did not ask the Soviet Union for permission to reoccupy Sharm el-Sheikh and close the Gulf of Aqaba to Israel, and the Israelis did not ask the United States for permission to fight in order to reopen it. The war by proxy may be the safest species of small, local conflicts, but it is hardly safe. By not implicating the armed forces of a great power directly, it does enable that power to extricate itself more gracefully than would otherwise be possible. But the war by proxy still remains the most dangerous game of armed conflict the great powers are playing today.

APPENDIX 1

Aide-mémoire *Handed to Israeli Ambassador*
Abba Eban by Secretary of State John Foster Dulles
FEBRUARY 11, 1957

The United Nations General Assembly has sought specifically, vigorously, and almost unanimously, the prompt withdrawal from Egypt of the armed forces of Britain, France and Israel. Britain and France have complied unconditionally. The forces of Israel have been withdrawn to a considerable extent but still hold Egyptian territory at Sharm el-Sheikh at the entrance to the Gulf of Aqaba. They also occupy the Gaza strip which is territory specified by the Armistice arrangements to be occupied by Egypt.

We understand that it is the position of Israel that (1) it will evacuate its military forces from the Gaza strip provided Israel retains the civil administration and police in some relationship to the United Nations; and (2) it will withdraw from Sharm el-Sheikh if continued freedom of passage through the Straits is assured.

With respect to (1) the Gaza strip—it is the view of the United States that the United Nations General Assembly has no authority to require of either Egypt or Israel a substantial modification of the Armistice Agreement, which, as noted, now gives Egypt the right and responsibility of occupation. Accordingly, we believe that Israeli withdrawal from Gaza should be prompt and unconditional, leaving the future of the Gaza strip to be worked out through the efforts and good offices of the United Nations.

We recognize that the area has been a source of armed infiltration and reprisals back and forth contrary to the Armistice Agreement and is a source of great potential danger because of the presence there of so large a number of Arab refugees—about 200,000. Accordingly, we believe that the United Nations General Assembly and the Secretary General should seek that the United Nations Emergency Force, in the exercise of its mission, move into this area and be on the boundary between Israel and the Gaza strip.

The United States will use its best efforts to help to assure this result, which we believe is contemplated by the Second Resolution of February 2, 1957.

With respect to (2) the Gulf of Aqaba and access thereto —the United States believes that the Gulf comprehends international waters and that no nation has the right to prevent free and innocent passage in the Gulf and through the Straits giving access thereto. We have in mind not only commercial usage, but the passage of pilgrims on religious missions, which should be fully respected.

The United States recalls that on January 28, 1950, the Egyptian Ministry of Foreign Affairs informed the United States that the Egyptian occupation of the two islands of Tiran and Senafir at the entrance of the Gulf of Aqaba was only to protect the islands themselves against possible damage or violation and that "this occupation being in no way conceived in a spirit of obstructing in any way innocent passage through the stretch of water separating these two islands from the Egyptian coast of Sinai, it follows that this passage, the only practicable one, will remain free as in the past, in conformity with international practice and recognized principles of the law of nations."

In the absence of some overriding decision to the contrary, as by the International Court of Justice, the United States, on behalf of vessels of United States registry, is prepared to exercise the right of free and innocent passage and to join with others to secure general recognition of this right.

It is of course clear that the enjoyment of a right of free and innocent passage by Israel would depend upon its prior withdrawal in accordance with the United Nations Resolutions. The United States has no reason to assume that any littoral state would under these circumstances obstruct the right of free and innocent passage.

The United States believes that the United Nations General Assembly and the Secretary General should, as a precautionary measure, seek that the United Nations Emergency Force move into the Straits area as the Israeli forces are withdrawn. This again we believe to be within the contemplation of the Second Resolution of February 2, 1957.

(3) The United States observes that the recent resolutions of the United Nations General Assembly call not only for the prompt and unconditional withdrawal of Israel behind the Armistice lines but call for other measures.

We believe, however, that the United Nations has properly established an order of events and an order of urgency and that the first requirement is that forces of invasion and occupation should withdraw.

The United States is prepared publicly to declare that it will use its influence, in concert with other United Nations members, to the end that, following Israel's withdrawal, these other measures will be implemented.

We believe that our views and purposes in this respect are shared by many other nations and that a tranquil future for Israel is best assured by reliance upon that fact, rather than by an occupation in defiance of the overwhelming judgment of the world community.

APPENDIX 2

Letter from President Dwight D. Eisenhower
to Prime Minister David Ben Gurion
MARCH 2, 1957

MY DEAR MR. PRIME MINISTER: I was deeply gratified at the decision of your Government to withdraw promptly and fully behind the Armistice lines as set out by your Foreign Minister in her address of yesterday to the General Assembly. I venture to express the hope that the carrying out of these withdrawals will go forward with the utmost speed.

I know that this decision was not an easy one. I believe, however, that Israel will have no cause to regret having thus conformed to the strong sentiment of the world community as expressed in the various United Nations Resolutions relating to withdrawal.

It has always been the view of this Government that after the withdrawal there should be a united effort by all of the nations to bring about conditions in the area more stable, more tranquil, and more conducive to the general welfare than those which existed heretofore. Already the United Nations General Assembly has adopted Resolutions which presage such a better future. Hopes and expectations based thereon were voiced by your Foreign Minister and others. I believe that it is reasonable to entertain such hopes and expectations and I want you to know that the United States, as a friend of all the countries of the area and as a loyal member of the United Nations, will seek that such hopes prove not to be vain.

I am, my dear Mr. Prime Minister,
Sincerely,

DWIGHT D. EISENHOWER

Private Memorandum of Secretary General
Dag Hammarskjöld
AUGUST 5, 1957

As the decision on the UNEF [United Nations Emergency Force] was taken under Chapter VI [of the United Nations Charter] it was obvious from the beginning that the resolution did in no way limit the sovereignty of the host state. This was clear both from the resolution of the General Assembly and from the second and final report on the emergency force. Thus, neither the General Assembly nor the Secretary-General, acting for the General Assembly, created any right for Egypt, or gave any right to Egypt, in accepting consent as a condition for the presence and functioning of the UNEF on Egyptian territory. Egypt had the right, and the only problem was whether that right in this context should and could in some way be limited.

My starting point in the consideration of this last-mentioned problem—the limitation of Egypt's sovereign right in the interest of political balance and stability in the UNEF operation —was the fact that Egypt had spontaneously endorsed the General Assembly resolution of 5 November [creating the force] and by endorsing that resolution had consented to the presence of the UNEF for certain tasks. They could thus not ask the UNEF to withdraw before the completion of the tasks without running up against their own acceptance of the resolution on the force and its tasks.

The question arose in relation to Egypt first in a cable received 9 November from Burns* covering an interview the

* Lt. Gen. E. L. M. Burns, Chief of Staff of the United Nations Truce Supervision Organization. In November 1956, he was appointed commander of the United Nations Emergency Force.

same day with Fawzi.* In that interview Egypt had requested clarification of the question how long it was contemplated that the force would stay in the demarcation line area. To this I replied the same day: "A definite reply is at present impossible, but the emergency character of the force links it to the immediate crisis envisaged in the resolution of 2 November [calling for truce] and its liquidation. In case of different views as to when the crisis does not any longer warrant the presence of the troops, the matter will have to be negotiated with the parties." In a further cable to Burns the same day I said, however, also that "as the United Nations force would come with Egypt's consent, they cannot stay nor operate unless Egypt continues to consent."

On 10 November Ambassador Loutfi† under instruction, asked me "whether it was recognized that an agreement is necessary for their [UNEF's] remaining in the canal area" once their task in the area had been completed. I replied that it was my view that such an agreement would then be necessary.

On 11 November Ambassador Loutfi saw me again. He then said that it must be agreed that when the Egyptian consent is no more valid, the UN force should withdraw. To this I replied that I did not find that a withdrawal of consent could be made before the tasks which had justified the entry, had been completed; if, as might happen, different views on the degree of completion of the tasks prescribed proved to exist, the matter should be negotiated.

The view expressed by Loutfi was later embodied in an *aide-mémoire,* dated the same day, where it was said: "The Egyptian Government takes note of the following: A. It being agreed that consent of Egypt is indispensable for entry and presence of the UN forces in any part of its territory, if such consent no longer persists, these forces shall withdraw."

I replied to this in a memo dated 12 November in which I said: "I have received your *aide-mémoire* setting out the under-

* Mahmud Fawzi, Egyptian Foreign Minister.
† Omar Loutfi, then chief Egyptian delegate at the United Nations.

standing on the basis of which the Egyptian Government accepts my announcing today that agreement on the arrival in Egypt of the United Nations force has been reached. I wish to put on record my interpretation of two of these points." Regarding the point quoted above in the Egyptian *aide-mémoire,* I then continued: "I want to put on record that the conditions which motivate the consent to entry and presence, are the very conditions to which the tasks established for the force in the General Assembly resolution [requesting preparations for establishment of the force], 4 November, are directed. Therefore, I assume it to be recognized that as long as the task, thus prescribed, is not completed, the reasons for the consent of the government remain valid, and that a withdrawal of this consent before completion of the task would run counter to the acceptance by Egypt of the decision of the General Assembly. I read the statement quoted in the light of these considerations. If a difference should develop, whether or not the reasons for the arrangement are still valid, the matter should be brought up for negotiation with the United Nations."

This explanation of mine was sent to the Egyptian mission after my telephone conversation in the morning of the 12th with Dr. Fawzi where we agreed on publication of our agreement on the entry of the UNEF into Egypt. In view of the previous exchanges, I had no reason to believe that my statement would introduce any new difficulty. I also counted on the fact that Egypt probably by then was so committed as to be rather anxious not to reopen the discussion. However, I recognized to myself that there was an element of gambling involved which I felt I simply had to take in view of the danger that further delays might cause Egypt to change its mind, accept volunteers and throw our approaches overboard.

However, the next morning, 13 November, I received a message from Dr. Fawzi to the effect that the Government of Egypt could not subscribe to my interpretation of the question of consent and withdrawal, as set out on 12 November, and therefore, in the light of my communication of that date, "felt impelled to consider that the announced agreements should remain inoperative until all misunderstandings were cleared up." The Government reiterated in this context its view that if its consent no longer persisted, the UNEF should withdraw.

I replied to this communication—which caused a further delay of the transportation of troops to Egypt by at least twenty-four hours—in a cable sent immediately on receipt of the communication. In drafting my reply I had a feeling that it now was a must to get the troops in and that I would be in a position to find a formula, saving the face of Egypt while protecting the UN stand, once I would discuss the matter personally with President Nasser.

In the official reply 13 November I said that my previous statements had put forward my personal opinion that "the reasons" for consent remained valid as long as the task was not completed. I also said that for that reason a withdrawal of consent leading to the withdrawal of the force before the task was completed (as previously stated) in my view, "although within the rights of the Egyptian Government would go against its acceptance of the basic resolution of the General Assembly." I continued by saying that my reference to negotiation was intended to indicate only that the question of withdrawal should be a matter of discussion to the extent that different views were held as to whether the task of the General Assembly was fulfilled or not. I referred in this respect to my stand as explained already in my message of 9 November, as quoted above.

I commented upon the official reply in a special personal message to Fawzi, sent at the same time, where I said that we "both had to reserve our freedom of action, but that, all the same, we could go ahead, hoping that a controversial situation would not arise." "If arrangements would break down on this issue" (withdrawal only on completion of the tasks), "I could not avoid going to the General Assembly" (with the conflict which had developed between us on this question of principle) "putting it to their judgment to decide what could or could not be accepted as an understanding. This situation would be a most embarrassing one for all but I would fear the political repercussions, as obviously very few would find it reasonable that recognition of your freedom of action should mean that you, after having permitted the force to come, might ask it to withdraw at a time when the very reasons which had previously prompted you to accept were still obviously valid." I ended by saying that I trusted that Fawzi on the basis of this personal message could help me by "putting the stand I had to take on my own rights, in the right perspective." The letter to Fawzi thus made it clear that if the Government did not accept my stand on withdrawal as a precondition for further steps, the matter would be raised in the Assembly.

On the basis of these two final communications from me, Egypt gave green lights for the arrival of the troops, thus, in fact, accepting my stand and letting it supersede their own communication 13 November.

In my effort to follow up the situation, which prevailed after the exchange in which different stands had been maintained by Egypt and by me, I was guided by the consideration that Egypt constitutionally had an undisputed right to request the withdrawal of the troops, even if initial consent had been given, but that, on the other hand, it should be possible on the basis of my own stand as finally tacitly accepted, to force them into an agreement in which they limited their freedom of action as to withdrawal by making a request for withdrawal dependent upon the completion of the task—a question which, in the UN, obviously would have to be submitted to interpretation by the General Assembly.

The most desirable thing, of course, would have been to tie Egypt by an agreement in which they declared, that withdrawal should take place only if so decided by the General Assembly. But in this naked form, however, the problem could never have been settled. I felt that the same was true of an agreement to the effect that withdrawal should take place upon "agreement on withdrawal" between the UN and the Egyptian Government. However, I found it worthwhile to try a line, very close to the second one, according to which Egypt would declare to the United Nations that it would exert all its sovereign rights with regard to the troops on the basis of a good faith interpretation of the tasks of the force. The United Nations should make a reciprocal commitment to maintain the force as long as the task was not completed. If such a dual statement was introduced in an agreement between the parties, it would be obvious that the procedure in case of a request from Egypt for the withdrawal of UNEF would be as follows. The matter would at once be brought before the General Assembly. If the General Assembly found that the task was completed, everything would be all right. If they found that the task was not completed and Egypt, all the same, maintained its stand and enforced the withdrawal, Egypt would break the agreement with the United Nations. Of course Egypt's freedom of action could under no circumstances be limited but by some kind of agreement. The device I used meant only that instead of limiting their rights by a basic understanding requesting an agreement *directly concerning withdrawal,* we created an obligation to reach agreement on the fact that the tasks were completed, and, thus, *the conditions for a withdrawal established.*

I elaborated a draft text for an agreement along the lines I had in mind during the night between 15 and 16 November in Capodichino [Italy]. I showed the text to Fawzi at our first talk on 16 November and I discussed practically only this issue with Nasser for seven hours in the evening and night of 17 November. Nasser, in this final discussion, where the text I had proposed was approved with some amendments, showed that he very fully understood that, by limiting their freedom of action in the way I proposed, they would take a very serious step, as it would mean that the question of the extent of the task would become decisive for the relations between Egypt and the United Nations and would determine Egypt's political freedom of action. He felt, not without justification, that the definition given of the task in the UN texts was very loose and that, tying the freedom of action of Egypt to the concept of the task—

which had to be interpreted also by the General Assembly—
and doing so in a written agreement, meant that he accepted
a far-reaching and unpredictable restriction. To shoot the text
through in spite of Nasser's strong wish to avoid this, and his
strong suspicion of the legal construction—especially of the
possible consequences of differences of views regarding the task
—I felt obliged, in the course of the discussion, to threaten
three times, that unless an agreement of this type was made, I
would have to propose the immediate withdrawal of the troops.
If any proof would be necessary for how the text of the agreement was judged by President Nasser, this last mentioned fact
tells the story.

It is obvious that, with a text of the content mentioned approved by Egypt, the whole previous exchange of views was
superseded by a formal and explicit recognition by Egypt of the
stand I had taken all through, in particular on 9 and 12 November. The previous exchange of cables cannot any longer have
any interpretative value as only the text of the agreement was
put before the General Assembly and approved by it with the
concurrence of Egypt and as its text was self-contained and
conclusive. All further discussion, therefore, has to start from
the text of the agreement, which is to be found in document
A/3375. The interpretation of the text must be the one set out
above.

APPENDIX 4

Report of Secretary General U Thant on the
Withdrawal of the United Nations Emergency Force

MAY 18, 1967

1. This special report is submitted in accordance with paragraph 4 of General Assembly resolution 1125 (XI) of 2 February 1957.

2. On 18 May 1967, at 12 noon, I received through the Permanent Representative of the United Arab Republic to the United Nations the following message from Mr. Mahmoud Riad, Minister for Foreign Affairs of the United Arab Republic:

> The Government of the United Arab Republic has the honour to inform Your Excellency that it has decided to terminate the presence of the United Nations Emergency Force from the territory of the United Arab Republic and Gaza strip.
>
> Therefore, I request that the necessary steps be taken for the withdrawal of the Force as soon as possible.
>
> I avail myself of this opportunity to express to Your Excellency my gratitude and warm regards.

3. I replied to the above message in the early evening of 18 May as follows:

> I have the honour to acknowledge your letter to me of 18 May conveying the message from the Minister of Foreign Affairs of the United Arab Republic concerning the United Nations Emergency Force. Please be so kind as to transmit to the Foreign Minister the following message in reply:
>
> Dear Mr. Minister,
>
> Your message informing me that your Government no longer consents to the presence of the United Nations Emergency Force on the territory of the United Arab Republic,

that is to say in Sinai, and in the Gaza strip, and requesting that the necessary steps be taken for its withdrawal as soon as possible, was delivered to me by the Permanent Representative of the United Arab Republic at noon on 18 May.

As I have indicated to your Permanent Representative on 16 May, the United Nations Emergency Force entered Egyptian territory with the consent of your Government and in fact can remain there only so long as that consent continues. In view of the message now received from you, therefore, your Government's request will be complied with and I am proceeding to issue instructions for the necessary arrangements to be put in train without delay for the orderly withdrawal of the Force, its vehicles and equipment and for the disposal of all properties pertaining to it. I am, of course, also bringing this development and my actions and intentions to the attention of the UNEF Advisory Committee and to all Governments providing contingents for the Force. A full report covering this development will be submitted promptly by me to the General Assembly, and I consider it necessary to report also to the Security Council about some aspects of the current situation in the area.

Irrespective of the reasons for the action you have taken, in all frankness, may I advise you that I have serious misgivings about it for, as I have said each year in my annual reports to the General Assembly on UNEF, I believe that this Force has been an important factor in maintaining relative quiet in the area of its deployment during the past ten years and that its withdrawal may have grave implications for peace.

With warm personal regards.

4. Instructions relating to the withdrawal of UNEF were cabled by me to the Force Commander in the evening of 18 May.

5. As background, the General Assembly will recall that in resolution 1125 (XI) the General Assembly considered "that, after full withdrawal of Israel from the Sharm el-Sheikh and Gaza areas, the scrupulous maintenance of the Armistice Agreement requires the placing of the United Nations Emergency Force on the Egyptian-Israel armistice demarcation line and the implementation of other measures as proposed in the

Secretary-General's report, with due regard to the considerations set out therein with a view to assist in achieving situations conducive to the maintenance of peaceful conditions in the area." The General Assembly further requested the Secretary-General, in paragraph 4 of resolution 1125 (XI), "in consultation with the parties concerned, to take steps to carry out these measures and to report, as appropriate, to the General Assembly." Since the eleventh session of the General Assembly the Secretary-General has reported to the Assembly annually on the Force.

6. The general considerations which I have had in mind and the sequence of events leading up to the present situation are set out in an *aide-mémoire* of 17 May which I handed to the Permanent Representative of the United Arab Republic at 5:30 p.m. on 17 May, the text of which reads as follows:

1. The Secretary-General of the United Nations requests the Permanent Representative of the United Arab Republic to the United Nations to convey to his Government the Secretary-General's most serious concern over the situation that has arisen with regard to the United Nations Emergency Force in the past twenty-four hours as a result of the demands upon it made by United Arab Republic military authorities and of certain actions of United Arab Republic troops in the area.

2. Before engaging in detail, the Secretary-General wishes to make the following general points entirely clear:

(a) He does not in any sense question the authority of the Government of the United Arab Republic to deploy its troops as it sees fit in United Arab Republic territory or territory under the control of the United Arab Republic.

(b) In the sectors of Gaza and Sinai, however, it must be recognized that the deployment of troops of the United Arab Republic in areas in which UNEF troops are stationed and carrying out their functions may have very serious implications for UNEF, its functioning and its continued presence in the area.

(c) The Commander of UNEF cannot comply with any requests affecting the disposition of UNEF troops emanating from any source other than United Nations Headquarters, and the orders delivered to General Rikhye on 16 May by military officers of the United Arab Republic were not right procedurally and quite rightly were disregarded by General Rikhye.

(d) UNEF has been deployed in Gaza and Sinai for more than ten years of the purpose of maintaining quiet along the Armistice Demarcation Line and the International Frontier. It has served this purpose with much distinction. It went into the area and has remained there with the full consent of the Government of the United Arab Republic. If that consent should be withdrawn or so qualified as to make it impossible for the Force to function effectively, the Force, of course, will be withdrawn.

3. The following is the sequence of events which have given rise to the present crisis:

(a) At 2200 hours LT on 16 May Brigadier Eiz-El-Din Mokhtar handed to General Rikhye, the Commander of UNEF, the following letter:

> To your information, I gave my instructions to all UAR Armed Forces to be ready for action against Israel the moment it might carry out any aggressive action against any Arab country. Due to these instructions our troops are already concentrated in Sinai on our eastern borders. For the sake of complete security of all UN troops which install OPs along our borders, I request that you issue your orders to withdraw all these troops immediately. I have given my instructions to our Commander of the eastern zone concerning this subject. Inform back the fulfilment of this request. Yours, Farik Awal: (M. Fawzy) COS of UAR Armed Forces.

(b) The Commander of UNEF replied that he had noted the contents of General Fawzy's letter and would report immediately to the Secretary-General for instructions, since he had no authority to withdraw any troops of UNEF, or in any other way to redeploy UNEF troops, except on instructions from the Secretary-General.

(c) On learning of the substance of General Fawzy's letter to General Rikhye, the Secretary-General asked the Permanent Representative of the United Arab Republic to the United Nations to see him immediately. The Permanent Representative of the United Arab Republic came to the Secretary-General's office at 1845 hours on 16 May. The Secretary-General requested him to communicate with his Government with the utmost urgency and to transmit to them his views, of which the following is a summary:

(i) The letter addressed to the Commander of UNEF was not right procedurally since the Commander of UNEF could not take orders affecting his command from a source other than the Secretary-General. General Rikhye was therefore correct in his insistence on taking no action until he received instructions from the Secretary-General.

(ii) The exact intent of General Fawzy's letter needed clarification. If it meant the temporary withdrawal of UNEF troops from the Line or from parts of it, it would be unacceptable because the purpose of the United Nations Force in Gaza and Sinai is to prevent a recurrence of fighting, and it cannot be asked to stand aside in order to enable the two sides to resume fighting. If it was intended to mean a general withdrawal of UNEF from Gaza and Sinai, the communication should have been addressed to the Secretary-General from the Government of the United Arab Republic and not to the Commander of UNEF from the Chief of Staff of the Armed Forces of the United Arab Republic.

(iii) If it was the intention of the Government of the United Arab Republic to withdraw the consent which it gave in 1956 for the stationing of UNEF on the territory of the United Arab Republic and in Gaza it was, of course, entitled to do so. Since, however, the basis for the presence of UNEF was an agreement made directly between President Nasser and Dag Hammarskjöld as Secretary-General of the United Nations, any request for the withdrawal of UNEF must come directly to the Secretary-General from the Government of the United Arab Republic. On receipt of such a request, the Secretary-General would order the withdrawal of all UNEF troops from Gaza and Sinai, simultaneously informing the General Assembly of what he was doing and why.

(iv) A request by the United Arab Republic authorities for

a temporary withdrawal of UNEF from the Armistice Demarcation Line and the International Frontier, or from any parts of them, would be considered by the Secretary-General as tantamount to a request for the complete withdrawal of UNEF from Gaza and Sinai, since this would reduce UNEF to ineffectiveness.

(d) The Secretary-General informed the Commander of UNEF of the position as outlined above, as explained to the Permanent Representative of the United Arab Republic, and instructed him to do all that he reasonably could to maintain all UNEF positions pending further instructions.

(e) At 0800 hours Z on 17 May, the Commander of UNEF reported that on the morning of 17 May, 30 soldiers of the Army of the United Arab Republic had occupied El Sabha in Sinai and that their troops were deployed in the immediate vicinity of the UNEF Observation Post there. Three armoured cars of the United Arab Republic were located near the Yugoslav UNEF camp at El Sabha and detachments of 15 soldiers each had taken up positions north and south of the Yugoslav camp at El Amr. All UNEF Observation Posts along the Armistice Demarcation Line and International Frontier were manned as usual.

(f) At 1030 hours Z on 17 May, the Commander of UNEF reported that troops of the United Arab Republic had occupied the UNEF Observation Post on El Sabha and that the Yugoslav UNEF camps at El Quseima and El Sabha were now behind the positions of the Army of the United Arab Republic. The Commander of UNEF informed the Chief of the United Arab Republic Liaison Service of these developments, expressing his serious concern at them. The Chief of the United Arab Republic Liaison Service agreed to request the immediate vacation of the Observation Post at El Sabha by troops of the United Arab Republic and shortly thereafter reported that orders to this effect had been given by the United Arab Republic military authorities. He requested, however, that to avoid any future misunderstandings the Yugoslav Observation Post at El Sabha should be immediately withdrawn to El Quseima camp. The Commander replied that any such withdrawal would require the authorization of the Secretary-General.

(g) At 1200 hours Z, the Chief of the United Arab Republic Liaison Service conveyed to the Commander of UNEF a request from General Muhammed Fawzy, Chief of Staff of the Armed Forces of the United Arab Republic, for the withdrawal of UNEF Yugoslav detachments in the Sinai within twenty-four hours. He added that the Commander of UNEF might take forty-eight hours or so to withdraw the UNEF detachment from Sharm el-Sheikh.

(h) At 1330 hours Z, the Commander of UNEF reported that a sizable detachment of troops of the United Arab Republic was moving into the UNEF area at El Kuntilla.

4. The Secretary-General is obliged to state that UNEF cannot remain in the field under the conditions described in the foregoing paragraphs. The function of UNEF has been to assist in maintaining quiet along the Line by acting as a deterrent to infiltration and as a buffer between the opposing forces. It can discharge neither of these functions if it is removed from the Line and finds itself stationed behind forces of the United Arab Republic. In other words, UNEF, which has contributed so greatly to the relative quiet which has prevailed in the area in which it has been deployed for more than ten years, cannot now be asked to stand aside in order to become a silent and helpless witness to an armed confrontation between the parties. If, therefore, the orders to the troops of the United Arab Republic referred to above are maintained, the Secretary-General will have no choice but to order the withdrawal of UNEF from Gaza and Sinai as expeditiously as possible.

5. The Secretary-General wishes also to inform the Permanent Representative of the United Arab Republic that as of now, on the basis of the fully reliable reports received from the Chief of Staff of the United Nations Truce Supervision Organization in Palestine, there have been no recent indications of troop movements or concentrations along any of the Lines which should give rise to undue concern.

6. The Secretary-General requests the Permanent Representative of the United Arab Republic to transmit the contents of this *aide-mémoire* with utmost urgency to his Government.

7. At the same time the following *aide-mémoire* dated 17 May was handed by me to the Permanent Representative of the United Arab Republic:

It will be recalled that in an *aide-mémoire* attached to the report of the Secretary-General on basic points for the presence and functioning in Egypt of the United Nations Emergency Force[1] it was recorded that:

1. *Official Records of the General Assembly, Eleventh Session, Annexes,* agenda item 66, document A/3375.

    1. The Government of Egypt declares that, when exercising its sovereign rights on any matter concerning the presence and functioning of UNEF, it will be guided, in good faith, by its acceptance of General Assembly resolution 1000 (ES-I) of 5 November 1956.

The *aide-mémoire* also records that:

    2. The United Nations takes note of this declaration of the Government of Egypt and declares that the activities of UNEF will be guided, in good faith, by the task established for the Force in the aforementioned resolution; in particular, the United Nations, understanding this to correspond to the wishes of the Government of Egypt, reaffirms its willingness to maintain UNEF until its task is completed.

The General Assembly, in resolution 1121 (XI) of 24 November 1956, noted with approval the contents of the *aide-mémoire* referred to above.

The Minister for Foreign Affairs of Egypt, in concluding on behalf of the Government of Egypt the agreement of 8 February 1957 concerning the status of the United Nations Emergency Force in Egypt, recalled:

    . . . the declaration of the Government of Egypt that, when exercising its sovereign powers on any matter concerning the presence and functioning of the United Nations Emergency Force, it would be guided, in good faith, by its acceptance of the General Assembly resolution of 5 November 1956. . . .

8. As a result of the situation described above, I held an informal meeting with the representatives of the countries providing contingents to UNEF in the late afternoon of 17 May. I informed them of the situation as then known and there was an exchange of views.

9. Since the first *aide-mémoire* was written the following developments have been reported by the Commander of UNEF:

(a) Early on 18 May, the sentries of the UNEF Yugoslav detachment were forced out of their observation post on the International Frontier near El Kuntilla camp. At 1220 hours GMT on 18 May 1967, soldiers of the United Arab Republic forced UNEF soldiers of the Yugoslav contingent to withdraw from the observation post on the International Frontier in front of El Amr camp, and later officers of the United Arab Republic visited El Amr camp and asked the UNEF Yugoslav platoon to withdraw within fifteen minutes.

(b) At 1210 hours GMT on 18 May, officers of the United Arab Republic visited the Yugoslav camp at Sharm el-Sheikh and informed the Commanding Officer that they had come to take over the camp and the UNEF observation post at Ras Nasrani, demanding a reply within fifteen minutes.

(c) At 1430 hours GMT on 18 May, the UNEF Yugoslav detachment at El Quseima camp reported that two artillery shells, apparently ranging rounds from the United Arab Republic artillery, had burst between the UNEF Yugoslav camps at El Quseima and El Sabha.

(d) At 0857 hours GMT on 18 May, a UNEF aircraft carrying Major-General Rikhye, the Commander of UNEF, on a flight from El Arish to Gaza was intercepted west of the Armistice Demarcation Line by two Israel military aircraft which tried to make the UNEF aircraft follow them to the Israel side of the Line to land, and went so far as to fire several warning shots. The pilot of the United Nations aircraft, on instructions from the UNEF Commander, ignored these efforts and proceeded to land at Gaza. I have strongly protested this incident to the Government of Israel through the Permanent Representative of Israel to the United Nations. The Chief of Staff of the Israel Defence Forces has since conveyed regrets for this incident to Major-General Rikhye.

10. Late in the afternoon of 18 May, I convened a meeting of the UNEF Advisory Committee, set up under the terms of paragraphs 6, 8 and 9 of resolution 1001 (ES-I) of 7 November 1956, and the representatives of three countries not mem-

bers of the Advisory Committee but providing contingents to UNEF to inform them of developments and to consult them on the situation.

11. The exchange of notes between the Minister for Foreign Affairs of the United Arab Republic and the Secretary-General, quoted at the beginning of this report, explains the position which I have found myself compelled to adopt under the resolutions of the General Assembly and the agreements reached between the Secretary-General of the United Nations and the Egyptian authorities as the basis for the entry of UNEF into the territory of the United Arab Republic in November 1956, and its subsequent deployment in Gaza and Sinai in 1957.

12. I have taken this position for the following main reasons:

(a) The United Nations Emergency Force was introduced into the territory of the United Arab Republic on the basis of an agreement reached in Cairo between the Secretary-General of the United Nations and the President of Egypt, and it therefore has seemed fully clear to me that since United Arab Republic consent was withdrawn it was incumbent on the Secretary-General to give orders for the withdrawal of the Force. The consent of the host country is a basic principle which has applied to all United Nations peace-keeping operations.

(b) In practical fact, UNEF cannot remain or function without the continuing consent and co-operation of the host country.

(c) I have also been influenced by my deep concern to avoid any action which would either compromise or endanger the contingents which make up the Force. The United Nations Emergency Force is, after all, a peace-keeping and not an enforcement operation.

(d) In the face of the request for the withdrawal of the Force, there seemed to me to be no alternative course of action which could be taken by the Secretary-General without putting in question the sovereign authority of the Government of the United Arab Republic within its own territory.

13. I cannot conclude this report without expressing the deepest concern as to the possible implications of the latest developments for peace in the area. For more than ten years UNEF, acting as a buffer between the opposing forces of Israel and the United Arab Republic on the Armistice Demarcation Line in Gaza and the International Frontier in Sinai, has been the principal means of maintaining quiet in the area. Its removal inevitably restores the armed confrontation of the United Arab Republic and Israel and removes the stabilizing influence of an international force operating along the boundaries between the two nations. Much as I regret this development, I have no option but to respect and acquiesce in the request of the Government of the United Arab Republic. I can only express the hope that both sides will now exercise the utmost calm and restraint in this new situation, which otherwise will be fraught with danger.

14. Finally, I must express the highest appreciation to the Governments of all the Members of the United Nations which have supported UNEF and especially to those which have provided the military contingents which made up the Force. The appreciation of the United Nations is also due to the many thousand officers and men who have served so loyally and with such distinction in UNEF. The Force at its inception represented an extraordinary innovation in the efforts of the world community to find improved methods of keeping the peace. For more than ten years it has fulfilled its functions with a far greater degree of success than could have been hoped for. It is, in fact, the model upon which many hopes for the future effectiveness of the United Nations in peace-keeping have been based. Its termination at this particular time raises serious anxiety as to the maintenance of peace in the area in which it is operating. In this anxious time, therefore, I feel it my duty to appeal not only to the parties directly affected by the withdrawal of UNEF to do all in their power to keep the peace, but also to all the Members of the United Nations to intensify

their efforts both for the maintenance of peace in this particular situation and for the improvement of the capacity of the organization to maintain peace. It goes without saying that I shall continue to do all within my power towards the attainment of both these objectives.

Report of Secretary General
U Thant
MAY 19, 1967

1. I have felt it to be an obligation to submit this report in order to convey to members of the Council my deep anxiety about recent developments in the Near East and what I consider to be an increasingly dangerous deterioration along the borders there.

2. The members of the Council will be aware of the Special Report on the United Nations Emergency Force which I made to the General Assembly on 18 May 1967 (A/6669).

3. I am very sorry to feel obliged to say that in my considered opinion the prevailing state of affairs in the Near East as regards relations between the Arab States and Israel, and among the Arab States themselves, is extremely menacing.

4. There has been a steady deterioration along the line between Israel and Syria, particularly with regard to disputes over cultivation rights in the Demilitarized Zone, since the first of the year. In this regard I may point to my reports to the Council of 15 January 1967 (S/7683) and of 8 May 1967 (S/7877). In late January the Chief of Staff of the United Nations Truce Supervision Organization in Palestine, Lt. General Odd Bull, obtained the agreement of Israel and Syria to attend an emergency and extraordinary meeting of the Israel-Syrian Mixed Armistice Commission on an agreed agenda item on cultivation problems. Three meetings were actually held but the agreed agenda item was not discussed because both parties insisted on first bringing up broader issues. It has not been possible to achieve a resumption of these meetings

owing to an impasse over a position taken firmly by Syria. In consequence, General Bull, on my advice (S/7877), is now trying to initiate separate discussions with the two parties in order to work out practical cultivation arrangements affecting disputed lands along the line.

5. It was precisely in the effort to avert serious armed clashes such as that which occurred on 7 April 1967 that so much emphasis has been given by UNTSO's Chief of Staff to the need for discussion and agreement on cultivation arrangements, whether achieved within or outside ISMAC. In the absence of such an agreement, tension along the line continues high and the possibility of new armed clashes in disputed areas is ever-present.

6. A number of factors serve to aggravate the situation to an unusual degree, increasing tension and danger.

7. El Fatah activities, consisting of terrorism and sabotage, are a major factor in that they provoke strong reactions in Israel by the Government and population alike. Some recent incidents of this type have seemed to indicate a new level of organization and training of those who participate in these actions. It is clear that the functions and resources of UNTSO do not enable it to arrest these activities. Although allegations are often made, to the best of my knowledge there is no verified information about the organization, central direction and originating source of these acts, which have occurred intermittently in the vicinity of Israel's lines with Jordan, Lebanon and Syria. All three of the latter Governments have officially disclaimed responsibility for these acts and those who perpetrate them. I am not in a position to say whether any or all of the Governments concerned have done everything they reasonably can to prevent such activities across their borders. The fact is that they do recur with disturbing regularity.

8. Intemperate and bellicose utterances, by other officials and non-officials, eagerly reported by Press and radio, are unfortunately more or less routine on both sides of the lines in the Near East. In recent weeks, however, reports emanating from

Israel have attributed to some high officials in that State statements so threatening as to be particularly inflammatory in the sense that they could only heighten emotions and thereby increase tensions on the other side of the lines.

9. There have been in the past few days persistent reports about troop movements and concentrations, particularly on the Israel side of the Syrian border. These have caused anxiety and at times excitement. The Government of Israel very recently has assured me that there are no unusual Israel troop concentrations or movements along the Syrian line, that there will be none and that no military action will be initiated by the armed forces of Israel unless such action is first taken by the other side. Reports from UNTSO Observers have confirmed the absence of troop concentrations and significant troop movements on both sides of the line.

10. The decision of the Government of the United Arab Republic to terminate its consent for the continued presence of the United Nations Emergency Force on United Arab Republic territory in Sinai and on United Arab Republic controlled territory in Gaza came suddenly and was unexpected. The reasons for this decision have not been officially stated, but they were clearly regarded as overriding by the Government of the United Arab Republic. It is certain that they had nothing to do with the conduct of UNEF itself or the way in which it was carrying out the mandate entrusted to it by the General Assembly and accepted by the Government of the United Arab Republic when it gave its consent for the deployment of UNEF within its jurisdiction. There can be no doubt, in fact, that UNEF has discharged its responsibilities with remarkable effectiveness and great distinction. No United Nations peace-keeping operation can be envisaged as permanent or semi-permanent. Each one must come to an end at some time or another. UNEF has been active for ten and a half years and that is a very long time for any country to have foreign troops, even under an international banner, operating autonomously on its soil. On the other hand, it can be said that the

timing of the withdrawal of UNEF leaves much to be desired because of the prevailing tensions and dangers throughout the area. It also adds one more frontier on which there is a direct confrontation between the military forces of Israel and those of her Arab neighbours.

11. It is well to bear in mind that United Nations peace-keeping operations such as UNEF, and this applies in fact to all peace-keeping operations thus far undertaken by the United Nations, depend for their presence and effectiveness not only on the consent of the authorities in the area of their deployment but on the co-operation and goodwill of those authorities. When, for example, the United Arab Republic decided to move its troops up to the line, which it had a perfect right to do, the buffer function which UNEF had been performing was eliminated. Its continued presence was thus rendered useless, its position untenable, and its withdrawal became virtually inevitable. This was the case even before the official request for the withdrawal had been received by me.

12. It is all too clear that there is widespread misunderstanding about the nature of United Nations peace-keeping operations in general and UNEF in particular. As I pointed out in my Special Report of 18 May 1967 to the General Assembly (A/6669, paragraph 12 (c)) "The United Nations Emergency Force is, after all, a peace-keeping and not an enforcement operation." This means, of course, that the operation is based entirely on its acceptance by the governing authority of the territory on which it operates and that it is not in any sense related to Chapter VII of the Charter. It is a fact beyond dispute that neither UNEF nor any other United Nations peace-keeping operation thus far undertaken would have been permitted to enter the territory involved if there had been any suggestion that it had the right to remain there against the will of the governing authority.

13. The order for the withdrawal of UNEF has been given. The actual process of withdrawal will be orderly, deliberate, and dignified and not precipitate.

14. I do not believe that any of the Governments concerned are so careless of the welfare of their own people or of the risks of a spreading conflict as to deliberately embark on military offensives across their borders, unless they become convinced, rightly or wrongly, that they are threatened. Nevertheless, there is good reason to fear that the withdrawal of UNEF will give rise to increased danger along the Armistice Demarcation Line and the International Frontier between Israel and the United Arab Republic. The presence of UNEF has been a deterrent and restraining influence along both lines. There are some particularly sensitive areas involved, notably Sharm el-Sheikh and Gaza. The former concerns the Strait of Tiran. In the Gaza strip there are 307,000 refugees and the substantial Palestine Liberation Army must also be taken into account.

15. It is true to a considerable extent that UNEF has allowed us for ten years to ignore some of the hard realities of the underlying conflict. The Governments concerned, and the United Nations, are now confronted with a brutally realistic and dangerous situation.

16. The Egyptian-Israel Mixed Armistice Commission (EIMAC), established by the Egyptian-Israel General Armistice Agreement, remains in existence with its headquarters at Gaza, and could, as it did prior to the establishment of UNEF, provide a limited form of United Nations presence in the area, as in the case of the other Mixed Armistice Commissions which are served by UNTSO. The Government of Israel, however, has denounced the EIMAC and for some years has refused to have anything to do with it. The United Nations has never accepted as valid this unilateral action by the Government of Israel. It would most certainly be helpful in the present situation if the Government of Israel were to reconsider its position and resume its participation in EIMAC.

17. Similarly, I may repeat what I have said in the past, that it would be very helpful to the maintenance of quiet along the Israel-Syria line if the two parties would resume their participa-

tion in ISMAC, both in the current emergency session and in the regular sessions.

18. Since the announcement of the decision of the Government of the United Arab Republic with regard to UNEF, tension in the area has mounted. Troop movements on both sides have been observed, but as of the evening of 19 May these do not seem to have attained alarming proportions. Although one brief shooting incident on 19 May has been reported, I believe it can be said that as of this moment there is no indication on either side of the line of any major action of an offensive nature, but the confrontation along the line between the armed forces of the two countries which has been avoided for more than ten years now quickly begins to reappear. Unless there is very great restraint on both sides of the line, one can readily envisage a series of local clashes across the line which could easily escalate into heavy conflict.

19. I do not wish to be alarmist but I cannot avoid the warning to the Council that in my view the current situation in the Near East is more disturbing, indeed, I may say more menacing, than at any time since the fall of 1956.

APPENDIX 6

Report of Secretary General
U Thant
MAY 26, 1967

1. In my report of 19 May 1967 (S/7896), which I submitted to the Security Council following the receipt on 18 May 1967 of the official request of the Government of the United Arab Republic for the withdrawal of the United Nations Emergency Force (UNEF), I described the general situation in the Near East at present as "more disturbing, indeed, . . . more menacing, than at any time since the fall of 1956." I can only reiterate this assessment.

2. It has been alleged in some quarters that the prompt compliance with the request for the withdrawal of the Force is a primary cause of the present crisis in the Near East. This ignores the fact that the underlying basis for this and other crisis situations in the Near East is the continuing Arab-Israel conflict which has been present all along, and of which the crisis situation created by the unexpected request for the withdrawal of UNEF is the latest expression. In my special report to the General Assembly (A/6669), in paragraph 12, I gave the main reasons for the position that I have taken on this issue. In my report to the Security Council on 19 May 1967 (S/7896), I restated the basis for my decision and pointed out that there was a "widespread misunderstanding about the nature of United Nations peace-keeping operations in general and UNEF in particular." In view of the evident persistence of this misunderstanding and of various recent public statements by some responsible leaders, I feel obliged once again, before proceeding with my report, to restate briefly the grounds

for the position which I have taken on the withdrawal of UNEF.

3. UNEF was introduced into the territory of the United Arab Republic on the basis of an agreement between the Secretary-General of the United Nations and the President of Egypt. The consent of the host country, in this as in other peace-keeping operations, was the basis for its presence on the territory of the United Arab Republic. When that consent was withdrawn, the essential part of the basis of UNEF's presence ceased to exist.

4. As stated in my special report to the General Assembly (A/6669), I consulted with the UNEF Advisory Committee on 18 May 1967. The Committee did not move, as it was its right to do under the terms of paragraph 9 of General Assembly resolution 1001 (ES-I), to request the convening of the General Assembly on the situation which had arisen. It was after this meeting of the Advisory Committee, on the evening of 18 May, that I transmitted my reply to the Government of the United Arab Republic concerning the withdrawal of UNEF.

5. My decision in this matter was based upon both legal and practical considerations. It is a practical fact that neither UNEF nor any other United Nations peace-keeping operation could function or even exist without the continuing consent and co-operation of the host country. Once the consent of the host country was withdrawn and it was no longer welcome, its usefulness was ended. In fact, the movement of UAR Forces up to the Line in Sinai even before the request for withdrawal was received by me had already made the effective functioning of UNEF impossible. I may say here that the request received by me on 18 May was the only request received from the Government of the United Arab Republic, since the cryptic letter to Major-General Rikhye from General Fawzi on 16 May was both unclear and unacceptable. Furthermore, I had very good reason to be convinced of the earnestness and the determination of the Government of the United Arab Republic in requesting

the withdrawal of UNEF. It was therefore obvious to me that the position of the personnel of UNEF would soon become extremely difficult, and even dangerous, if the decision for the withdrawal of the Force was delayed, while the possibility for its effective action had already been virtually eliminated. Moreover, if the request were not promptly complied with, the Force would quickly disintegrate due to the withdrawal of individual contingents.

6. It may be relevant to note here that UNEF functioned exclusively on the United Arab Republic side of the Line in a zone from which the armed forces of the United Arab Republic had voluntarily stayed away for over ten years. It was this arrangement which allowed UNEF to function as a buffer and as a restraint on infiltration. When this arrangement lapsed United Arab Republic troops moved up to the Line as they had every right to do.

7. If UNEF had been deployed on both sides of the Line as originally envisaged in pursuance of the General Assembly resolution, its buffer function would not necessarily have ended. However, its presence on the Israel side of the Line has never been permitted. The fact that UNEF was not stationed on the Israel side of the Line was a recognition of the unquestioned sovereign right of Israel to withhold its consent for the stationing of the Force. The acquiescence in the request of the United Arab Republic for the withdrawal of the Force after ten and a half years on United Arab Republic soil was likewise a recognition of the sovereign authority of the United Arab Republic. In no official document relating to UNEF has there been any suggestion of a limitation of this sovereign authority.

8. In order to discuss the situation with the Government of the United Arab Republic, and especially in order to examine with that Government the situation created by the withdrawal of UNEF, I decided to advance the date of a visit to Cairo which I had planned some time ago for the beginning of July. I arrived in Cairo on the afternoon of 23 May and left Cairo

on the early afternoon of 25 May to return to United Nations Headquarters.

9. During my stay in Cairo I had discussions with President Gamal Abdel Nasser and Mr. Mahmoud Riad, the Minister of Foreign Affairs. They explained to me the position of the Government of the United Arab Republic, which is substantially as set forth in the speech given by President Nasser to the United Arab Republic Air Force Advance Command on 22 May 1967 which has been reported fully in the Press. President Nasser and Foreign Minister Riad assured me that the United Arab Republic would not initiate offensive action against Israel. Their general aim, as stated to me, was for a return to the conditions prevailing prior to 1956 and to full observance by both parties of the provisions of the General Armistice Agreement between Egypt and Israel.

10. The decision of the Government of the United Arab Republic to restrict shipping in the Strait of Tiran, of which I learned while en route to Cairo, has created a new situation. Free passage through the Strait is one of the questions which the Government of Israel considers most vital to her interests. The position of the Government of the United Arab Republic is that the Strait is territorial waters in which it has a right to control shipping. The Government of Israel contests this position and asserts the right of innocent passage through the Strait. The Government of Israel has further declared that Israel will regard the closing of the Strait of Tiran to Israel flagships and any restriction on cargoes of ships of other flags proceeding to Israel as a *casus belli*. While in Cairo, I called to the attention of the Government of the United Arab Republic the dangerous consequences which could ensue from restricting innocent passage of ships in the Strait of Tiran. I expressed my deep concern in this regard and my hope that no precipitate action would be taken.

11. A legal controversy existed prior to 1956 as to the extent of the right of innocent passage by commercial vessels through the Strait of Tiran and the Gulf of Aqaba. Since March

1957, when UNEF forces were stationed at Sharm el-Sheikh and Ras Nasrani at the mouth of the Gulf of Aqaba, there has been no interference with shipping in the Strait of Tiran.

12. It is not my purpose here to go into the legal aspects of this controversy or to enter into the merits of the case. At this critical juncture I feel that my major concern must be to try to gain time in order to lay the basis for a detente. The important immediate fact is that, in view of the conflicting stands taken by the United Arab Republic and Israel, the situation in the Strait of Tiran represents a very serious potential threat to peace. I greatly fear that a clash between the United Arab Republic and Israel over this issue, in the present circumstances, will inevitably set off a general conflict in the Near East.

13. The freedom of navigation through the Strait of Tiran is not, however, the only immediate issue which is endangering peace in the Near East. Other problems, such as sabotage and terrorist activities and rights of cultivation in disputed areas in the Demilitarized Zone between Israel and Syria, will, unless controlled, almost surely lead to further serious fighting.

14. In my view, a peaceful outcome to the present crisis will depend upon a breathing spell which will allow tension to subside from its present explosive level. I therefore urge all the parties concerned to exercise special restraint, to forgo belligerence and to avoid all other actions which could increase tension, to allow the Council to deal with the underlying causes of the present crisis and to seek solutions.

15. There are other possible courses of action which might contribute substantially to the reduction of tension in the area. In paragraph 16 of my report to the Security Council on 19 May (S/7896) I referred to the possibility of the Egypt-Israel Mixed Armistice Commission (EIMAC) providing a limited form of United Nations presence in the area. In that report I stated that "it would most certainly be helpful in the present situation if the Government of Israel were to reconsider its position and resume its participation in EIMAC." I suggest

that the Council consider this possible approach also during its search for ways out of the present crisis. This form of United Nations presence could to some extent fill the vacuum left by the withdrawal of UNEF.

16. In paragraph 17 of my previous report to the Council I also suggested that "it would be very helpful to the maintenance of quiet along the Israel-Syria line if the two parties would resume their participation in ISMAC, both in the current emergency session and in the regular sessions," and I would wish on this occasion to repeat that suggestion.

17. It also would be useful for the Council to recall that, by its resolution 73 (1949) of 11 August 1949, the Council found that:

. . . the Armistice Agreements constitute an important step towards the establishment of permanent peace in Palestine. . . .

and reaffirmed:

. . . the order contained in its resolution 54 (1948) to the Governments and authorities concerned, pursuant to Article 40 of the Charter of the United Nations, to observe an unconditional cease-fire and, bearing in mind that the several Armistice Agreements include firm pledges against further acts of hostility between the parties and also provide for their supervision by the parties themselves, relies upon the parties to ensure the continued application and observance of these Agreements. . . .

18. In my discussion with officials of the United Arab Republic and Israel I have mentioned possible steps which could be taken by mutual consent and which would help to reduce tension. I shall of course continue to make all possible efforts to contribute to a solution of the present crisis. The problems to be faced are complex and the obstacles are formidable. I do not believe however that we can allow ourselves to despair.

19. It should be kept always in mind that in spite of the extreme difficulties of the situation, the United Nations has played an essential and important role for more than eighteen years in maintaining at least some measure of peace in the Near

East. In that task it has encountered many setbacks, frustrations, crises, conflicts and even war, but the effort continues unabated. We are now confronted with new and threatening circumstances, but I still believe that with the co-operation of all parties concerned the United Nations, and the Security Council in particular, must continue to seek, and eventually to find, reasonable, peaceful and just solutions.

APPENDIX 7

Letter of Dr. Ralph J. Bunche
to The New York Times,
JUNE 11, 1967

June 9, 1967

Sir,

In his article entitled "Cairo: Quiet Flows the Nile" of Sunday, 4 June, Mr. James Reston states that the Egyptians he has been talking to "even deny that they planned to get rid of the United Nations troops at the mouth of Aqaba. This, they say, was proposed by the Secretary-General of the United Nations on the ground that if the United Nations couldn't keep its troops in one part of the crisis area, it wouldn't keep them in another part." This statement is repeated in Mr. Reston's article in your issue of 5 June, in which it is described as "the argument from the official side of Cairo."

If only for the sake of historical accuracy, I wish to make the following observations:

(1) Whatever may have been said to Mr. Reston in Cairo, or by whom, I can assure you that there has not been the slightest hint of such a position here, and with good reason, for there is not a shred of truth to it. In critical times such as these, of course, it is common in official and unofficial circles alike, to seek scapegoats (to a shameful degree at present in the United States) and to indulge in what may be called deception, if one wishes to be polite about it.

(2) The letter received by the Commander of the United Nations Emergency Force (UNEF) from the Chief of Staff of the United Arab Republic Army on the night of 16 May demanded the withdrawal of "all United Nations troops which

installed Observation Posts along our borders." This unquestionably included Sharm el-Sheikh which was, in fact, a United Nations Observation Post.

(3) As reported by the Secretary-General on 18 May to the General Assembly, this message to General Rikhye was quickly followed by a movement of United Arab Republic troops up to the line in Sinai, and by a demand from the Chief of Staff of the United Arab Republic Army at midday local time on 17 May for withdrawal within twenty-four hours of all UNEF detachments in Sinai, specifically including Sharm el-Sheikh. In fact, United Arab Republic troops arrived to take over the United Nations camp and positions at Sharm el-Sheikh and Ras Nasrani at 1210 hours GMT on 18 May, demanding a response from the UNEF troops there within fifteen minutes. They did not get it, and the UNEF troops remained there for six more days, although they were unable to function.

(4) The official request for the withdrawal of UNEF was received by the Secretary-General at 12 noon New York Time on 18 May, i.e. some four hours *after* the actual arrival of United Arab Republic troops at Sharm el-Sheikh.

(5) The reason for the Secretary-General's position that UNEF could not accept an order to withdraw from one part of the line and remain on another part was that to do this would in fact make UNEF a party to the resumption of war by opening the door to a direct military confrontation between Israel and the United Arab Republic. Once the United Arab Republic decided to move its troops to any part of the line, which they could have done at any time during the past ten years, UNEF's presence ceased to have any useful function.

The line that had to be covered by UNEF, incidentally, was 295 miles long while the total strength of the Force was 3400 (1800 on the line), with personal arms for self-defence only. At Sharm el-Sheikh, 32 men were stationed.

[Dr. Bunche is Under-Secretary for Special Political Affairs of the United Nations.]

APPENDIX 8

Report of the Secretary General on the Withdrawal of the United Nations Emergency Force

JUNE 26, 1967

ANNEX

Cable Containing Instructions for the Withdrawal of UNEF Sent by the Secretary-General to the Commander of UNEF on 18 May 1967 at 2230 Hours New York Time

INTRODUCTION

1. This report on the withdrawal of the United Nations Emergency Force (UNEF) is submitted because, as indicated in my statement on 20 June 1967 to the fifth emergency special session of the General Assembly (1527th plenary meeting), important questions have been raised concerning the actions taken on the withdrawal of UNEF. These questions merit careful consideration and comment. It is in the interest of the United Nations, I believe, that this report should be full and

175

frank, in view of the questions involved and the numerous statements that have been made, both public and private, which continue to be very damaging to the United Nations and to its peace-keeping role in particular. Despite the explanations already given in the several reports on the subject which have been submitted to the General Assembly and to the Security Council, misunderstandings and what, I fear, are misrepresentations, persist, in official as well as unofficial circles, publicly and behind the scenes.

2. A report of this kind is not the place to try to explain why there has been so much and such persistent and grossly mistaken judgement about the withdrawal of UNEF. It suffices to say here that the shattering crisis in the Near East inevitably caused intense shock in many capitals and countries of the world, together with deep frustration over the inability to cope with it. It is, of course, not unusual in such situations to seek easy explanations and excuses. When, however, this tactic involves imputing responsibility for the unleashing of major hostilities, it is, and must be, a cause for sober concern. The objective of this report is to establish an authentic, factual record of actions and their causes.

3. The emphasis here, therefore, will be upon facts. The report is intended to be neither a polemic nor an apologia. Its sole purpose is to present a factually accurate picture of what happened and why. It will serve well the interests of the United Nations, as well as of historical integrity, if this presentation of facts can help to dissipate some of the distortions of the record which, in some places, apparently have emanated from panic, emotion and political bias.

CHRONOLOGY OF RELEVANT ACTIONS

4. Not only events but dates, and even the time of day, have an important bearing on this exposition. The significant events and actions and their dates and times are therefore set forth below.

16 May 1967

5. *2000 hours GMT (2200 hours Gaza local time)*. A message from General Fawzi, Chief of Staff of the United Arab Republic Armed Forces, was received by the Commander of UNEF, Major-General Rikhye, requesting withdrawal of "all UN troops which install OPs along our borders" (A/6730, para. 6, sub-para. 3 (a)). Brigadier Mokhtar, who handed General Fawzi's letter to the Commander of UNEF, told General Rikhye at the time that he must order the immediate withdrawal of United Nations troops from El Sabha and Sharm el-Sheikh on the night of 16 May since United Arab Republic armed forces must gain control of these two places that very night. The UNEF Commander correctly replied that he did not have authority to withdraw his troops from these positions on such an order and could do so only on instructions from the Secretary-General; therefore, he must continue with UNEF operations in Sinai as hitherto. Brigadier Mokhtar told the Commander of UNEF that this might lead to conflict on that night (16 May) between United Arab Republic and UNEF troops, and insisted that the Commander issue orders to UNEF troops to remain confined to their camps at El Sabha and Sharm el-Sheikh. General Rikhye replied that he could not comply with this request. He did, of course, inform the contingent commanders concerned of these developments. He also informed United Nations Headquarters that he proposed to continue with UNEF activities as established until he received fresh instructions from the Secretary-General.

6. *2130 hours GMT (1730 hours New York time)*. The Secretary-General received at this time the UNEF Commander's cable informing him of the above-mentioned message from General Fawzi. The UNEF Commander was immediately instructed to await further instructions from the Secretary-General and, pending this later word from him, to "be firm in maintaining UNEF position while being as understanding and

as diplomatic as possible in your relations with local UAR officials."

7. *2245 hours GMT (1845 hours New York time)*. The Permanent Representative of the United Arab Republic visited the Secretary-General at this time at the latter's urgent request. The Secretary-General requested the Permanent Representative to communicate with his Government with the utmost urgency and to transmit to it his views (A/6730, para. 6, sub-para. 3 (c)). In particular, the Secretary-General requested the Permanent Representative to obtain his Government's clarification of the situation, pointing out that any request for the withdrawal of UNEF must come directly to the Secretary-General from the Government of the United Arab Republic.

8. *2344 hours GMT*. The UNEF Commander further reported at this time that considerable military activity had been observed in the El Arish area since the afternoon of 16 May 1967.

17 May 1967

9. *0800 hours GMT (0400 hours New York time)*. The Commander of UNEF reported then that on the morning of 17 May, thirty soldiers of the Army of the United Arab Republic had occupied El Sabha in Sinai and that United Arab Republic troops were deployed in the immediate vicinity of the UNEF observation post there. Three armoured cars of the United Arab Republic were located near the Yugoslav UNEF camp at El Sabha and detachments of fifteen soldiers each had taken up positions north and south of the Yugoslav contingent's camp at El Amr. All UNEF observation posts along the armistice demarcation line and the international frontier were manned as usual, but in some places United Arab Republic troops were also at the line.

10. *1030 hours GMT (0630 hours New York time)*. The Commander of UNEF reported then that troops of the United Arab Republic had occupied the UNEF observation post at

El Sabha and that the Yugoslav UNEF camps at El Quseima and El Sabha were now behind the positions of the army of the United Arab Republic. The Commander of UNEF informed the Chief of the United Arab Republic Liaison Staff of these developments, expressing his serious concern at them. The Chief of the United Arab Republic Liaison Staff agreed to request the immediate evacuation of the observation post at El Sabha by United Arab Republic troops and shortly thereafter reported that orders to this effect had been given by the United Arab Republic military authorities. He requested, however, that to avoid any future misunderstandings, the Yugoslav observation post at El Sabha should be withdrawn immediately to El Quseima camp. The Commander replied that any such withdrawal would require the authorization of the Secretary-General.

11. *1200 hours GMT (0800 hours New York time).* The Chief of the United Arab Republic Liaison Staff at this time conveyed to the Commander of UNEF a request from General Muhammed Fawzi, Chief of Staff of the Armed Forces of the United Arab Republic, for the withdrawal of the Yugoslav detachments of UNEF in the Sinai within twenty-four hours. He added that the UNEF Commander might take "forty-eight hours or so" to withdraw the UNEF detachment from Sharm el-Sheikh. The Commander of UNEF replied that any such move required instructions from the Secretary-General.

12. *1330 hours GMT.* The Commander of UNEF then reported that a sizable detachment of troops of the United Arab Republic was moving into the UNEF area at El Kuntilla.

13. *2000 hours GMT (1600 hours New York time).* The Secretary-General at this date held an informal meeting in his office with the representatives of countries providing contingents to UNEF to inform them of the situation as then known. There was an exchange of views. The Secretary-General gave his opinion on how he should and how he intended to proceed, observing that if a formal request for the withdrawal of UNEF were to be made by the Government of the United Arab Re-

public, the Secretary-General, in his view, would have to comply with it, since the Force was on United Arab Republic territory only with the consent of the Government and could not remain there without it. Two representatives expressed serious doubts about the consequences of agreeing to a peremptory request for the withdrawal of UNEF and raised the questions of consideration of such a request by the General Assembly and an appeal to the United Arab Republic not to request the withdrawal of UNEF. Two other representatives stated the view that the United Arab Republic was entitled to request the removal of UNEF at any moment and that that request would have to be respected regardless of what the General Assembly might have to say in the matter, since the agreement for UNEF's presence had been concluded between the then Secretary-General and the Government of Egypt. A clarification of the situation from the United Arab Republic should therefore be awaited.

14. *2150 hours GMT (1750 hours New York time)*. The Secretary-General at this time saw the Permanent Representative of the United Arab Republic and handed to him an *aide-mémoire,* the text of which is contained in paragraph 6 of document A/6730. The Secretary-General also gave to the Permanent Representative of the United Arab Republic an *aide-mémoire* calling to the attention of his Government the "good faith" accord, the text of which is contained in paragraph 7 of document A/6730.

18 May 1967

15. *1321 hours GMT (0921 hours New York time)*. The Commander of UNEF reported at this time that his Liaison Officer in Cairo had been informed by an ambassador of one of the countries providing contingents to UNEF that the Foreign Minister of the United Arab Republic had summoned the representatives of nations with troops in UNEF to the Ministry for Foreign Affairs and informed them that UNEF had terminated its tasks in the United Arab Republic and in the Gaza

strip and must depart from the above territory forthwith. This information was confirmed by representatives of some of these countries at the United Nations.

16. Early on 18 May the UNEF sentries proceeding to man the normal observation post at El Sabha in Sinai were prevented from entering the post and from remaining in the area by United Arab Republic soldiers. The sentries were then forced to withdraw. They did not resist by use of force since they had no mandate to do so.

17. *1100 hours GMT*. United Arab Republic soldiers at this time forced Yugoslav UNEF sentries out of their observation post on the international frontier in front of El Kuntilla Camp. One hour later, United Arab Republic officers arrived at the water point and asked UNEF soldiers to withdraw the guard.

18. *1220 hours GMT*. At this hour, United Arab Republic soldiers entered the UNEF observation post on the international frontier in front of El Amr Camp and forced the Yugoslav soldiers to withdraw. Later, two United Arab Republic officers visited El Amr Camp and asked the UNEF platoon to withdraw within fifteen minutes.

19. *1210 hours GMT*. United Arab Republic officers then visited the Yugoslav camp at Sharm el-Sheikh and informed the Commanding Officer that they had come to take over the camp and the UNEF observation post at Ras Nasrani, demanding a reply within fifteen minutes. The contingent commander replied that he had no instructions to hand over the positions.

20. *1430 hours GMT*. The UNEF Yugoslav detachment at El Quseima camp reported that two artillery shells, apparently ranging rounds from the United Arab Republic artillery, had burst between the UNEF Yugoslav camps at El Quseima and El Sabha.

21. *1030 hours New York time*. The Secretary-General met at this time with the Permanent Representative of Israel who gave his Government's views on the situation, emphasizing that the UNEF withdrawal should not be achieved by a uni-

lateral United Arab Republic request alone and asserting Israel's right to a voice in the matter. The question of stationing UNEF on the Israel side of the line was raised by the Secretary-General and this was declared by the Permanent Representative of Israel to be entirely unacceptable to his Government.

22. *1600 hours GMT (12 noon New York time)*. At this hour the Secretary-General received through the Permanent Representative of the United Arab Republic the following message from Mr. Mahmoud Riad, Minister of Foreign Affairs of the United Arab Republic:

> The Government of the United Arab Republic has the honour to inform Your Excellency that it has decided to terminate the presence of the United Nations Emergency Force from the territory of the United Arab Republic and Gaza strip.
>
> Therefore, I request that the necessary steps be taken for the withdrawal of the Force as soon as possible.
>
> I avail myself of this opportunity to express to Your Excellency my gratitude and warm regards.

At the same meeting the Permanent Representative of the United Arab Republic informed the Secretary-General of the strong feeling of resentment in Cairo at what was there considered to be attempts to exert pressure and to make UNEF an "occupation force." The Secretary-General expressed deep misgivings about the likely disastrous consequences of the withdrawal of UNEF and indicated his intention to appeal urgently to President Nasser to reconsider the decision. Later in the day, the representative of the United Arab Republic informed the Secretary-General that the Foreign Minister had asked the Permanent Representative by telephone from Cairo to convey to the Secretary-General his urgent advice that the Secretary-General should not make an appeal to President Nasser to reconsider the request for withdrawal of UNEF and that, if he did so, such a request would be sternly rebuffed. The Secretary-General raised the question of a possible visit by him to Cairo and was shortly thereafter informed that such a visit as soon as possible would be welcomed by the Government of the United Arab Republic.

23. *1700 hours New York time.* The Secretary-General met with the UNEF Advisory Committee, set up under the the terms of paragraphs 6, 8 and 9 of resolution 1001 (ES-I) of 7 November 1956, and the representatives of three countries not members of the Advisory Committee but providing contingents to UNEF, to inform them of developments and particularly the United Arab Republic's request for UNEF's withdrawal, and to consult them for their views on the situation. At this meeting, one of the views expressed was that the United Arab Republic's demand for the immediate withdrawal of UNEF from United Arab Republic territory was not acceptable and that the ultimate responsibility for the decision to withdraw rested with the United Nations acting through the Security Council or the General Assembly. The holders of this view therefore urged further discussion with the Government of the United Arab Republic as well as with other Governments involved. Another position was that the Secretary-General had no choice but to comply with the request of the Government of the United Arab Republic, one representative stating that the moment the request for the withdrawal of UNEF was known his Government would comply with it and withdraw its contingent. A similar position had been taken in Cairo by another Government providing a contingent. No proposal was made that the Advisory Committee should exercise the right vested in it by General Assembly resolution 1001 (ES-I) to request the convening of the General Assembly to take up the situation arising from the United Arab Republic communication. At the conclusion of the meeting, it was understood that the Secretary-General had no alternative other than to comply with the United Arab Republic's demand, although some representatives felt the Secretary-General should previously clarify with that Government the meaning in its request that withdrawal should take place "as soon as possible." The

Secretary-General informed the Advisory Committee that he intended to reply promptly to the United Arab Republic, and to report to the General Assembly and to the Security Council on the action he had taken. It was for the Member States to decide whether the competent organs should or could take up the matter and to pursue it accordingly.

24. After the meeting of the Advisory Committee, at approximately 1900 hours New York time on 18 May, the Secretary-General replied to the message from the Minister for Foreign Affairs of the United Arab Republic through that Government's Permanent Representative as follows:

I have the honour to acknowledge your letter to me of 18 May conveying the message from the Minister of Foreign Affairs of the United Arab Republic concerning the United Nations Emergency Force. Please be so kind as to transmit to the Foreign Minister the following message in reply:

Dear Mr. Minister,
Your message informing me that your Government no longer consents to the presence of the United Nations Emergency Force on the territory of the United Arab Republic, that is to say in Sinai, and in the Gaza Strip, and requesting that the necessary steps be taken for its withdrawal as soon as possible, was delivered to me by the Permanent Representative of the United Arab Republic at noon on 18 May.

As I have indicated to your Permanent Representative on 16 May, the United Nations Emergency Force entered Egyptian territory with the consent of your Government and in fact can remain there only so long as that consent continues. In view of the message now received from you, therefore, your Government's request will be complied with and I am proceeding to issue instructions for the necessary arrangements to be put in train without delay for the orderly withdrawal of the Force, its vehicles and equipment and for the disposal of all properties pertaining to it. I am, of course, also bringing this development and my actions and intentions to the attention of the UNEF Advisory Committee and to all Governments providing contingents for the Force. A full report covering this development will be submitted promptly by me to the General Assembly, and I consider it necessary to report also to the Security Council about some aspects of the current situation in the area.

Irrespective of the reasons for the action you have taken, in all frankness, may I advise you that I have serious misgivings about it for, as I have said each year in my annual reports to the General Assembly on UNEF, I believe that this Force has been an important factor in maintaining relative quiet in the area of its deployment during the past ten years and that its withdrawal may have grave implications for peace.

With warm personal regards,

U THANT

Please accept, Sir, the assurances of my highest consideration.

It is to be noted that the decision notified to the Government of the United Arab Republic in this letter was in compliance with the request to withdraw the Force. It did not, however, signify the actual withdrawal of the Force which, in fact, was to remain in the area for several more weeks.

25. Formal instructions relating to the withdrawal of UNEF were sent to the UNEF Commander by the Secretary-General on the night of 18 May (see annex).

26. Also on the evening of 18 May the Secretary-General submitted his special report to the General Assembly (A/6730).

27. On 19 May the Secretary-General issued his report to the Security Council on recent developments in the Near East (S/7896).

19 May 1967

28. *1130 hours New York time.* The Secretary-General again received the Permanent Representative of Israel who gave him a statement from his Government concerning the withdrawal of UNEF, strongly urging the Secretary-General to avoid condoning any changes in the *status quo* pending the fullest and broadest international consultation.

29. On the afternoon of 22 May, the Secretary-General departed from New York, arriving in Cairo on the afternoon of 23 May. He left Cairo on the afternoon of 25 May, arriving back in New York on 26 May (see S/7906). While en route

to Cairo during a stop in Paris, the Secretary-General learned that on this day President Nasser had announced his intention to reinstitute the blockade against Israel in the Strait of Tiran.

17 June 1967

30. The withdrawal of UNEF was completed. Details of the actual withdrawal and evacuation of UNEF are given in document A/6730/Add.2.

MAIN POINTS AT ISSUE

31. Comment is called for on some of the main points at issue even prior to the consideration of the background and basis for the stationing of UNEF on United Arab Republic territory.

The Causes of the Present Crisis

32. It has been said rather often in one way or another that the withdrawal of UNEF is a primary cause of the present crisis in the Near East. This is, of course, a superficial and over-simplified approach. As the Secretary-General pointed out in his report of 26 May 1967 to the Security Council (S/7906), this view "ignores the fact that the underlying basis for this and other crisis situations in the Near East is the continuing Arab-Israel conflict which has been present all along and of which the crisis situation created by the unexpected withdrawal of UNEF is the latest expression." The Secretary-General's report to the Security Council of 19 May 1967 (S/7896) described the various elements of the increasingly dangerous situation in the Near East prior to the decision of the Government of the United Arab Republic to terminate its consent for the presence of UNEF on its territory.

33. The United Nations Emergency Force served for more than ten years as a highly valuable instrument in helping to maintain quiet along the line between Israel and the United Arab Republic. Its withdrawal revealed in all its depth and danger the undiminishing conflict between Israel and her Arab neighbours. The withdrawal also made immediately acute the

problem of access for Israel to the Gulf of Aqaba through the Strait of Tiran—a problem which had been dormant for over ten years only because of the presence of UNEF. But the presence of UNEF did not touch the basic problem of the Arab-Israel conflict—it merely isolated, immobilized and covered up certain aspects of that conflict. At any time in the last ten years either of the parties could have reactivated the conflict and if they had been determined to do so UNEF's effectiveness would automatically have disappeared. When, in the context of the whole relationship of Israel with her Arab neighbours, the direct confrontation between Israel and the United Arab Republic was revived after a decade by the decision of the United Arab Republic to move its forces up to the line, UNEF at once lost all usefulness. In fact, its effectiveness as a buffer and as a presence had already vanished, as can be seen from the chronology given above, even before the request for its withdrawal had been received by the Secretary-General from the Government of the United Arab Republic. In recognizing the extreme seriousness of the situation thus created, its true cause, the continuing Arab-Israel conflict, must also be recognized. It is entirely unrealistic to maintain that that conflict could have been solved, or its consequences prevented, if a greater effort had been made to maintain UNEF's presence in the area against the will of the Government of the United Arab Republic.

The Decision on UNEF's Withdrawal

34. The decision to withdraw UNEF has been frequently characterized in various quarters as "hasty," "precipitous," and the like, even, indeed, to the extent of suggesting that it took President Nasser by surprise. The question of the withdrawal of UNEF is by no means a new one. In fact, it was the negotiations on this very question with the Government of Egypt which, after the establishment of UNEF by the General Assembly, delayed its arrival while it waited in a staging area at Capodichino airbase, Naples, Italy, for several days in November 1956. The Government of Egypt, understandably, did not wish

to give permission for the arrival on its soil of an international force, unless it was assured that its sovereignty would be respected and a request for withdrawal of the Force would be honoured. Over the years, in discussions with representatives of the United Arab Republic, the subject of the continued presence of UNEF has occasionally come up, and it was invariably taken for granted by United Arab Republic representatives that if their Government officially requested the withdrawal of UNEF the request would be honoured by the Secretary-General. There is no record to indicate that this assumption was ever questioned. Thus, although the request for the withdrawal of UNEF came as a surprise, there was nothing new about the question of principle nor about the procedure to be followed by the Secretary-General. It follows that the decision taken by him on 18 May 1967 to comply with the request for the withdrawal of the Force was seen by him as the only reasonable and sound action that could be taken. The actual withdrawal itself, it should be recalled, was to be carried out in an orderly, dignified, deliberate and not precipitate manner over a period of several weeks. The first troops in fact left the area only on 29 May.

The Possibility of Delay

35. Opinions have also been frequently expressed that the decision to withdraw UNEF should have been delayed pending consultations of various kinds, or that efforts should have been made to resist the United Arab Republic's request for UNEF's withdrawal, or to bring pressure to bear on the Government of the United Arab Republic to reconsider its decision in this matter. In fact, as the chronology given above makes clear, the effectiveness of UNEF, in the light of the movement of United Arab Republic troops up to the line and into Sharm el-Sheikh, had already vanished before the request for withdrawal was received. Furthermore, the Government of the United Arab Republic had made it entirely clear to the Secretary-General that an appeal for reconsideration of the withdrawal decision

would encounter a firm rebuff and would be considered as an attempt to impose UNEF as an "army of occupation." Such a reaction, combined with the fact that UNEF positions on the line had already been effectively taken over by United Arab Republic troops in pursuit of their full right to move up to the line in their own territory, and a deep anxiety for the security of UNEF personnel should an effort be made to keep UNEF in position after its withdrawal had been requested, were powerful arguments in favour of complying with the United Arab Republic request, even supposing there had not been other overriding reasons for accepting it.

36. It has been said that the decision to withdraw UNEF precipitated other consequences such as the reinstitution of the blockade against Israel in the Strait of Tiran. As can be seen from the chronology, the UNEF positions at Sharm el-Sheikh on the Strait of Tiran (manned by thirty-two men in all) were in fact rendered ineffective by United Arab Republic troops before the request for withdrawal was received. It is also pertinent to note that in response to a query from the Secretary-General as to why the United Arab Republic had announced its reinstitution of the blockade in the Strait of Tiran while the Secretary-General was actually en route to Cairo on 22 May, President Nasser explained that his Government's decision to resume the blockade had been taken some time before U Thant's departure and it was considered preferable to make the announcement before rather than after the Secretary-General's visit to Cairo.

The Question of Consultations

37. It has been said also that there was not adequate consultation with the organs of the United Nations concerned or with the Members before the decision was taken to withdraw the Force. The Secretary-General was, and is, firmly of the opinion that the decision for withdrawal of the Force, on the request of the host Government, rested with the Secretary-General after consultation with the Advisory Committee on

UNEF, which is the organ established by the General Assembly for consultation regarding such matters. This was made clear by Secretary-General Hammarskjöld, who took the following position on 26 February 1957 in reply to a question about the withdrawal of the Force from Sharm el-Sheikh:

> An indicated procedure would be for the Secretary-General to inform the Advisory Committee on the United Nations Emergency Force, which would determine whether the matter should be brought to the attention of the Assembly.[1]

The Secretary-General consulted the Advisory Committee before replying to the letter of 18 May 1967 from the United Arab Republic requesting withdrawal. This consultation took place within a few hours after receipt of the United Arab Republic request, and the Advisory Committee was thus quickly informed of the decision which the Secretary-General had in mind to convey in his reply to the Foreign Minister of the United Arab Republic. As indicated in the report to the Security Council of 26 May 1967:

> The Committee did not move, as it was its right to do under the terms of paragraph 9 of General Assembly resolution 1001 (ES-I) to request the convening of the General Assembly on the situation which had arisen. (S/7906, para. 4)

38. Before consulting the Advisory Committee on UNEF, the Secretary-General had also consulted the Permanent Representatives of the seven countries providing the contingents of UNEF and informed them of his intentions. This, in fact, was more than was formally required of the Secretary-General in the way of consultation.

39. Obviously, many Governments were concerned about the presence and functioning of UNEF and about the general situation in the area, but it would have been physically impossible to consult all of the interested representatives within any

1. *Official Records of the General Assembly, Eleventh Session, Annexes,* agenda item 66, document A/3563, annex I, B, 2.

reasonable time. This was an emergency situation requiring urgent action. Moreover, it was perfectly clear that such consultations were sure to produce sharply divided counsel, even if they were limited to the permanent members of the Security Council. Such sharply divided advice would have complicated and exacerbated the situation, and, far from relieving the Secretary-General of the responsibility for the decision to be taken, would have made the decision much more difficult to take.

40. It has been said that the final decision on the withdrawal of UNEF should have been taken only after consideration by the General Assembly. This position is not only incorrect but also unrealistic. In resolution 1000 (ES-I) the General Assembly established a United Nations command for an emergency international force. On the basis of that resolution the Force was quickly recruited and its forward elements flown to the staging area at Naples. Thus, though established, it had to await the permission of the Government of Egypt to enter Egyptian territory. That permission was subsequently given by the Government of Egypt as a result of direct discussions between Secretary-General Hammarskjöld and President Nasser of Egypt. There is no official United Nations document on the basis of which any case could be made that there was any limitation on the authority of the Government of Egypt to rescind that consent at its pleasure, or which would indicate that the United Arab Republic had in any way surrendered its right to ask for and obtain at any time the removal of UNEF from its territory. This point is elaborated later in this report (see paras. 71-80 below).

41. As a practical matter, there would be little point in any case in taking such an issue to the General Assembly unless there would be reasonable certainty that that body could be expected expeditiously to reach a substantive decision. In the prevailing circumstances, the question could have been validly raised as to what decision other than the withdrawal of UNEF could have been reached by the Assembly once United Arab

Republic consent for the continued presence of UNEF was withdrawn.

42. As regards the practical possibility of the Assembly considering the request for UNEF's withdrawal, it is relevant to observe that the next regular session of the General Assembly was some four months off at the time the withdrawal request was made. The special session of the General Assembly which was meeting at the time could have considered the question, according to rule 19 of the Assembly's rules of procedure, only if two thirds or eighty-two members voted for the inclusion of the item in the agenda. It is questionable, to say the least, whether the necessary support could have been mustered for such a controversial item. There could have been no emergency special session since the issue was not then before the Security Council, and therefore the condition of lack of unanimity did not exist.

43. As far as consultation with or action by the Security Council was concerned, the Secretary-General reported to the Council on the situation leading up to and created by the withdrawal of UNEF on 19 May 1967 (S/7896). In that report he characterized the situation in the Near East as "extremely menacing." The Council met for the first time after this report on 24 May 1967, but took no action.

44. As has already been stated, the Advisory Committee did not make any move to bring the matter before the General Assembly, and no representative of any Member Government requested a meeting of either the Security Council or the General Assembly immediately following the Secretary-General's reports (A/6730 and S/7896). In this situation, the Secretary-General himself did not believe that any useful purpose would be served by his seeking a meeting of either organ, nor did he consider that there was basis for him to do so at that time. Furthermore, the information available to the Secretary-General did not lead him to believe that either the General Assembly or the Security Council would have decided that UNEF should remain on United Arab Republic territory, by force if neces-

sary, despite the request of the Government of the United Arab Republic that it should leave.

Practical Factors Influencing the Decision

45. Since it is still contended in some quarters that the UNEF operation should somehow have continued after the consent of the Government of the United Arab Republic to its presence was withdrawn, it is necessary to consider the factors, quite apart from constitutional and legal considerations, which would have made such a course of action entirely impracticable.

46. The consent and active co-operation of the host country is essential to the effective operation and, indeed, to the very existence, of any United Nations peace-keeping operation of the nature of UNEF. The fact is that UNEF had been deployed on Egyptian and Egyptian-controlled territory for over ten and a half years with the consent and co-operation of the Government of the United Arab Republic. Although it was envisaged in pursuance of General Assembly resolution 1125 (XI) of 2 February 1957 that the Force would be stationed on both sides of the line, Israel exercised its sovereign right to refuse the stationing of UNEF on its side, and the Force throughout its existence was stationed on the United Arab Republic side of the line only.

47. In these circumstances, the true basis for UNEF's effectiveness as a buffer and deterrent to infiltration was, throughout its existence, a voluntary undertaking by local United Arab Republic authorities with UNEF, that United Arab Republic troops would respect a defined buffer zone along the entire length of the line in which only UNEF would operate and from which United Arab Republic troops would be excluded. This undertaking was honoured for more than a decade, and this Egyptian co-operation extended also to Sharm el-Sheikh, Ras Nasrani and the Strait of Tiran. This undertaking was honoured although UNEF had no authority to challenge the right of United Arab Republic troops to be present anywhere on their own territory.

48. It may be pointed out in passing that over the years UNEF dealt with numerous infiltrators coming from the Israel as well as from the United Arab Republic side of the line. It would hardly be logical to take the position that because UNEF has successfully maintained quiet along the line for more than ten years, owing in large measure to the co-operation of the United Arab Republic authorities, that Government should then be told that it could not unilaterally seek the removal of the Force and thus in effect be penalized for the long co-operation with the international community it had extended in the interest of peace.

49. There are other practical factors relating to the above-mentioned arrangement which are highly relevant to the withdrawal of UNEF. First, once the United Arab Republic troops moved up to the line to place themselves in direct confrontation with the military forces of Israel, UNEF had, in fact, no further useful function. Secondly, if the Force was no longer welcome, it could not as a practical matter remain in the United Arab Republic, since the friction which would almost inevitably have arisen with that Government, its armed forces and with the local population would have made the situation of the Force both humiliating and untenable. It would even have been impossible to supply it. UNEF clearly had no mandate to try to stop United Arab Republic troops from moving freely about on their own territory. This was a peace-keeping force, not an enforcement action. Its effectiveness was based entirely on voluntary co-operation.

50. Quite apart from its position in the United Arab Republic, the request of that Government for UNEF's withdrawal automatically set off a disintegration of the Force, since two of the Governments providing contingents quickly let the Secretary-General know that their contingents would be withdrawn, and there can be little doubt that other such notifications would not have been slow in coming if friction had been generated through an unwillingness to comply with the request for withdrawal.

51. For all the foregoing reasons, the operation, and even the continued existence of UNEF on United Arab Republic territory, after the withdrawal of United Arab Republic consent, would have been impossible, and any attempt to maintain the Force there would without question have had disastrous consequences.

LEGAL AND CONSTITUTIONAL CONSIDERATIONS AND THE QUESTION OF CONSENT FOR THE STATIONING OF UNEF ON UNITED ARAB REPUBLIC TERRITORY

52. Legal and constitutional considerations were, of course, of great importance in determining the Secretary-General's actions in relation to the request of the Government of the United Arab Republic for the withdrawal of UNEF. Here again, a chronology of the relevant actions in 1956 and 1957 may be helpful.

53. *4 November 1956.* The General Assembly, at its first emergency special session in resolution 998 (ES-I), requested "the Secretary-General to submit to it within forty-eight hours a plan for the setting up, with the consent of the nations concerned, of an emergency international United Nations Force to secure and supervise the cessation of hostilities. . . ."

54. *5 November 1956.* The General Assembly, in its resolution 1000 (ES-I), established a United Nations Command for an emergency international Force, and, *inter alia,* invited the Secretary-General "to take such administrative measures as may be necessary for the prompt execution of the actions envisaged in the present resolution."

55. *7 November 1956.* The General Assembly, by its resolution 1001 (ES-I), *inter alia,* approved the guiding principles for the organization and functioning of the emergency international United Nations Force and authorized the Secretary-General "to take all other necessary administrative and executive action."

56. *10 November 1956.* Arrival of advance elements of UNEF at staging area in Naples.

57. *8-12 November 1956.* Negotiations between Secretary-General Hammarskjöld and the Government of Egypt on entry of UNEF into Egypt.

58. *12 November 1956.* Agreement on UNEF entry into Egypt announced and then postponed, pending clarification, until 14 November.

59. *15 November 1956.* Arrival of advance elements of UNEF in Abu Suweir, Egypt.

60. *16 November to 18 November 1956.* Negotiations between Secretary-General Hammarskjöld and President Nasser in Cairo on the presence and functioning of UNEF in Egypt and co-operation with Egyptian authorities, and conclusion of an *"aide-mémoire* on the basis for the presence and functioning of UNEF in Egypt" (the so-called "good faith accord").[2]

61. *24 January 1957.* The Secretary-General in a report to the General Assembly[3] suggested that the Force should have units stationed on both sides of the armistice demarcation line and that certain measures should be taken in relation to Sharm el-Sheikh. On *2 February 1957,* the General Assembly, by its resolution 1125 (XI), noted with appreciation the Secretary-General's report and considered that "after full withdrawal of Israel from the Sharm el-Sheikh and Gaza areas, the scrupulous maintenance of the Armistice Agreement required the placing of the United Nations Emergency Force on the Egyptian-Israel armistice demarcation line and the implementation of other measures as proposed in the Secretary-General's report, with due regard to the considerations set out therein with a view to assist in achieving situations conducive to the maintenance of peaceful conditions in the area."

62. *7 March 1957.* Arrival of UNEF in Gaza.

63. *8 March 1957.* Arrival of UNEF elements at Sharm el-Sheikh.

2. Ibid., document A/3375, annex.
3. Ibid., document A/3512.

64. In general terms the consent of the host country to the presence and operation of the United Nations peace-keeping machinery is a basic prerequisite of all United Nations peace-keeping operations. The question has been raised whether the United Arab Republic had the right to request unilaterally the withdrawal "as soon as possible" of UNEF from its territory or whether there were limitations on its rights in this respect. An examination of the records of the first emergency special session and the eleventh session of the General Assembly is relevant to this question.

65. It is clear that the General Assembly and the Secretary-General from the very beginning recognized, and in fact emphasized, the need for Egyptian consent in order that UNEF be stationed or operate on Egyptian territory. Thus, the initial resolution 998 (ES-I) of 4 November 1956 requested the Secretary-General to submit a plan for the setting up of an emergency force, "with the consent of the nations concerned." The "nations concerned" obviously included Egypt (now the United Arab Republic), the three countries (France, Israel and the United Kingdom) whose armies were on Egyptian soil and the States contributing contingents to the Force.

66. The Secretary-General, in his report to the General Assembly of 6 November 1956, stated, *inter alia:*

9. Functioning, as it would, on the basis of a decision reached under the terms of the resolution 337 (V) "Uniting for peace," the Force, if established, would be limited in its operations to the extent that consent of the parties concerned is required under generally recognized international law. While the General Assembly is enabled to *establish* the Force with the consent of those parties which contribute units to the Force, it could not request the Force to be *stationed* or *operate* on the territory of a given country without the consent of the Government of that country.[4]

4. Ibid., *First Emergency Special Session, Annexes,* agenda item 5, document A/3302, para. 9.

67. He noted that the foregoing did not exclude the possibility that the Security Council could use such a Force within the wider margins provided under Chapter VII of the United Nations Charter. He pointed out, however, that it would not be necessary to elaborate this point further, since no use of the Force under Chapter VII, with the rights in relation to Member States that this would entail, had been envisaged.

68. The General Assembly in its resolution 1001 (ES-I) of 7 November 1956 expressed its approval of the guiding principles for the organization and functioning of the emergency international United Nations Force as expounded in paragraphs 6 to 9 of the Secretary-General's report. This included the principle of consent embodied in paragraph 9.

69. The need for Egypt's consent was also stated as a condition or "understanding" by some of the States offering to contribute contingents to the Force.

70. It was thus a basic legal principle arising from the nature of the Force, and clearly understood by all concerned, that the consent of Egypt was a prerequisite to the stationing of UNEF on Egyptian territory, and it was a practical necessity as well in acquiring contingents for the Force.

The "Good Faith" Aide-Mémoire of 20 November 1956

71. There remains to be examined whether any commitments were made by Egypt which would limit its pre-existing right to withdraw its consent at any time that it chose to do so. The only basis for asserting such limitation could be the so-called "good faith" *aide-mémoire* which was set out as an annex to a report of the Secretary-General submitted to the General Assembly on 20 November 1956.

72. The Secretary-General himself did not offer any interpretation of the "good faith" *aide-mémoire* to the General Assembly or make any statement questioning the remarks made by the Foreign Minister of Egypt in the General Assembly the following week (see paragraph 74 below). It would appear,

however, that in an exchange of cables he had sought to obtain the express acknowledgement from Egypt that its consent to the presence of the Force would not be withdrawn before the Force had completed its task. Egypt did not accept this interpretation but held to the view that if its consent was no longer maintained the Force should be withdrawn. Subsequent discussions between Mr. Hammarskjöld and President Nasser resulted in the "good faith" *aide-mémoire*.

73. An interpretative account of these negotiations made by Mr. Hammarskjöld in a personal and private paper entitled *"aide-mémoire,"* dated 5 August 1957, some eight and a half months after the discussions, has recently been made public by a private person who has a copy. It is understood that Mr. Hammarskjöld often prepared private notes concerning significant events under the heading *"aide-mémoire."* This memorandum is not in any official record of the United Nations nor is it in any of the official files. The General Assembly, the Advisory Committee on UNEF and the Government of Egypt were not informed of its contents or existence. It is not an official paper and has no standing beyond being a purely private memorandum of unknown purpose or value, in which Secretary-General Hammarskjöld seems to record his own impressions and interpretations of his discussions with President Nasser. This paper, therefore, cannot affect in any way the basis for the presence of UNEF on the soil of the United Arab Republic as set out in the official documents, much less supersede those documents.

Position of Egypt

74. It seems clear that Egypt did not understand the "good faith" *aide-mémoire* to involve any limitation on its right to withdraw its consent to the continued stationing and operation of UNEF on its territory. The Foreign Minister of Egypt, speaking in the General Assembly on 27 November 1956, one week after the publication of the "good faith" *aide-mémoire*

and three days following its approval by the General Assembly, said:

> We still believe that the General Assembly resolution of 7 November 1956 still stands, together with its endorsement of the principle that the General Assembly could not request the United Nations Emergency Force to be stationed or to operate on the territory of a given country without the consent of the Government of the country. This is the proper basis on which we believe, together with the overwhelming majority of this Assembly, that the United Nations Emergency Force could be stationed or could operate in Egypt. It is the only basis on which Egypt has given its consent in this respect.[5]

He then added:

> . . . as must be abundantly clear, this Force has gone to Egypt to help Egypt, with Egypt's consent; and no one here or elsewhere can reasonably or fairly say that a fire brigade, after putting out a fire, would be entitled or expected to claim the right of deciding not to leave the house.[6]

Analysis of the "Task" of the Force

75. In the "good faith" *aide-mémoire* the Government of Egypt declared that, "when exercising its sovereign rights on any matters concerning the presence and functioning of UNEF, it will be guided, in good faith, by its acceptance of General Assembly resolution 1000 (ES-I) of 5 November 1956."

76. The United Nations in turn declared "that the activities of UNEF will be guided, in good faith, by the task established for the Force in the aforementioned resolutions [1000 (ES-I) and 997 (ES-I)]; in particular, the United Nations, understanding this to correspond to the wishes of the Government of Egypt, reaffirms its willingness to maintain UNEF until its task is completed."

77. It must be noted that, while Egypt undertook to be

5. *Official Records of the General Assembly, Eleventh Session, Plenary Meetings,* 597th meeting, para. 48.
6. Ibid., para. 50.

guided in *good faith* by its acceptance of General Assembly resolution 1000 (ES-I), the United Nations also undertook to be guided in *good faith* by the task established for the Force in resolutions 1000 (ES-I) and 997 (ES-I). Resolution 1000 (ES-I), to which the declaration of Egypt referred, established a United Nations Command for the Force "to secure and supervise the cessation of hostilities in accordance with all the terms" of resolution 997 (ES-I). It must be recalled that at this time Israel forces had penetrated deeply into Egyptian territory and that forces of France and the United Kingdom were conducting military operations on Egyptian territory. Resolution 997 (ES-I) urged as a matter of priority that all parties agree to an immediate cease-fire, and halt the movement of military forces and arms into the area. It also urged the parties to the armistice agreements promptly to withdraw all forces behind the armistice lines, to desist from raids across the armistice lines, and to observe scrupulously the provisions of the armistice agreements. It further urged that, upon the cease-fire being effective, steps be taken to reopen the Suez Canal and restore secure freedom of navigation.

78. While the terms of resolution 997 (ES-I) cover a considerable area, the emphasis in resolution 1000 (ES-I) is on *securing and supervising the cessation of hostilities*. Moreover, on 6 November 1956 the Secretary-General, in his second and final report on the plan for an emergency international United Nations Force, noted that "the Assembly intends that the Force should be of a temporary nature, the length of its assignment being determined by the needs arising out of the present conflict." [7] Noting further the terms of resolution 997 (ES-I) he added that "the functions of the United Nations Force would be, when a cease-fire is being established, to enter Egyptian territory with the consent of the Egyptian Government, in order to help maintain quiet during and after the withdrawal of non-Egyptian troops, and to secure compliance with the other terms

7. Ibid., *First Emergency Special Session, Annexes,* agenda item 5, document A/3302, para. 8.

established in the resolution of 2 November 1956" (997 (ES-I)).[8]

79. In a cable delivered to Foreign Minister Fawzi on 9 or 10 November 1956, in reply to a request for clarification as to how long it was contemplated that the Force should stay in the demarcation line area, the Secretary-General stated: "A definite reply is at present impossible but the emergency character of the Force links it to the immediate crises envisaged in resolution 2 November [997 (ES-I)] and its liquidation." This point was confirmed in a further exchange of cables between the Secretary-General and Dr. Fawzi on 14 November 1956.

80. The Foreign Minister of Egypt (Dr. Fawzi) gave his understanding of the task of the Force in a statement to the General Assembly on 27 November 1956:

> Our clear understanding—and I am sure it is the clear understanding of the Assembly—is that this Force is in Egypt only in relation to the present attack against Egypt by the United Kingdom, France and Israel, and for the purposes directly connected with the incursion of the invading forces into Egyptian territory. The United Nations Emergency Force is in Egypt, not as an occupation force, not as a replacement for the invaders, not to clear the Canal of obstructions, not to resolve any question or settle any problem, be it in relation to the Suez Canal, to Palestine or to any other matter; it is not there to infringe upon Egyptian sovereignty in any fashion or to any extent, but, on the contrary, to give expression to the determination of the United Nations to put an end to the aggression committed against Egypt and to the presence of the invading forces in Egyptian territory.[9]

81. In letters dated 3 November 1956 addressed to the Secretary-General, the representatives of both France and the United Kingdom had proposed very broad functions for UNEF, stating on behalf of their Governments that military action could be stopped if the following conditions were met:

8. Ibid., para. 12.
9. Ibid., *Eleventh Session, Plenary Meetings,* 597th meeting, para. 49.

(a) Both the Egyptian and Israel Governments agree to accept a United Nations Force to keep the peace.

(b) The United Nations decides to constitute and maintain such a Force until an Arab-Israel peace settlement is reached and until satisfactory arrangements have been agreed in regard to the Suez Canal, both agreements to be guaranteed by the United Nations.

(c) In the meantime, until the United Nations Force is constituted, both combatants agree to accept forthwith limited detachments of Anglo-French troops to be stationed between the combatants.[10]

These broad functions for the Force were not acceptable to the General Assembly, however, as was pointed out in telegrams dated 4 November 1956 from Secretary-General Dag Hammarskjöld to the Minister for Foreign Affairs of France and the Secretary of State for Foreign Affairs of the United Kingdom.[11]

82. Finally, it is obvious that the task referred to in the "good faith" *aide-mémoire* could only be the task of the Force as it had been defined in November 1956 when the understanding was concluded. The "good faith" undertaking by the United Nations would preclude it from claiming that the Egyptian agreement was relevant or applicable to functions which the Force was given at a much later date. The stationing of the Force on the armistice demarcation line and at Sharm el-Sheikh was only determined in pursuance of General Assembly resolution 1125 (XI) of 2 February 1957. The Secretary-General, in his reports relating to this decision, made it clear that the further consent of Egypt was essential with respect to these new functions.[12] Consequently, the understanding recorded in the "good faith" *aide-mémoire* of 20 November 1956 could not have been, itself, a commitment with respect to functions

10. Ibid., *First Emergency Special Session, Annexes,* documents A/3268 and A/3269.
11. Ibid., document A/3284, annexes 2 and 4.
12. Ibid., *Eleventh Session, Annexes,* agenda item 66, documents A/3512, para. 20, and A/3527, para. 5.

only determined in February and March 1957. It is only these later tasks that the Force had been performing during the last ten years—tasks of serving as a buffer and deterring infiltrators which went considerably beyond those of securing and supervising the cessation of hostilities provided in the General Assembly resolutions and referred to in the "good faith" *aide-mémoire*.

The Stationing of UNEF on the Armistice Demarcation Line and at Sharm el-Sheikh

83. There remains to examine whether Egypt made further commitments with respect to the stationing of the Force on the armistice demarcation line and at Sharm el-Sheikh. Israel, of course, sought to obtain such commitments, particularly with respect to the area around Sharm el-Sheikh.

84. For example, in an *aide-mémoire* of 4 February 1957,[13] the Government of Israel sought clarification as to whether units of the United Nations Emergency Force would be stationed along the western shore of the Gulf of Aqaba in order to act as a restraint against hostile acts, and would remain so deployed until another effective means was agreed upon between the parties concerned for ensuring permanent freedom of navigation and the absence of belligerent acts in the Strait of Tiran and the Gulf of Aqaba. The Secretary-General pointed out that such "clarification" would require "Egyptian consent." He stated:

> The second of the points in the Israel *aide-mémoire* requests a "clarification" which, in view of the position of the General Assembly, could go beyond what was stated in the last report only after negotiation with Egypt. This follows from the statements in the debate in the General Assembly, and the report on which it was based, which make it clear that the stationing of the Force at Sharm el-Sheikh, under such terms as those mentioned in the question posed by Israel, would require Egyptian consent.[14]

13. Ibid., document A/3527, annex I.
14. Ibid., document A/3527, para. 5.

205 / A P P E N D I X 8

85. It is clear from the record that Egypt did not give its consent to Israel's proposition. The Secretary-General's report of 8 March 1957 [15] recorded "arrangements for the complete and unconditional withdrawal of Israel in accordance with the decision of the General Assembly." There is no agreement on the part of Egypt to forgo its rights with respect to the granting or withdrawing of its consent to the continued stationing of the Force on its territory. On the contrary, at the 667th plenary meeting of the General Assembly on 4 March 1957, the Foreign Minister of Egypt stated:

At our previous meeting I stated that the Assembly was unanimous in expecting full and honest implementation of its resolutions calling for immediate and unconditional withdrawal by Israel. I continue to submit to the Assembly that this position —which is the only position the Assembly can possibly take— remains intact and entire. Nothing said by anyone here or elsewhere could shake this fact or detract from its reality and its validity, nor could it affect the fullness and the lawfulness of Egypt's rights and those of the Arab people of the Gaza Strip.[16]

86. The Foreign Minister of Israel, in her statement at the 666th meeting of the General Assembly, on 1 March 1957, asserted that an assurance had been given that any proposal for the withdrawal of UNEF from the Gulf of Aqaba area would come first to the Advisory Committee on UNEF (see paragraphs 95–98 below).

Question of the Stationing of UNEF on Both Sides of the Armistice Demarcation Line

87. Another point having significance with respect to the undertakings of Egypt is the question of the stationing of UNEF on both sides of the armistice demarcation line. The Secretary-General, in his report of 24 January 1957 to the

15. Ibid., document A/3568.
16. Ibid., *Eleventh Session, Plenary Meetings,* 667th meeting, para. 240.

General Assembly,[17] suggested that the Force should have units stationed also on the Israel side of the armistice demarcation line. In particular, he suggested that units of the Force should at least be stationed in the El Auja demilitarized zone[18] which had been occupied by the armed forces of Israel. He indicated that if El Auja were demilitarized in accordance with the Armistice Agreement and units of UNEF were stationed there, a condition of reciprocity would be the Egyptian assurance that Egyptian forces would not take up positions in the area in contravention of the Armistice Agreement.[19] However, Israel forces were never withdrawn from El Auja and UNEF was not accepted at any point on the Israel side of the line.

88. Following the Secretary-General's report, the General Assembly on 2 February 1957 adopted resolution 1125 (XI), in which it noted the report with appreciation and considered:

> . . . that, after full withdrawal of Israel from the Sharm el-Sheikh and Gaza areas, the scrupulous maintenance of the Armistice Agreement requires the placing of the United Nations Emergency Force on the Egyptian-Israel armistice demarcation line and the implementation of other measures as proposed in the Secretary-General's report, with due regard to the considerations set out therein with a view to assist in achieving situations conducive to the maintenance of peaceful conditions in the area.

89. On 11 February 1957, the Secretary-General stated in a report to the General Assembly that, in the light of the implication of Israel's question concerning the stationing of

17. Ibid., *Eleventh Session, Annexes,* agenda item 66, document A/3512.
18. Article VIII of the Egyptian-Israel General Armistice Agreement provides, *inter alia,* that an area comprising the village of El Auja and vicinity, as defined in the article, shall be demilitarized and that both Egyptian and Israel armed forces shall be totally excluded therefrom. The article further provides that on the Egyptian side of the frontier, facing the El Auja area, no Egyptian defensive positions shall be closer to El Auja than El Qouseima and Abou Aoueigila.
19. *Official Records of the General Assembly, Eleventh Session, Annexes,* agenda item 66, document A/3512, paras. 15–22.

UNEF at Sharm el-Sheikh (see paragraph 84 above), he "considered it important . . . to learn whether Israel itself, in principle, consents to a stationing of UNEF units on its territory in implementation of the functions established for the Force in the basic decisions and noted in resolution 1125 (XI) where it was indicated that the Force should be placed 'on the Egyptian-Israel armistice demarcation line.' " [20] No affirmative response was ever received from Israel. In fact, already on 7 November 1956 the Prime Minister of Israel, Mr. Ben Gurion, in a speech to the Knesset, stated, *inter alia,* "On no account will Israel agree to the stationing of a foreign force, no matter how called, in her territory or in any of the territories occupied by her." In a note to correspondents of 12 April 1957 a "United Nations spokesman" stated:

> Final arrangements for the UNEF will have to wait for the response of the Government of Israel to the request by the General Assembly that the Force be deployed also on the Israeli side of the Armistice Demarcation Line.

90. In a report dated 9 October 1957 to the twelfth session of the General Assembly,[21] the Secretary-General stated:

> Resolution 1125 (XI) calls for placing the Force "on the Egyptian-Israel armistice demarcation line," but no stationing of UNEF on the Israel side has occurred to date through lack of consent by Israel.

91. In the light of Israel's persistent refusal to consent to the stationing and operation of UNEF on its side of the line in spite of General Assembly resolution 1125 (XI) of 2 February 1957 and the efforts of the Secretary-General, it is even less possible to consider that Egypt's "good faith" declaration made in November 1956 could constitute a limitation of its rights with respect to the continued stationing and operation

20. Ibid., document A/3527, para. 5.
21. Ibid., *Twelfth Session, Annexes,* agenda item 65, document A/3694, para. 15.

of UNEF on Egyptian territory in accordance with the resolution of 2 February 1957.

92. The representative of Israel stated at the 592nd meeting of the General Assembly, on 23 November 1956:

> If we were to accept one of the proposals made here—namely, that the Force should separate Egyptian and Israel troops for as long as Egypt thought it convenient and should then be withdrawn on Egypt's unilateral request—we would reach a reduction to absurdity. Egypt would then be in a position to build up, behind the screen of this Force, its full military preparations and, when it felt that those military preparations had reached their desired climax, to dismiss the United Nations Emergency Force and to stand again in close contact and proximity with the territory of Israel. This reduction to absurdity proves how impossible it is to accept in any matter affecting the composition or the functions of the Force the policies of the Egyptian Government as the sole or even the decisive criterion.[22]

93. The answer to this problem which is to be found in resolution 1125 (XI) of 2 February 1957 is not in the form of a binding commitment by Egypt which the record shows was never given, but in the proposal that the Force should be stationed on both sides of the line. Israel in the exercise of its sovereign right did not give its consent to the stationing of UNEF on its territory and Egypt did not forgo its sovereign right to withdraw its consent at any time.

Role of the UNEF Advisory Committee

94. General Assembly resolution 1001 (ES-I) of 7 November 1956, by which the Assembly approved the guiding principles for the organization and functioning of UNEF, established an Advisory Committee on UNEF under the chairmanship of the Secretary-General. The Assembly decided that the Advisory Committee, in the performance of its duties, should be empowered to request, through the usual procedures,

22. Ibid., *Eleventh Session, Plenary Meetings,* 592nd meeting, para. 131.

the convening of the General Assembly and to report to the Assembly whenever matters arose which, in its opinion, were of such urgency and importance as to require consideration by the General Assembly itself.

95. The memorandum of important points in the discussion between the representative of Israel and the Secretary-General on 25 February 1957 recorded the following question raised by the representative of Israel:

> In connexion with the duration of UNEF's deployment in the Sharm el-Sheikh area, would the Secretary-General give notice to the General Assembly of the United Nations before UNEF would be withdrawn from the area, with or without Egyptian insistence, or before the Secretary-General would agree to its withdrawal? [23]

96. The response of the Secretary-General was recorded as follows:

> On the question of notification to the General Assembly, the Secretary-General wanted to state his view at a later meeting. An indicated procedure would be for the Secretary-General to inform the Advisory Committee on the United Nations Emergency Force, which would determine whether the matter should be brought to the attention of the Assembly.[24]

97. On 1 March 1957 the Foreign Minister of Israel stated at the 666th plenary meeting of the General Assembly:

> My Government has noted the assurance embodied in the Secretary-General's note of 26 February 1957 [A/3363, annex] that any proposal for the withdrawal of the United Nations Emergency Force from the Gulf of Aqaba area would first come to the Advisory Committee on the United Nations Emergency Force, which represents the General Assembly in the implementation of its resolution 997 (ES-I) of 2 November 1956. This procedure will give the General Assembly an opportunity

23. Ibid., *Eleventh Session, Annexes,* agenda item 66, document A/3563, annex I, A, 2.
24. Ibid., annex I, B, 2.

to ensure that no precipitate changes are made which would have the effect of increasing the possibility of belligerent acts.[25]

98. In fact, the 25 February 1957 memorandum does not go as far as the interpretation given by the Foreign Minister of Israel. In any event, however, it gives no indication of any commitment by Egypt, and so far as the Secretary-General is concerned it only indicates that a procedure would be for the Secretary-General to inform the Advisory Committee which would determine whether the matter should be brought to the attention of the General Assembly. This was also the procedure provided in General Assembly resolution 1001 (ES-I). It was, furthermore, the procedure followed by the Secretary-General on the withdrawal of UNEF.

OBSERVATIONS

99. A partial explanation of the misunderstanding about the withdrawal of UNEF is an evident failure to appreciate the essentially fragile nature of the basis for UNEF's operation throughout its existence. UNEF in functioning depended completely on the voluntary co-operation of the host Government. Its basis of existence was the willingness of Governments to provide contingents to serve under an international command and at a minimum of cost to the United Nations. It was a symbolic force, small in size, with only 3400 men, of whom 1800 were available to police a line of 295 miles at the time of its withdrawal. It was equipped with light weapons only. It had no mandate of any kind to open fire except in the last resort in self-defence. It had no formal mandate to exercise any authority in the area in which it was stationed. In recent years it experienced an increasingly uncertain basis of financial support, which in turn gave rise to strong annual pressures for reduction in its strength. Its remarkable success for more than a decade, despite these practical weaknesses, may have led to wrong conclusions about its nature, but it has also pointed the

25. Ibid., *Eleventh Session, Plenary Meetings,* 666th meeting, para. 8.

way to a unique means of contributing significantly to international peace-keeping.

Cable Containing Instructions for the Withdrawal of UNEF Sent by the Secretary-General to the Commander of UNEF on 18 May 1967, at 2230 hours New York Time

The following instructions are to be put in effect by you as of date and time of their receipt and shall remain operative until and unless new instructions are sent by me.

1. UNEF is being withdrawn because the consent of the Government of the United Arab Republic for its continued deployment on United Arab Republic territory and United Arab Republic-controlled territory has been rescinded.

2. Date of the commencement of the withdrawal of UNEF will be 19 May when the Secretary-General's response to the request for withdrawal will be received in Cairo by the Government of the United Arab Republic, when also the General Assembly will be informed of the action taken and the action will become public knowledge.

3. The withdrawal of UNEF is to be orderly and must be carried out with dignity befitting a Force which has contributed greatly to the maintenance of quiet and peace in the area of its deployment and has earned widespread admiration.

4. The Force does not cease to exist or to lose its status or any of its entitlements, privileges and immunities until all of its elements have departed from the area of its operation.

5. It will be a practical fact that must be reckoned with by the Commander that as of the date of the announcement of its withdrawal the Force will no longer be able to carry out its established functions as a buffer and as a deterrent to infiltration. Its duties, therefore, after 19 May and until all elements have been withdrawn, will be entirely nominal and concerned primarily with devising arrangements and implementation of arrangements for withdrawal and the morale of the personnel.

6. The Force, of course, will remain under the exclusive command of its United Nations Commander and is to take no orders from any other source, whether United Arab Republic or national.

7. The Commander, his headquarters staff and the contingent commanders shall take every reasonable precaution to ensure the continuance of good relations with the local authorities and the local population.

8. In this regard, it should be made entirely clear by the Commander to the officers and other ranks in the Force that there is no discredit of the Force in this withdrawal and no humiliation involved for the reason that the Force has operated very successfully and with, on the whole, co-operation from the Government on the territory of an independent sovereign State for over ten years, which is a very long time; and, moreover, the reasons for the termination of the operation are of an overriding political nature, having no relation whatsoever to the performance of the Force in the discharge of its duties.

9. The Commander and subordinate officers must do their utmost to avoid any resort to the use of arms and any clash with the forces of the United Arab Republic or with the local civilian population.

10. A small working team will be sent from Headquarters by the Secretary-General to assist in the arrangements for, and effectuation of, the withdrawal.

11. The Commander shall take all necessary steps to protect United Nations installations, properties and stores during the period of withdrawal.

12. If necessary, a small detail of personnel of the Force or preferably of United Nations security officers will be maintained as long as necessary for the protection of United Nations properties pending their ultimate disposition.

13. UNEF aircraft will continue flights as necessary in connexion with the withdrawal arrangements but observation flights will be discontinued immediately.

14. Elements of the Force now deployed along the line will

be first removed from the line, the IF and ADL, including Sharm el-Sheikh to their camps and progressively to central staging.

15. The pace of the withdrawal will of course depend upon the availability of transport by air, sea and ground to Port Said. The priority in withdrawal should of course be personnel and their personal arms and equipment first, followed by contingent stores and equipment.

16. We must proceed on the assumption that UNEF will have full co-operation of United Arab Republic authorities on all aspects of evacuation, and to this end a request will be made by me to the United Arab Republic Government through their Mission here.

17. As early as possible the Commander of UNEF should prepare and transmit to the Secretary-General a plan and schedule for the evacuation of troops and their equipment.

18. Preparation of the draft of the sections of the annual report by the Secretary-General to the General Assembly should be undertaken and, to the extent possible, completed during the period of the withdrawal.

19. In the interests of the Force itself and the United Nations, every possible measure should be taken to ensure against public comments or comments likely to become public on the withdrawal, the reasons for it and reactions to it.

Speech of President
Gamal Abdel Nasser
MAY 22, 1967

The entire country looks up to you today. The entire Arab nation supports you. It is clear that in these circumstances the entire people fully support you and consider the armed forces as their hope today. It is definite that the entire Arab nation also supports our armed forces in the present circumstances through which the entire Arab nation is passing.

What I wish to say is that we are now in 1967, and not in 1956 after the tripartite aggression. A great deal was said and all the secrets were ambiguous. Israel, its commanders and rulers, boasted a great deal after 1956. I have read every word written about the 1956 events, and I also know exactly what happened in 1956.

On the night of Oct. 29, 1956, the Israeli aggression against us began. Fighting began on Oct. 30. We received the Anglo-French ultimatum which asked us to withdraw several miles west of the Suez Canal.

On Oct. 31, the Anglo-French attack on us began. The air raids began at sunset on Oct. 31. At the same time, all our forces in Sinai were withdrawn completely to inside Egypt. Thus in 1956 we did not have an opportunity to fight Israel. We decided to withdraw before the actual fighting with Israel began.

Despite our decision to withdraw, Israel was unable to occupy any of our positions except after we left them. But Israel created a big uproar, boasted and said a great deal about the Sinai campaign and the Sinai battle.

Every one of you knows all the rubbish that was said. They probably believed it themselves.

Today, more than ten years after Suez, all the secrets have been exposed. The most important secret concerns Ben Gurion, when the imperialists brought him to France to employ him as a dog for imperialism to begin the operation.

Ben Gurion refused to undertake anything unless he was given a written guarantee that they would protect him from the Egyptian bombers and the Egyptian Air Force. All this is no longer secret. The entire world knows.

It was on this basis that France sent fighter planes to Ben Gurion, and it was also on this basis that Britain pledged to Ben Gurion to bomb Egyptian airfields within twenty-four hours after the aggression began.

This goes to show how much they took into account the Egyptian forces. Ben Gurion himself said he had to think about the Haifa-Jerusalem-Tel Aviv triangle, which contains one-third of Israel's population. He could not attack Egypt out of fear of the Egyptian Air Force and bombers.

At that time we had a few Ilyushin bombers. We had just acquired them to arm ourselves. Today we have many Ilyushins and others. There is a great difference between yesterday and today, between 1956 and 1967.

Why do I say all this? I say it because we are in a confrontation with Israel. Israel today is not backed by Britain and France as was the case in 1956. It has the United States, which supports it and supplies it with arms. But the world cannot again accept the plotting which took place in 1956.

Israel has been clamoring since 1956. It speaks of Israel's competence and high standard of training. It is backed in this by the West and the Western press. They capitalized on the Sinai campaign, where no fighting actually took place because we had withdrawn to confront Britain and France.

Today we have a chance to prove the fact. We have, indeed, a chance to make the world see matters in their true perspective. We are now face to face with Israel. In recent days Israel has been making threats of aggression and it has been boasting.

On May 12 a very impertinent statement was made. Anyone reading this statement must believe that these people are so boastful and deceitful that one simply cannot remain silent. The statement said that the Israeli commanders have announced they would carry out military operations against Syria in order to occupy Damascus and overthrow the Syrian Government.

On the same day, Israeli Premier Eshkol made a strongly threatening statement against Syria. At the same time, the commentaries said that Israel believed Egypt could not make a move because it was bogged down in Yemen.

Of course they say that we are bogged down in Yemen and have problems there. We are in Yemen. But they seem to believe the lies they have been saying all these years about our existence in Yemen. It is also possible that the Israelis believe such lies.

We are capable of bearing our duties in Yemen, and at the same time doing our national duty here in Egypt in defending our borders and in attacking if Israel attacks Arab country.

On May 13 we received accurate information that Israel was concentrating on the Syrian border huge armed forces of about 11 to 13 brigades. These forces were divided into two fronts, one south of Lake Tiberias and the other north of the lake.

The decision made by Israel at this time was to carry out an aggression against Syria as of May 17. On May 14 we took our measures, discussed the matter and contacted our Syrian brothers. The Syrians also had this information.

On this basis, Lieut. Gen. Muhammed Fawzi left for Syria to coordinate matters. We told them that we had decided that if Syria was attacked, Egypt would enter the battle from the first minute. This was the situation May 14. The forces began to move in the direction of Sinai to take up normal positions.

News agencies reported yesterday that these military movements must have been the result of a previously well-laid plan. And I say that the sequence of events determined the plan. We had no plan before May 13, because we believed that Israel would not dare attack any Arab country and that Israel would not have dared to make such an impertinent statement.

On May 16 we requested the withdrawal of the United Nations Emergency Force (UNEF) in a letter from Lieut. Gen. Muhammed Fawzi. We then requested the complete withdrawal of UNEF.

A big worldwide campaign, led by the United States, Britain and Canada, began opposing the withdrawal of UNEF from Egypt. Thus we felt that there were attempts to turn UNEF into a force serving neoimperialism.

It is obvious that UNEF entered Egypt with our approval and therefore cannot continue to stay in Egypt except with our approval. Until yesterday, a great deal was said about UNEF.

A campaign is also being mounted against the United Nations Secretary General because he made a faithful and honest decision and could not surrender to the pressure brought to bear upon him by the United States, Britain and Canada to make UNEF an instrument for implementing imperialism's plans.

It is quite natural—and I say this quite frankly—that had UNEF ignored its basic mission and turned to achieving the aims of imperialism, we would have regarded it as a hostile force and forcibly disarmed it. We are definitely capable of doing such a job.

I say this now not to discredit the UNEF but to those who have neoimperialist ideas and who want the United Nations to achieve their aims: There is not a single nation which truly respects itself and enjoys full sovereignty which could accept these methods in any form.

At the same time I say that the UNEF has honorably and faithfully carried out its duties. And the UN Secretary General refused to succumb to pressure. Thus he issued immediate orders to the UNEF to withdraw. Consequently, we laud the UNEF, which stayed ten years in our country serving peace.

And when they left—at a time when we found that the neoimperialist forces wanted to divert them from their basic aim —we gave them a cheerful sendoff and saluted them.

Our forces are now in Sinai, and we are in a state of complete mobilization in Gaza and Sinai. We note that there is a great deal of talk about peace these days. Peace, peace, international peace, international security, UN intervention and so on and so forth, which appears daily in the press.

Why is it that no one spoke about peace, the United Nations and security when on May 12 the Israeli Premier and the Israeli commanders made their statements that they would occupy Damascus, overthrow the Syrian region, strike vigorously at Syria and occupy a part of Syrian territory?

It was obvious that they approved of the statements made by the Israeli Premier and commanders.

There is talk about peace now. What is peace? If there is a true desire for peace, we say that we also work for peace.

But does peace mean that we should ignore the rights of the Palestinian people because of the lapse of time? Does peace mean that we should concede our rights because of the lapse of time? Nowadays they speak about a "UN presence in the region for the sake of peace." Does "UN presence in the region for peace" mean that we should close our eyes to everything?

The United Nations adopted a number of resolutions in favor of the Palestinian people. Israel implemented none of these resolutions. This brought no reaction from the United States.

Today U.S. Senators, members of the House of Representatives, the press and the entire world speak in favor of Israel, of the Jews. But nothing is said in favor of the Arabs.

The UN resolutions which are in favor of the Arabs were not implemented. What does this mean? No one is speaking in the Arab's favor. How does the United Nations stand with regard to the Palestinian people? How does it stand with regard to the tragedy which has continued since 1958?

The peace talk is heard only when Israel is in danger. But when Arab rights and the rights of the Palestinian people are lost, no one speaks about peace, rights or anything.

Therefore it is clear that an alliance exists between the Western powers—chiefly represented by the United States and Britain—and Israel. There is a political alliance. This political alliance prompts the Western powers to give military equipment to Israel.

Yesterday and the day before yesterday the entire world was speaking about Sharm el-Sheikh, navigation in the Gulf of Aqaba, the Eilat port. This morning I heard the BBC say that in 1956 Abdel Nasser pledged to open the Gulf of Aqaba.

Of course this is not true. It was copied from a British paper called the *Daily Mail*. No such thing happened. Abdel Nasser would never forfeit any UAR right. As I said, we would never give away a grain of sand from our soil or our country.

The armed forces' responsibility is now yours. The armed forces yesterday occupied Sharm el-Sheikh. What is the meaning of the armed forces' occupation of Sharm el-Sheikh? It is an affirmation of our rights and our sovereignty over the Aqaba Gulf. The Aqaba Gulf constitutes our Egyptian territorial waters. Under no circumstances will we allow the Israeli flag to pass through the Aqaba Gulf.

The Jews threatened war. We tell them: You are welcome, we are ready for war. Our armed forces and all our people are ready for war, but under no circumstances will we abandon any of our rights. This water is ours.

War might be an opportunity for the Jews—for Israel and Rabin* to test their forces against ours and to see that what they wrote about the 1956 battle and the occupation of Sinai was all a lot of nonsense.

Of course there is imperialism, Israel and reaction. Reaction casts doubt on everything, and so does the Islamic Alliance.

We all know that the Islamic Alliance is now represented by three states: the kingdom of Saudi Arabia, the kingdom of Jordan, and Iran. They are saying that the purpose of the Islamic Alliance is to unite the Moslems against Israel.

I would like the Islamic Alliance to serve the Palestine ques-

* Israeli Chief of Staff, Major General Yitzhak Rabin.

tion in only one way: by preventing the supply of oil to Israel. The oil which now reaches Israel through Eilat comes from one of the Islamic Alliance states. It goes to Eilat from Iran.

Who is supplying Israel with oil? The Islamic Alliance— Iran, an Islamic Alliance state.

Such is the Islamic Alliance. It is an imperialist alliance, and this means it sides with Zionism because Zionism is the main ally of imperialism.

The Arab world, which is now mobilized to the highest degree, knows all this. It knows how to deal with the imperialist agents, the allies of Zionism and the fifth column. They say they want to coordinate their plans with us. We cannot at all coordinate our plans with the Islamic Alliance members because it would mean giving our plans to the Jews and to Israel.

This is a serious battle. When we said we were ready for the battle, we meant that we would indeed fight if Syria or any other Arab state was subjected to aggression.

The armed forces are now everywhere. The army and all the forces are now mobilized, and so are the people. They are all behind you, praying for you day and night and feeling that you are the pride of their nation, of the Arab nation. This is the feeling of the Arab people in Egypt and outside Egypt. We are confident that you will honor the trust.

Every one of us is ready to die and not give away a grain of his country's sand. This, for us, is the greatest honor. It is the greatest honor for us to defend our country. We are not scared by imperialist, Zionist or reactionary campaigns.

We are independent, and we know the taste of freedom. We have built a strong national army and achieved our objectives. We are building our country.

There is currently a propaganda campaign, a psychological campaign and a campaign of doubt against us. We leave all this behind us and follow the course of duty and victory.

May God be with you!

APPENDIX 10

*Speech of President Gamal Abdel Nasser
to Central Council of International
Confederation of Arab Trade Unions*

MAY 26, 1967

For several years, many people have raised doubts about our intentions toward Palestine. But talk is easy and action is difficult—very difficult. We emerged wounded from the 1956 battle. Britain, Israel, and France attacked us then. We sustained heavy losses in 1956. Later, unity [with Syria] was realized. The 1961 secession occurred when we had just barely gotten completely together and firmly on our feet.

Later the Yemeni revolution broke out. We considered it our duty to rescue our brothers simply because of the principles and ideals which we advocated and still advocate. We awaited the proper day when we would be fully prepared and confident that we would adopt strong measures if we were to enter the battle with Israel. I say nothing aimlessly. One day two years ago, I stood up to say that we have no plan to liberate Palestine and that revolutionary action is our only course to liberate Palestine. I spoke at the summit conferences. The summit conferences were meant to prepare the Arab states to defend themselves. Recently we have felt strong enough that if we were to enter a battle with Israel, with God's help we could triumph. On this basis, we decided to take actual steps.

A great deal has been said in the past about the UN Emergency Force (UNEF). Many people blamed us for UNEF's presence. We were not strong enough. Should we have listened to them or built and trained our army instead while UNEF still existed? I said once that we could tell UNEF to leave

221

within half an hour. Once we were fully prepared we could ask UNEF to leave. And this is what has actually happened.

The same thing happened with regard to Sharm el-Sheikh. We were also attacked on this score by some Arabs. Taking over Sharm el-Sheikh meant confrontation with Israel. Taking such action also meant that we were ready to enter a general war with Israel. It was not a separate operation. Therefore, we had to take this fact into consideration when moving to Sharm el-Sheikh. The present operation was mounted on this basis.

Actually I was authorized by the Supreme Executive Committee [of the Arab Socialist Union] to implement this plan at the right time. The right time came when Syria was threatened with aggression. We sent reconnaissance planes over Israel. Not a single brigade was stationed opposite us on the Israeli side of the border. All Israeli brigades were confronting Syria. All but four brigades have now moved south to confront Egypt. Those four are still on the border with Syria. We are confident that once we have entered the battle we will triumph, God willing.

With regard to military plans, there is complete coordination of military action between us and Syria. We will operate as one army fighting a single battle for the sake of a common objective—the objective of the Arab nation. The problem today is not just Israel, but also those behind it. If Israel embarks on an aggression against Syria or Egypt, the battle against Israel will be a general one and not confined to one spot on the Syrian or Egyptian border. The battle will be a general one and our basic objective will be to destroy Israel. I probably could not have said such things five or even three years ago. If I had said such things and had been unable to carry them out my words would have been empty and valueless.

Today, some eleven years after 1956, I say such things because I am confident. I know what we have here in Egypt and what Syria has. I also know that other states—Iraq, for instance—has sent its troops to Syria; Algeria will send troops;

Kuwait also will send troops. They will send armoured and infantry units. This is Arab power. This is the true resurrection of the Arab nation, which at one time was probably in despair. Today people must know the reality of the Arab world. What is Israel? Israel today is the United States. The United States is the chief defender of Israel. As for Britain, I consider it America's lackey. Britain does not have an independent policy. Wilson always follows Johnson's steps and says what he wants him to say. All Western countries take Israel's view.

The Gulf of Aqaba was a closed waterway prior to 1956. We used to search British, U.S., French, and all other ships. After the tripartite aggression—and we all know the tripartite plot—we left the area to UNEF, which came here under a UN resolution to make possible the withdrawal of Britain, France and Israel. The Jews say they opened the maritime route. I say they told lies and believed their own lies. We withdrew because the British and the French attacked us. This battle was never just between us and Israel. I have recently been with the armed forces. All the armed forces are ready for a face to face battle between the Arabs and Israel. Those behind Israel are also welcome.

APPENDIX 11

Press Conference of President
Gamal Abdel Nasser in Presidential Palace (excerpts)
MAY 28, 1967

The problem all of us are experiencing now and are concerned about—all of us, statesmen, journalists, and the multitudes of peoples—is neither the problem of the Tiran Straits nor the withdrawal of the UN Emergency Force (UNEF). All these are side issues of a bigger and more serious problem—the problem of the aggression which has taken place and continues to take place on the Arab homeland of Palestine and the continuous threat posed by that aggression against all Arab countries. This is the original problem.

Those who think that the crucial issues of nations and peoples can die and succumb to the symptoms of old age with the passage of time are grossly mistaken. Individuals may succumb to the symptoms of old age, including forgetfulness, but peoples are immortal, juvenescent, and eternally young. This is specially true in this case as aggression is not over. It continues to take place and in fact tries to affect and dominate a wider area.

We completely refuse to confine our concern to the subject of the Tiran Straits or the withdrawal of UNEF. In our opinion neither topic is open to question. The Tiran Straits are Egyptian territorial waters and Egypt has the right of sovereignty over them. No power no matter how powerful—and I am saying this quite clearly so that every side will know its position—can affect or circumvent the rights of Egyptian sovereignty. Any attempt of this kind will be an aggression against the Egyptian people and the entire Arab nation and will result in unimaginable damage to the aggressors.

The subject of the withdrawal of UNEF is also not open to question. UNEF came to our territory in the circumstances of the tripartite aggression, the disgraceful collusion which destroyed the moral and material reputation of all the perpetrators. All the secrets of the collusion have been unearthed. They condemn the plotters and brand them with contempt. As I have already said, UNEF came to our territory on our approval and its continued existence here depends on this approval. We have withdrawn our approval and the UN Secretary General has faithfully, honestly, and honorably responded to our request. The question of UNEF is now completely over and is no longer open for discussion.

The circumstances in which we requested the withdrawal of UNEF are also known to all of you. Syria was threatened. There was a plan to invade Syria. Measures had been taken and a date set for the implementation of this plan. In the meantime, the voices of Israeli officials were heard openly calling for an advance on Damascus. Naturally, we could not stand idly by while Syria was being threatened with invasion. We could not allow this to be done to Syria or to any Arab country. Therefore, the UAR armed forces had to move to positions from which they could effectively deter aggression. Many natural developments followed our action. These developments were a surprise for everyone except those who had disseminated biased propaganda against the Arab nation. They were now caught in the trap they had laid for others. They lied and lied until they believed themselves. Reality therefore took them by surprise.

We do not believe that any sincere man can describe any measure we have taken in the past two weeks as an aggression or even find in it any trace of aggression. Our forces went to Sinai to deter aggression. We have exercised in the Tiran Straits the rights of Egyptian sovereignty. Any interference with these rights will itself be an aggression. Why? This takes us back to the source, origin, reality, and core of the problem. Israel was created by imperialism and by the forces which seek to dominate the Arab nation. We are not the only ones who say this. It is said by others who are today defending the Israeli aggression. They say it on every occasion. Nearly word for word, they say they have created Israel and are responsible for its security. They have given Israel the biggest part of Arab Palestine. After this first and biggest aggression, they continued supporting its aggressive plan.

* * * *

QUESTION: Mr. President: You said that if Israel is threatening war you are prepared for it and you say to Israel, "welcome." Is your confidence due to your reading of the international political situation, or does it stem from your belief in the military supremacy of the UAR armed forces?

ANSWER: In answering this question, I would say that in its threats in the past few years, Israel has gone beyond every limit. The most recent thing was the Israeli Premier's threat to attack Syria and his war threats. Israel has been continuously threatening war. On 12 May this threat reached an extent that no one would accept. It was the duty of every Arab to respond to this threat. Therefore, I said that if Israel wanted to threaten war—which it actually did—then Israel is welcome.

In my opinion, Israel fell into the trap of a false victory in 1956. In that year we did not fight Israel, we fought against Anglo-French aggression. We withdrew our forces from Sinai in order to face Britain and France. One day we stood in the face of Israel with a small force, and on that day Israel was unable to penetrate any Egyptian position. In spite of that, the American press published articles glorifying the Israeli Army, the Israeli might, and so forth. This was all nonsense. We also read books—even verse was written about the 1956 campaign.

Today we are alone face to face with Israel, and if Israel wants to try war I would again say to it, "welcome." Today we are different than in 1956. In 1956 we withdrew our army from Sinai in order to face Britain. In the Suez war Israel colluded with France and Britain. Today our army has returned to Sinai to its original positions. We are now in 1967. While taking this action we, of course, choose the time and the place to talk. We choose the time and place to say, "welcome." Actually, the timing was determined for us by the Israeli Prime Minister, although we were prepared for it. This answers the first part of the question. As for the question of military supremacy, we believe of course that our armed forces are capable of carrying out their duty with honor, strength, and sincerity.

*   *   *   *

QUESTION: Mr. President, the recent political decisions taken by the UAR Government and implemented militarily last week, plus the corresponding measures taken by the Israeli side, have certainly increased the danger of a military conflict in the Middle East, even if these decisions were regarded as a reaction to the Israeli threats against Syria. Does UAR policy aim at taking a final decision now regarding Israel's existence, and, if this is not the case, what in your opinion should be done to preserve peace in the area?

ANSWER: We have taken these measures to restore things to what they were before. Now we are waiting to see what Israel will do next. Should Israel provoke us or any other Arab country, such as Syria, we are all prepared to face it. If Israel chooses war, then, as I have said, it is welcome to it. A great uproar has been created in the world by the United States, which is the creator and protector of Israel. It is trying to complicate and exaggerate things.

*   *   *   *

QUESTION: If there is war between the Arab states and Israel, do you think it could possibly remain limited to the states of the area only?

ANSWER: Of course, I cannot predict the future. However, if there is a war between only Israel and us, I think it will be limited to this area alone.

*   *   *   *

QUESTION: Mr. President, will you tell us why Egypt has chosen this particular moment to ask for the withdrawal of the UNEF and to impose a blockade on the Gulf of Aqaba?

ANSWER: I did not choose this time. It was Israeli Prime Minister Eshkol alone who chose this time. The matter has always been on our mind, but we did not choose the time. As I said before, when Eshkol threatened to march on Damascus, when Eshkol threatened to occupy Syria and to overthrow the national regime in Syria, it became our duty to come forward to help our Arab brothers. Thus we had to ask for the withdrawal of the UNEF, and since the UNEF withdrew it was inevitable for us to go to the Gulf of Aqaba and restore the pre-1956 conditions there.

* * * *

QUESTION: Under what circumstances would Your Excellency consider the question of lifting the ban on Israeli ships in the Gulf of Aqaba?

ANSWER: Under no circumstances. Israel's ships shall not pass in Egyptian territorial water. This is a position from which I will not budge one inch.

* * * *

QUESTION: Does Your Excellency the President see any chance of reaching a settlement which would achieve permanent peace between the Arab states and Israel in light of the current situation?

ANSWER: I have also spoken about this. Today's talk is not about a settlement and the achievement of peace between the Arab states and Israel. The point is that Israel is based on aggression. Where are the rights of the Palestine people? The rights of the Palestine people must be regained. It is impossible to reach a settlement regarding the current situation. We will remain patient, ten, or more years until we achieve the rights of the Palestine people. As I have said before, the Arab people are not a people who easily forget. They are a people who have a civilization and a history, and they must achieve their aim.

*   *   *   *

QUESTION: The President has often said that the Arabs will decide the time and place of war with Israel. Does Your Excellency feel that the present moment is well chosen in view of the predictions that present U.S.-Soviet relations are not as cordial as they were a few weeks ago and are not characterized by sharp confrontation (as heard), and that therefore this situation might be suitable for Egypt since its aim is to keep the big powers out of the conflict?

ANSWER: What has happened so far is that we were faced with Israeli threats. The Israeli prime minister stated he wants to occupy Syria, to occupy Damascus, and to change the national government in Syria. Are we prepared to deal with this situation? We definitely are: Our armed forces and our people are ready to deal with the situation.

The idea is not to bring about a confrontation between the United States and Soviet Union. Under no circumstances do we wish such a thing to happen, because this would mean a war affecting the entire world. It would mean a nuclear war. We have never considered this or wished it to happen. At the same time, we cannot allow the Israeli prime minister to threaten us and say that he will march on us and occupy us. Such threats have been made. There was no reaction in the United States to these threats. No one denounced them. Not a single paper in the United States denounced these threats. Of course, as far as time and place are concerned, we are now fully prepared for the confrontation. As I have already said, if Israel attacks any Arab country, we will not allow it to fight on a single front. It will be a full-scale war.

*   *   *   *

QUESTION: Is Egypt's decision regarding Israeli shipping in the Gulf of Aqaba irreversible?

ANSWER: I have already answered this question. The decision is irreversible.

*   *   *   *

QUESTION: Do you see any improvement in the Middle East situation today compared with a week ago, before U Thant's visit?

ANSWER: I do not see any improvement. We have regained our rights, removed UNEF, returned to the Gulf of Aqaba, and resumed our sovereignty there. Some people are threatening us with war while others are threatening us with aggression. We are waiting. We are leaving the initiative to them. Whoever wants to fight us may please come forward and do so. We are prepared to fight back.

QUESTION: Mr. President, do you expect an attack by Israel or by the United States or by both of them in collusion in the near future?

ANSWER: I expect anything. As for an attack by Israel, we expect it every day. In 1956 we were expecting an attack by France and Britain but never imagined that they—particularly Britain—would collude with Israel. But the unexpected happened; Britain colluded with Israel; Israel attacked us when we thought the attack would come from Britain. Today we expect anything.

QUESTION: Mr. President, now that the last territorial gains which Israel achieved in the 1956 Suez war have been eliminated, do you see any hope of negotiating a general settlement for the Palestine problem, and what conditions would the UAR attach to such negotiations?

ANSWER: As I have said, Israel's existence in itself is an aggression. The last territorial gains which Israel achieved in the 1956 Suez war have now been eliminated, but we do not see any hope for negotiating a general settlement of the Palestine problem. This is because none of the 1948 and 1959 UN resolutions have been implemented. All the Western countries, including the United States and Britain, speak about Israel's rights and take a partial stand. None of them speak about the Arabs and Arab rights or the rights of the Palestinians in their country and property. How then can we speak about a general settlement of the Palestine problem? I believe that the Palestinian people must retrieve their rights.

*   *   *   *

QUESTION: Do you believe that war with Israel is inevitable at this time, and do you imagine, from your own experience, that Israel will not reply violently to the closure of the Tiran Straits?

ANSWER: War with Israel has existed since 1948. We have been expecting Israeli aggression ever since. We have regained the rights which were ours in 1956. As I have already said, we have left the next move to Israel. Whether it wants to reply to our exercising our rights with violence or nonviolence, we are prepared. Our sons, our army, the whole Arab nation are prepared.

*   *   *   *

QUESTION: Has the UAR taken into consideration the possibility of the United States intervening militarily in favor of Israel?

ANSWER: I do not take the United States into consideration in my reckoning. If I took into consideration the United States, the Sixth Fleet, the Seventh Fleet, and the American generals I would not be able to do anything. We would not be able to move. We do not take the United States into consideration. If it intervenes we must defend ourselves and our rights. But if I were to calculate the power of the United States and my power I would quit, because I calculate that the United States is superior to me in land, sea, and air. I do not take this into consideration at all. If the United States intervenes, that is another question. In that case we must defend ourselves. No power, however big, can defeat any people determined to defend itself, its right to live, and its country's sovereignty.

*   *   *   *

*Speech of President Gamal Abdel Nasser
to Members of National Assembly (excerpts)*
MAY 29, 1967

The circumstances through which we are now passing are in fact difficult ones because we are not only confronting Israel but also those who created Israel and who are behind Israel. We are confronting Israel, and the West as well—the West which created Israel and which despised us, the Arabs, and which ignored us before and after 1948. They had no regard whatsoever for our feelings, our hopes in life, or our rights. The West completely ignored us, and the Arab nation was unable to check the West's stand.

Then came the events of 1956—the Suez battle. We all know what happened in 1956. When we stood to demand our rights, Britain, France, and Israel opposed us and we were faced with the tripartite aggression. We did, however, resist and proclaimed that we would fight to the last drop of our blood. God gave us success and God's victory was great. Subsequently we were able to stand and to build. Now, eleven years after 1956, we are restoring things to what they were in 1956. This is from the material aspect. In my opinion this material aspect is but a small part, whereas the spiritual aspect is the great side of the issue. The spiritual aspect involves the renaissance of the Arab nation, the revival of the Palestine question, and the restoration of confidence to every Arab and to every Palestinian. This is on the basis that if we were able to restore conditions to what they were before 1956, God will surely help and urge us to restore the situation to what it was in 1948.

Brothers: Arab revolt, upheaval, and commotion which we

now see taking place in every Arab country are not only because we have returned to the Gulf of Aqaba or rid ourselves
of the UN Emergency Force (UNEF), but because we have
restored Arab honor and renewed Arab hopes. Israel used to
boast a great deal and the Western powers, headed by the
United States and Britain, used to ignore and even despise us
and consider us of no value. But now that the time has come—
and I have already said in the past that we will decide the time
and place and now allow them to decide—we must be ready for
triumph and not for a recurrence of the 1948 comedies. We
shall triumph, God willing.

Preparations have already been made. We are now ready to
confront Israel. They have claimed many things about the 1956
Suez war, but no one believed them after the secrets of the 1956
collusion were uncovered—that mean collusion in which Israel
took part. Now we are ready for the confrontation. We are now
ready to deal with the entire Palestine question. The issue now
at hand is not the Gulf of Aqaba, the Straits of Tiran, or the
withdrawal of UNEF, but the rights of the Palestinian people.
It is the aggression which took place in Palestine in 1948 with
the collaboration of Britain and the United States. It is the
expulsion of the Arabs from Palestine, the usurpation of their
rights, and the plunder of their properties. It is the disavowal of
all the UN resolutions in favor of the Palestinian people.

The issue today is far more serious than they say. They want
to confine the issue to the Straits of Tiran, UNEF, and the right
of passage. We say: We demand the full rights of the Palestinian people. We say this out of our belief that Arab rights cannot
be squandered, because the Arabs throughout the Arab world
are demanding these Arab rights. We are not afraid of the
United States and its threats, of Britain and its threats, or of the
entire Western world and its partiality to Israel. The United
States and Britain are partial to Israel and are giving no consideration to the Arabs, to the entire Arab Nation.

They are giving no consideration to one hundred million
Arabs. Why? Because we have made them believe that we can-

not distinguish between friend and foe. We must make them know that we know who our foes are and who our friends are and treat them accordingly.

If the United States and Britain are partial to Israel, we must say that our enemy is not only Israel but also the United States and Britain and treat them as such. If the Western powers disavow our rights and ridicule and despise us, we the Arabs must teach them to respect us and take us seriously. Otherwise, all our talk about Palestine, the Palestinian people, and Palestinian rights will be null and void and inconsequential. We must treat enemies as enemies and friends as friends. I said yesterday that the states that champion freedom and peace have supported us. I spoke about the support given us by India, Pakistan, Afghanistan, Yugoslavia, Malaysia, the Chinese People's Republic, and the Asian and African states.

After my statements yesterday, I met with War Minister Shamseddin Badran and learned from him what took place in Moscow. I wish to tell you today that the Soviet Union is a friendly power and stands by us as a friend. In all our dealings with the Soviet Union—and I have been dealing with the USSR since 1955—it has not made a single request of us. The USSR has never interfered in our policy or internal affairs. This is the USSR as we have always known it. Actually, it is we that made urgent requests of the USSR. Last year, we asked for wheat and they sent it to us. When I also asked for all kinds of weapons, they gave them to us. When I met with Shamseddin Badran yesterday he handed me a message from Soviet Premier Kosygin saying that the USSR supports us in this battle and will not allow any power to intervene until matters were restored to what they were in 1956.

*   *   *   *

APPENDIX 13

Address of President Gamal Abdel Nasser
to the Nation
JUNE 9, 1967

We all know how the crisis began in the first half of last May. There was an enemy plan to invade Syria, and the statements by his politicians and his military commanders declared that frankly. The evidence was ample.

The sources of our Syrian brothers and our own reliable information were categorical on this.

Even our friends in the Soviet Union told the parliamentary delegation which was visiting Moscow early last month that there was a calculated intention. It was our duty not to accept this in silence. In addition to its being a question of Arab brotherhood, it was also a matter of national security. Who starts with Syria will finish with Egypt.

So our armed forces moved to our frontiers.

Following this came the withdrawal of the United Nations forces, then the return of our forces to the Sharm el-Sheikh position which commands the Tiran Straits and which the Israeli enemy used as one of the results of the tripartite aggression on us in 1956.

The passage of the enemy flag in front of our forces was intolerable and so were other matters connected with the most precious aspirations of the Arab nation.

Our estimates of the enemy's strength were precise. They showed us that our armed forces had reached a level of equipment and training at which they were capable of deterring and repelling the enemy.

We realized that the possibility of an armed clash existed,

and we accepted the risk. There were several factors before us, nationalist, Arab and international. These included a message from President Lyndon Johnson of the United States which was handed to our ambassador in Washington on May 26 asking us for restraint and not to be the first to open fire. Otherwise we would face serious consequences.

The same night the Soviet Ambassador asked to see me urgently at 3:30 a.m. and told me that the Soviet Government strongly requested we should not be the first to open fire.

On the morning of last Monday, June 5, the enemy struck. If we say now it was a stronger blow than we had expected we must say at the same time, and with assurance, that it was much stronger than his resources allowed.

Also, British aircraft raided in broad daylight positions on the Syrian and Egyptian front, in addition to operations by a number of American aircraft reconnoitering some of our positions. The inevitable result was that our land forces, fighting a most violent and brave battle in the open desert, found that their air cover was inadequate in face of decisive superiority.

It can be said without fear or exaggeration that the enemy was operating an air force three times its normal strength.

This was also faced by the forces of the Jordanian Arab Army, which fought a valiant battle under the command of King Hussein who, to be just, and honest to him, adopted a fine attitude. I confess that my heart bled as I followed the battles of his gallant army in Jerusalem and other positions on the western coast [of the Dead Sea] on a night in which the enemy and the powers plotting with him massed at least forty aircraft to operate over the Jordanian Army.

It was clear from the very first there were other forces behind him which came to settle their accounts with the Arab nationalist movement.

There were significant surprises:

1. The enemy we expected to come from the east and north came from the west. This showed he had facilities beyond his own resources and exceeding the estimate of his strength.

2. The enemy attacked, at one go, all the military and civil airfields in the United Arab Republic. This meant he was relying on something more than his normal strength to protect his skies from any retaliation from us. The enemy was also fighting on other Arab fronts with other assistance.

3. The evidence of imperialist collusion with the enemy is clear. It sought to benefit from the lesson of the former open collusion of 1956, this time concealing itself cunningly. What is now established is that American and British aircraft carriers were off the enemy's shores, helping his war effort.

There were magnificent and honorable battles.

The Algerian people and their great leader, Houari Boumedienne, gave without reservation to the battle.

The Iraqi people and their loyal leader, Abderrahman Arif, also gave without reservation.

The Syrian Army fought heroically, supported by the forces of the great Syrian people and under the leadership of their nationalist government.

The peoples and government of the Sudan, Kuwait, Yemen, Lebanon, Tunisia and Morocco adopted honorable attitudes.

The New York Times, June 10, 1967 (Reuters)

APPENDIX 14

Speech of President Gamal Abdel Nasser
at Cairo University Auditorium (excerpts)
JULY 23, 1967 *

The first point that should be clear before us all is that we were not the first to create the Middle East crisis. We all know that this crisis started with Israel's attempt to invade Syria. It is certain that Israel in this attempt was not working for its own interests; it was rather working for the interest of the powers which could not countenance the Arab revolutionary movement any longer.

The information we had about the invasion of Syria came from different sources. We had information from our Syrian brothers to the effect that Israel had mobilized eighteen brigades. We investigated this information and confirmed that Israel was mobilizing no less than thirteen brigades on Syrian borders.

Our parliamentary delegation which was headed by Anwar el-Sadat and which was visiting Moscow at the time was informed by our Soviet friends that the invasion of Syria was about to take place. But what could we do? We could have maintained silence, we could have waited, we could have only issued verbal statements and cables of support. But if this country had accepted to handle the situation in that way it would have given up its mission, role and personality.

There are some agreements between us and Syria; there was a joint defense pact between us. We do not consider our agreements with Arab countries or any other countries mere

* Official Egyptian Translation.

ink on paper. We consider these agreements sacred and therefore, we should abide by them. There was something between
us and Syria which exists between us and any Arab country—
something greater and more lasting than agreements or treaties.
There was and there will be strong faith in joint struggle and
common destiny.

Thus we were forced to move and take action in order to
confront the danger threatening Syria. This was made even
more imperative by the fact that the statements of the Israeli
political and military leaders and their overt threats against
Syria at that time were all openly and clearly referred to both
in the press and at the United Nations; there was not the least
doubt concerning the information we had, and consequently
we were not allowed time for waiting or for hesitation.

The second point is that our moves entailed certain practical consequences. First of all, we demanded the withdrawal
of the United Nations emergency forces. Then we once again
exercised the right of Egyptian sovereignty over the Gulf of
Aqaba. We had been pressed many times prior to that date by
our Arab brothers to take this move. Naturally, the move had
many effects both regionally and internationally.

The third point is that our move gave us the initiative in
repelling the danger threatening Syria. When we did this, however, we were fully aware, especially from an international
point of view, that we could not strike the first blow in a military operation. If we had done so, however, we would have
exposed ourselves to dangerous consequences—consequences
which would have been more dangerous than we could meet.
In fact we would have had to confront direct military action
and such action could well be launched under the pretext that
we had struck the first blow in the battle.

In this respect, I want to draw your attention to some important points.

The first point is the American warnings. You have probably read about them. The Counsellor of the American President summoned our Ambassador at a late hour in the night

in Washington and told him that Israel had information that we would mount an attack, adding that this would expose us to a dangerous situation. He asked us to retain self-control and said that the Americans were doing the same thing with Israel to have it maintain self-control. There was the message which we received from U.S. President Johnson in which he spoke about the United Nations and appealed to us to have self-control.

The second point, I have perhaps mentioned before. The Soviet Ambassador, in the following day, requested a meeting with me and conveyed to me a message from the Soviet Prime Minister asking us to have self-control and telling me about a message he had sent to the Israeli Prime Minister telling him that any action on the part of Israel would expose the world to grave dangers.

The third point, is that the entire world was against the opening of war. French President de Gaulle was clear when he said that France would adopt its stand on the basis of "who fired the first shot."

The fourth point is that we have been subjected to a diplomatic deception, to serious political fraud. We never imagined that such a fraud could be carried out by a major country, a major power. This political swindle came from the U.S. in the form of the U.S. President's message, his appeals, his requests for us to cooperate with the UN Secretary-General U Thant, his preparedness to dispatch his Vice-President and to discuss with us all matters and questions in order to help the entire world out of the crisis.

The UN Secretary-General came. We cooperated with the UN Secretary-General to the maximum degree. He asked us for a respite for the Gulf of Aqaba question and we agreed.

He said he wanted some time to give everybody a breathing space. The first point was that no Israeli ships were to go through the Gulf and at the same time we were not to carry out inspection.

We accepted this point and considered it a proposed solution from the UN Secretary-General. Then came an envoy of the U.S. President. He proposed that one of the Vice-Presidents fly to the U.S., meet the U.S. President and explain the situation to him.

I agreed on this. I then wrote to the U.S. President and told him that I welcomed the visit to Cairo of the U.S. Vice-President and, in the meantime, I was prepared to send Vice-President Zakaria Mohieddin to Washington to meet you [President Johnson] and explain to you the Arab standpoint.

Next day came their reply in which they welcomed Mohieddin's meeting with the U.S. President. They requested us to fix the date and we set Tuesday, June 6, as the date.

We all know that the aggression started on June 5. What does this mean? We did not imagine that the explosion would come so soon.

The fifth point is that we realized that we were in the dark about something and that it would not be late in revealing itself. It was clear that something had been afoot for a long time and, in fact, I had a presentiment two years ago that something was brewing against us since aid was cut off and the U.S. demanded that we should not develop our army and march forward with technical and military developments. When the troops were concentrated, my view was that there was only a twenty-per-cent possibility of war.

Before closing the Aqaba Gulf, we held a meeting of the Higher Executive Committee—the first time that took place in my home and discussed the question of closing that Gulf. At that meeting held on May 22, I told them that war chances were fifty per cent. At another meeting, I told them that war possibilities were eighty per cent. We met, all of us, at the Higher Executive Committee. It was clear that our work was defensive, that we would launch an offensive only if aggression were committed against Syria and that we should be on the alert.

At that meeting, nobody talked about attacking Israel, neither had there been any idea of launching an attack on

Israel. As I had explained, it was clear from all our analysis
that any offensive act against Israel would render us vulnerable
to big risks. The first of these was a U.S. attack on us in view
of U.S. declarations that it guaranteed the borders of the countries of the area. It was clear to us that the U.S.A., by saying
that it guaranteed those countries' borders and would not permit any changes in the area, did not mean the Arab states
but meant only Israel. It meant that if aggression were launched
against Israel, the U.S.A. would implement the declaration
formerly made by President Kennedy that the U.S.A. would
guarantee all the borders in this area.

On this basis, there was absolutely no question of opening
an offensive against Israel. Our whole operation at the Joint
Command was a defensive operation. What we took into account at the time was a process of prevention so that Israel
would not launch an aggression against Syria.

On May 23, we declared the closure of Aqaba Gulf to Israel
ships. The political changes in Israel at the beginning of June
and our close following of what was happening inside Israel
made us feel that the war was certainly going to take place.
What does this mean? It means that we never felt at ease at the
American diplomatic and political maneuvers. We were aware
that something was being engineered against us. We felt that
these designs would be put into effect very soon. On Friday,
June 2, I went to the High Command of the Armed Forces
and attended a meeting of the high military officials. I explained
to them my view point before I heard their explanation of the
situation. I stated at the meeting that it would not surprise me
to receive a blow from the enemy within forty-eight or seventy-
two hours—a blow that would never be delayed. I said this on
the basis of the developments that took place. I also said that
I expect that the aggression would take place on June 5 and
that the first blow would be dealt at our Air Force. What does
this mean? It means that we did not think lightly of the situation despite the diplomatic contacts that took place, the arrival
of the UN Secretary-General in Cairo and the consent of U.S.

President Johnson to send Zakaria Mohieddin to the United States.

Yet it was very clear that Israel would launch military action against us especially after the entry of Iraqi armed forces into Jordan in implementation of the Joint Defence Pact agreements.

When we come to the sixth point. Here we should acknowledge with complete honesty and with complete dignity that the military fight did not proceed the way we expected or desired. In fact, the battle proved the saying that no precaution could prevent a fatality.

*   *   *   *

The seventh point is related to the role played by America. Much of the role played by the U.S. is still vague and we know little about it. We have come to know all the secrets of 1956 only last year, that is to say, after ten years. We are not able to know all the secrets of the 1967 war now, but it is certain that the U.S. played a role, and much of it is still vague.

Nevertheless, there are a lot of questions to be raised. For instance, what is the political and diplomatic role played by the U.S.? Before the war, letters were sent to us asking restraint and even warning us that any action on our part might imperil the whole area. They offered to send the American Vice-President and they agreed on a visit to be made by Vice-President Zakaria Mohieddin to the United States to confer with President Johnson. All this was subterfuge to serve the ends of the Israeli aggression and the ends of an American plot against us laid down two years ago for the purpose of liquidating all the revolutionary regimes which refuse to be dragged into spheres of influence.

*   *   *   *

On the night of June 7, King Hussein had a telephone conversation with me during which he told me that four hundred planes were attacking the Jordanian front and that the radar networks in Jordan had registered this huge number of planes. From where did these planes come?

* * * *

The other question is why were there American planes over the front. On June 7, two planes carrying the American insignia were seen over our lines. At first, I did not believe it, but the information was correct and verified. Then, we issued a communiqué saying that American aircraft flew over our lines and front. We said that we believed the Americans are partners in the operation. We also said that there had been an air attack, with non-Israeli planes, on Jordan.

A message from President Johnson reached me at night. He had approached the Soviet head of state and asked that he send us a message for our relations with the United States were interrupted at the time. He said it was true that two U.S. planes flew over our lines, but they were on their way to rescue the U.S. spy ship *Liberty*.

* * * *

The United States was not surprised. American press reports are an evidence to this fact. The American magazine [*Life*] said Israel had told the American President that it favored aggression since it felt superior. It was also reported that the American President consulted his Chief of Staff and the Director of the Central Intelligence Agency who were of the Israeli opinion and that is why he gave the okay for the aggression.

Simultaneously, the Israelis secured pledges from the United States that if the Arabs attempted to enter Israel, the Sixth Fleet would prevent them. This was published by the press. Furthermore, the Israeli Premier Levi Eshkol expressed his gratitude to the American President for having told him that the Sixth Fleet was there to help Israel. When Eshkol told him that he might be busy on his ranch in Texas, he reassured him that the Sixth Fleet will protect them if the Arabs penetrated the borders of Israel. All this was published by the press.

* * * *

APPENDIX 15

Statements of Prime Minister
Levi Eshkol
MAY 12, 1967 *

"In view of the fourteen incidents of sabotage and infiltration perpetrated in the past month alone, Israel may have no other choice but to adopt suitable counter measures against the foci of sabotage and their abettors." This was declared by Israel's Prime Minister and Minister of Defence, Mr. Levi Eshkol, at a meeting of Mapai (the Israeli Labour Party) keymen, which took place on 12 May in Tel Aviv.

"Israel will continue to take action to prevent any and all attempts to perpetrate sabotage within her territory; Israel will continue to foil every scheme to divert the sources of the Jordan River and will defend its right to free navigation in the Red Sea,"—declared Israel's Prime Minister Levi Eshkol in an interview on *Kol Israel,* the National Broadcasting Service, on the eve of Memorial Day for those who fell in defence of Israel.

Mr. Eshkol added that peace and quiet would not reign on one side of the border alone; Israel would continue in the future, as in the past, to take all necessary steps to foil attempts of sabotage on Israeli territory under any form or pretext. "There will be no immunity for any State which aids and abets such acts," he stressed.

It was clear to Israel, he went on to say, that Syria was the focus of these acts of aggression. "However, Israel alone shall choose when, where and how to reply to the attacker."

* From the official Israeli *Weekly News Bulletin,* May 9–15, 1967, p. 20.

In connection with the Jordan River waters, Mr. Eshkol said: "Israel has in the past and will continue in the future to draw from the Jordan River only the amount of water due to her under the Johnston Plan—on condition that the Arab States will also confine themselves to the agreed partition of waters. In accordance with the Israel Government's declared policy, the Israel Defence Forces will continue to frustrate every plan aimed at diverting water from the Jordan sources, as this would constitute a direct infringement upon our territorial sovereignty."

In reply to a question concerning Israel's reaction to the recent threats to prevent free access to Israeli and Israel-bound shipping in the Red Sea, the Prime Minister emphasized that Israel would continue to thwart every attempt to interfere with shipping to and from Israel through the Red Sea, no matter by whom such attempts might be made.

In connection with alignment of forces in the Arab camp, Mr. Eshkol stated that nowadays it seemed as if Syria had taken upon herself the leadership in the battle against Israel. However, Syria's forces were not great, and "not without reason is she looking for protection among larger countries." Although this need not cause any alarm, "we shall go on manning our posts, ready for any possible deployment," he stated.

A P P E N D I X 16

Speech of Prime Minister
Levi Eshkol
MAY 13, 1967

The firm and persistent stand we have taken on behalf of our rights has strengthened the awareness among our neighbors that they will not be able to prevail against us in open combat. They recoil today from any frontal clash with Israel, and they postpone the date of such a confrontation to the remote future. Among the Arab rulers and their saboteur-minions, there are some who nowadays attempt to manifest their hostility to Israel in deeds, diligently in search of ways of attrition, subversion, and aggression against human lives. We have furnished proof that we shall not permit our borders to be opened to attack. We have proved that to their attempts to pick easy and exposed targets, we were able to respond at a place, time, and by a method of our own choosing. Thus, the saboteurs and their employers found out that they would not accomplish their aims this way. We do not recognize the limitations they endeavor to impose upon our acts of response. The Arab States and the nations of the world ought to know that any border which is tranquil from their side will also be quiet from our side. If they try to sow unrest on our border—unrest will come to theirs.*

* This is the only portion of the speech dealing with foreign policy.

Speech of Prime Minister
Levi Eshkol in the Knesset
MAY 22, 1967

Mr. Chairman, Members of the Knesset:

This session of the Knesset opens against the background of grave developments which took place during the past week on Egypt's border with Israel. I shall briefly review the chain of events.

During the night of May 15, 1967, news of the movement of Egyptian military forces into Sinai reached us from various sources. Military forces had been openly and demonstratively transferred, in broad daylight. Cairo explained that this step was taken in response to Israel's alleged preparations to attack Syria, and concentration of military forces on the northern frontier.

Upon learning of the Egyptian troop movements and the pretext offered to explain them, and before Egyptian forces had crossed the Suez Canal, we informed the UN that the allegations of Israeli troop concentrations in northern Israel were baseless. This statement was released for publication in the world press. Indeed, our statement was transmitted by the UN to Middle Eastern capitals, including Cairo. In his report to the Security Council on May 19, 1967, the UN Secretary-General states that UN observers verified the absence of Israeli troop concentrations and Israeli military movements on the northern frontier.

Nevertheless, Egyptian troop movements continued in the direction of Sinai, while mendacious propaganda continued to proceed from Cairo and Damascus concerning Israeli concentrations which had never taken place.

During the first days of Egyptian troop movements towards Sinai, authoritative political circles in the world capitals expressed the view that this was merely a propaganda move, devoid of any particular military significance.

The movement of Egyptian forces into Sinai gathered strength during the second half of last week, and today they are almost fully deployed in eastern Sinai and various positions throughout the peninsula.

Before May 14, the Egyptian force in Sinai consisted of less than two divisions, based mainly on infantry and some armour. Today, after reinforcements, Egyptian forces there are of a strength close to four divisions of infantry with armour. Furthermore, numerous artillery units have been brought up, and the Palestinian forces in the Gaza strip have been strengthened. Moreover, the Egyptian Air Force in the Sinai peninsula has also been reinforced.

All in all, the strength of Egyptian forces in Sinai has grown, according to our estimate, from thirty-five thousand to eighty thousand men. This is the first time that Egypt has brought forces of such dimensions into Sinai. With the increase of the Egyptian force and its advance into east Sinai, a graver international view is also being taken of Egypt's likely intentions and possible moves.

Members of the House:

While Egyptian forces advanced into east Sinai, the Chief of Staff of Egypt's armed forces informed the commander of the UN Emergency Force on Tuesday, May 16, as follows:

I have instructed all the armed forces of the United Arab Republic to be ready for action against Israel, as soon as Israel carries out any aggressive action against any Arab state. In the light of these instructions, our forces have already been concentrated in Sinai on our eastern border. In order to ensure the full safety of all UN forces deployed in observation posts along our borders, we request that the removal of these forces be ordered at once.

The Commander of the UN Emergency Force replied that he would at once report accordingly to the UN Secretary-General since he had no authority to withdraw any parts of the UN Emergency Force or to alter their deployment in any manner, unless instructed to do so by the Secretary-General.

From then on matters were dealt with by the UN Secretary-General; U Thant at once requested clarifications from the Egyptian representative at the UN, but at the same time he saw fit, for some reason, to announce on his own initiative that any request for the temporary removal of the UN Emergency Force from the border would be regarded as a demand for the complete evacuation of the Force from the Gaza strip and Sinai.

The UN Secretary-General's announcement was soon followed, on the very same day, by Egypt's official request for the complete evacuation of the UN force from Egyptian territory and from the Gaza strip.

The Secretary-General pointed out, it is true, in his reply on the same day, that the evacuation of the Force was liable to be of grave significance for the peace of the region, but to general surprise, he complied at once with the request for evacuation.

On Friday, May 19, the Commander of the UN Force, General Rikhye, informed the Israeli authorities that, as from 4:00 p.m. of the same day, the Force had ceased to carry out its functions and that it would remain in its bases and act only to ensure its own safety. This is the *only* official communication on this subject which Israel has received from the UN. Here I must point out that Israel was a party to this international arrangement, reached in 1957, but the Secretary-General did not see fit to consult Israel before he adopted his hasty decision. This past week was not the first time that Syrian sources spread mendacious reports of large-scale Israeli troop concentrations on the northern border for the purpose of attacking her.

Four times during the past two years the chief of the UN observers suggested a check on both sides of the border in connection with the allegations of threatening troop concentrations.

On March 17, 1965, the chief of UN observers proposed a review on the borders. Next day, Israel replied in the affirmative, while Syria failed to reply at all, and no check took place. On June 3, 1966, the UN made a similar request. Both sides agreed and the check was carried out.

On October 19, 1966, when the Syrians repeated their allegations, Israel, on her own initiative, proposed that the chief of UN observers should again carry out a similar check, which, indeed took place. On April 15, of this year, when Arab elements and others spread rumours of heavy Israeli troop concentrations, deployed for attack, the chief of the UN observers suggested to both parties that another check be carried out. On April 18, Israel expressed her consent. The check was not carried out owing to Syrian opposition.

Furthermore, after Syria had not enabled the implementation of such a check during the first week of May, she also failed to respond to the suggestion of the chairman of the Israel-Syrian Mixed Armistice Commission to obtain confirmation of the absence of Syrian troop concentrations on her border. Israel replied affirmatively to this request on the very same day.

To sum up: On May 15, the Egyptians explained that they had introduced their forces into Sinai on the strength of Syria's claim of alleged Israeli troop concentrations, deployed for an attack on Syria. In reality, however, Syria did all she possibly could in previous weeks to frustrate every UN endeavour to verify the true state of affairs, lest the spuriousness of her claims be revealed.

Indeed, the Secretary-General in his report to the Security Council of May 19, said, and I quote:

The Government of Israel has confirmed to me a few days ago that no unusual concentrations of Israeli forces or unusual military movements have taken place on the Syrian Armistice line.

He went on to say:

The reports of UN observers have verified the absence of troop concentrations and the absence of noteworthy military movements on both sides of the line.

Thus it transpires beyond any doubt that the Syrians have spread mendacious rumours which the Egyptians have clutched at and relied upon.

In the face of Syrian aggression we have tried, in vain, to exhaust all political measures of restraint. When acts of aggression continued and increased in gravity, we considered it necessary in certain cases to exercise our right of self-defence.

Nineteen incursions into Israel have taken place during the past six weeks. The UN Secretary-General himself, in his report to the Security Council of May 19, points out that these acts of terrorism and sabotage by El Fatah are a major factor in the deterioration of the situation to an unusual degree of tension and danger. "These acts provoke strong reactions in Israel by Government and people alike."

This appraisal is of great value for the comprehension of the basic causes of the growing tension in our region of late.

The Secretary-General goes on to state that several incidents have of late apparently indicated a new level of organization and training by those perpetrating sabotage and terrorist activities.

Members of the House:

The tension prevailing between Israel and the Arab countries has been influenced throughout the years by the state of inter-Arab relations and the relationship between the powers —against the background of their global and regional policies. All these factors are inextricably linked with each other.

In view of the mounting tension of late, the big powers ought to exercise their full influence in order to remove the danger of a conflagration in the Middle East.

Particular responsibility rests with the Soviet Union, which has friendly relations in Damascus and in Cairo, and which has not yet clearly disassociated herself from the policy of Damascus vis-à-vis Israel. It is only fitting that the declared policy of Soviet Russia, which advocates the settlement of controversies by negotiation—and not by violence—should also find expression in our region, without discrimination. This would further the maintenance of peace.

The concentrations of Egyptian forces in Sinai have reached proportions which increase the tension in our region and arouse world concern. The *status quo* must be restored on both sides of the border.

In the wake of the statements made by the UN Secretary-General, it is incumbent on UN members, and the big powers in particular, to declare in unmistakable terms their strongest opposition to the acts of sabotage carried out against a member state of the UN and to demand the complete cessation of such acts, which are contrary to international law and to the principles of the UN Charter.

International influence should be exerted to ensure continuation of the quiet which prevailed on the Egyptian-Israeli border since March 1957, by respecting the vital national and international rights of all states, including Israel.

The Secretary-General is leaving tonight for the Middle East, in order to contribute to the relaxation of tension and the consolidation of peace. We shall follow this visit, and its results, with interest.

I would like to say again to the Arab countries from this rostrum, particularly to Egypt and Syria, that we harbour no aggressive designs. We have no possible interest in violating either their security, their territory or their legitimate rights. Nor shall we interfere in any way in their internal affairs, their regimes, or their regional or international relations. We expect of them, according to the principles of reciprocity, the application of the same principles towards us.

Members of the Knesset:

During the early days of the movement of Egyptian forces towards Sinai, the view was expressed in various world capitals that it was a question of a purely demonstrative operation of no military significance. Others, of course, can adopt one interpretation or another. But we, to whose frontiers this force has approached, took the view that it was our duty to adopt all necessary steps to meet any possible development.

In view of the Egyptian concentrations on our borders and the evacuation of the UN Forces, I ordered a limited mobilization of reserves, which has been carried out according to plan.

On the completion of the limited mobilization, I visited the Israel Defence Forces units. The remarkable capacity of our Army, which has been fostered and perfected over the years, has reached a high level today. The Israel Defence Forces are capable today of meeting any test, with the same devotion, skill and capacity that they have demonstrated more than once in the past—and, knowing the facts as I do, I could say even more.

In conclusion I call upon all the peoples of the Middle East for reciprocal respect for the sovereignty, integrity and international rights of each of our countries. Israel, with complete confidence in her defensive capacity and her steadfastness of strength and spirit, expresses at this hour her readiness to participate in an effort to reinforce stability and advance peace in our region.

Statement of Prime Minister
Levi Eshkol in the Knesset (excerpt)
MAY 29, 1967

Following upon my statement to the Knesset last week about the security situation, I shall survey the main developments that have taken place in the area.

Two weeks ago, the Egyptian Army began to move its concentrations towards eastern Sinai, opposite Israel's frontier. Today, the main part of the Egyptian Army is concentrated in battle order in this area. On our northern frontier, Syria, Egypt's ally, is concentrating its army.

Parallel with this concentration the United Nations Emergency Force has been hastily evacuated from Sinai, the Gaza strip, and Sharm el-Sheikh. This force, which was established by the United Nations, entered Sinai and the Gaza strip at the time as part of an arrangement with Israel for the evacuation of her forces from Sinai and the Gaza strip. This evacuation was carried out on the basis of clear international undertakings for free passage in the Gulf of Aqaba and the cessation of infiltration from the Gaza strip. The withdrawal of the UN Force marks the removal of the symbol of the relative quiet that has reigned on the southern border for the past ten years.

The UN force constituted an expression of the will of the international community to ensure quiet on the border and free passage in the Straits. Nasser's agreement to the force's remaining in Sinai and the Strip expressed for ten years Egypt's readiness to undertake to preserve quiet on her border with Israel and to refrain from interference with free passage in the Straits. A week ago the ruler of Egypt announced the closing of the Straits to Israel shipping and ships carrying cargo to Israel. Since then he has several times repeated this statement and threats against anyone who should try to break this illegal blockade.

The Egyptian President has further proclaimed his intention and readiness to attack Israel for the purpose of destroying her. Yesterday, he went further and threatened to begin at once with extensive sabotage operations against Israel, her towns and villages, and her citizens. This very day attacks have been carried out against us from the Gaza strip.

These acts and declarations have altered the security and political situation in the area. The Government of Israel has, therefore, adopted a number of security and political initiatives with the aim of safeguarding Israel's vital interests. A precondition for safeguarding peace and our interests is our military strength. I, therefore, ordered, with the Government's agreement, the mobilization of the reserves of the Israel Defence Forces, and they are ready and prepared today to frustrate the enemy's designs in all sectors and on all our borders.

Members of the Knesset, the Government of Israel has repeatedly stated its determination to exercise its freedom of passage in the Straits of Tiran and the Gulf of Aqaba and defend it in case of need. This is a supreme national interest on which no concession is possible and no compromise is admissible. It is clear to us, and I feel that it is now clear to the nations of the world, that so long as the blockade exists peace is in danger.

It is this grave situation that obligates us particularly to find out first of all, and with great urgency, whether those governments that have undertaken to support and implement freedom of passage are prepared to translate their undertakings into the language of action in accordance with international law which the Egyptian ruler so criminally violates.

The Foreign Minister's brief visits to Paris, London and Washington were designed to clarify this question. He explained to the Presidents of the United States and France, and the

British Prime Minister, that it was a matter of a vital national interest which our country will unflinchingly protect. From the Foreign Minister's conversations we learned that all the governments with which he made contact desired that the *status quo* which has recently been violated should be respected. The President of the United States and the Prime Minister of Britain have made strong public statements on the subject.

There is special interest in the attitude of the United States, for its Government was the first to convey undertakings to Israel in 1957, in diplomatic exchanges, in letters from the President and the Secretary of State, and in public statements in the UN and other places.

After hearing President Johnson's statement of May 23, and the Foreign Minister's report of his talks in Washington, the Government was deeply impressed by the unambiguous stand of the United States in favour of the safeguarding of freedom of passage in these international waters. A similar attitude is expressed by the British Prime Minister, Mr. Harold Wilson, in his public statement and his talks with our Foreign Minister. Other maritime states have already informed us of their readiness to effectively support freedom of passage and we have been told that practical consultations on the subject are already taking place.

Under these conditions it is reasonable to expect that the states which support the principle of free passage should carry out and coordinate effective action in order to ensure that the Straits and the Gulf shall be open to the passage of the ships of all nations without discrimination within a short time. This expectation, which is founded on authorized and express statements, has had a strong influence on the attitude and decisions of the Israel Government at this stage. There is no doubt that the readiness to protect freedom of passage, which has been shown by great nations, has been influenced both by their attitude in principle and by their knowledge that the State of Israel will protect its rights.

It was our duty, first of all, to put international undertakings to the test. In the near future it will transpire whether this prospect is being realized. Israel's attitude in regarding the blocking of the Straits as an act of aggression against her remains fully in force. The Israel Government's statement at the United Nations General Assembly on 1 March 1957 still expresses our policy with complete accuracy.

We are now engaged in extensive political activity for the restoration of freedom of passage. This activity would not have been possible, and its prospects would have been dim, had it not been for our own strength and the justice of our claim. On the other hand, the ties which we have forged with other nations have helped, and will continue to help, to enhance our strength and protect our rights.

Members of the Knesset, the Egyptian ruler's statements about the closing of the Straits, about acts of violence, about his aggressive intentions and troop concentrations, have raised the tension in the area to a peak. Col. Nasser has created a position in which there is a danger of war.

On several occasions I have informed the Knesset and the nation of the growth in the power of the Israel Defence Forces. Today, our Army is at the zenith of its strength in manpower, fighting spirit and military equipment. We must devote our attention not only to ensuring the freedom of passage, but also to the danger of military aggression led by Egypt. No sensible person will find it difficult to understand that so long as there exists a massive concentration of the forces of Egypt and her allies in the neighborhood of our borders a conflagration could break out. The Israel Defence Forces will, therefore, remain mobilized at arms ready for any test, and if the necessity arises they have the strength to defeat the aggressors.

Egypt's measures constitute a threat to peace in the whole of our area. The Egyptian President's inflammatory declarations and threats implant illusions in the hearts of his excitable devotees. The Egyptian ruler should remember that this is not the first time that he has been borne on the wings of his imagination seeing himself a victor before he has gone out to war. He should remember that his disappointment was not long delayed, as we ourselves have witnessed.

*　　*　　*　　*

APPENDIX 19

Statement of Soviet Government

MAY 23, 1967

A situation giving rise to anxiety, from the viewpoint of the interests of peace and international security, has been taking shape in the Near East in recent weeks. After the armed attack by Israeli forces on the territory of the Syrian Arab Republic on 7 April of this year, Israel's ruling circles continued aggravating the atmosphere of military psychosis in this country. Leading statesmen, including Foreign Minister Eban, openly called for large-scale Israeli "punitive" operations against Syria and the striking of "a decisive blow" against her. The defence and foreign policy committees of the Knesset [Parliament] on 9 May granted the Government powers for military operations against Syria. Israeli troops moved to the frontiers of Syria were alerted. Mobilization was proclaimed in the country.

It is quite clear that Israel could not act in this way if it were not for the direct and indirect encouragement it had for its position from certain imperialist circles which seek to bring back colonial oppression to Arab lands. These circles regard Israel, in the present conditions, as the main force against Arab countries that pursue an independent national policy and resist pressure from imperialism.

Israeli extremists apparently hoped to take Syria by surprise and deal a blow at Syria alone. But they miscalculated. Showing solidarity with the courageous struggle of the Syrian people, who are upholding their independence and sovereign rights, Arab States—the United Arab Republic, Iraq, Algeria, Yemen,

261 / APPENDIX 19

Lebanon, Kuwait, Sudan, and Jordan—declared their determination to help Syria in the event of an attack by Israel.

The United Arab Republic, honouring its commitments as an ally for joint defence with Syria, took steps to contain the aggression. Considering that the presence of United Nations troops in the Gaza area and Sinai Peninsula would, in this situation, give Israel advantages for staging a military provocation against Arab countries, the Government of the United Arab Republic asked the United Nations to pull its troops out of this area. A number of Arab States voiced their readiness to place their armed forces at the disposal of the joint Arab command to repel Israeli aggression.

As is known, the Soviet Government warned the Government of Israel, in connexion with the armed provocation of 7 April, that Israel will bear the responsibility for the consequences of its aggressive policy. It appears that a reasonable approach has not yet triumphed in Tel Aviv. As a result, Israel is again to blame for a dangerous aggravation of tension in the Near East.

The question arises: What interests does the State of Israel serve by pursuing such a policy? If they calculate in Tel Aviv that Israel will play the role of a colonial overseer for the imperialist Powers over the peoples of the Arab East, there is no need to prove the groundlessness of such calculations in this age when the peoples of whole continents have shaken off the fetters of colonial oppression and are now building an independent life.

For decades the Soviet Union has been giving all-around assistance to the peoples of Arab countries in their just struggle for national liberation against colonialism and for the advancement of their economy.

But let no one have any doubts about the fact that, should anyone try to unleash aggression in the Near East, he would be met not only with the united strength of Arab countries but also with strong opposition to aggression from the Soviet Union and all peace-loving States.

It is the firm belief of the Soviet Government that the peoples have no interest in kindling a military conflict in the Middle East. It is only a handful of colonial oil monopolies and their hangers-on that can be interested in such a conflict. It is only the forces of imperialism, with Israel following along in the wake of their policy, that can be interested in it.

The Soviet Government keeps a close watch on the developments in the Near East. It proceeds from the fact that the maintenance of peace and security in the area directly adjacent to the Soviet borders touches upon the vital interests of the Soviet peoples. Taking due account of the situation, the Soviet Union is doing and will continue to do everything in its power to prevent a violation of peace and security in the Near East and to safeguard the legitimate rights of the peoples.

APPENDIX 20

Statement of President
Lyndon B. Johnson
MAY 23, 1967

In recent days, tension has again arisen along the armistice lines between Israel and the Arab states. The situation there is a matter of grave concern to the whole international community.

We earnestly support all efforts, in and outside the United Nations and through its appropriate organs, including the Secretary General, to reduce tensions and to restore stability. The Secretary General has gone to the Near East on his mission of peace with the hopes and prayers of men of good will everywhere.

The Near East links three continents. The birthplace of civilization and of three of the world's great religions, it is the home of some sixty million people; and the crossroads between East and West.

The world community has a vital interest in peace and stability in the Near East, one that has been expressed primarily through continuing United Nations actions and assistance over the past twenty years.

The United States, as a member of the United Nations, and as a nation dedicated to a world order based on law and mutual respect, has actively supported efforts to maintain peace in the Near East.

The danger, and it is a grave danger, lies in some miscalculation arising from a misunderstanding of the intentions and actions of others.

The Government of the United States is deeply concerned,

in particular, with three potentially explosive aspects of the present confrontation.

First, we regret that the general armistice agreements have failed to prevent warlike acts from the territory of one against another government, or against civilians, or territory, under control of another government.

Second, we are dismayed at the hurried withdrawal of the United Nations Emergency Force from Gaza and Sinai after more than ten years of steadfast and effective service in keeping the peace, without action by either the General Assembly or the Security Council. We continue to regard the presence of the United Nations in the area as a matter of fundamental importance and shall support its continuance with all possible vigor.

Third, we deplore the recent build-up of military forces and believe it a matter of urgent importance to reduce troop concentrations. The status of sensitive areas, as the Secretary General emphasized in his report to the Security Council, such as the Gaza strip and Gulf of Aqaba, is a particularly important aspect of the situation.

In this connection, I want to add that the purported closing of the Gulf of Aqaba to Israeli shipping has brought a new and grave dimension to the crisis. The United States considers the gulf to be an international waterway and feels that a blockade of Israeli shipping is illegal and potentially disastrous to the cause of peace. The right of free, innocent passage of the international waterway is a vital interest of the international community.

The Government of the United States is seeking clarification on this point. We have urged Secretary General Thant to recognize the sensitivity of the Aqaba question and to give it the highest priority in his discussions in Cairo.

To the leaders of all the nations of the Near East, I wish to say what three Presidents have said before—that the United States is firmly committed to the support of the political independence and territorial integrity of all the nations of the area.

The United States strongly opposes aggression by anyone in the area, in any form, overt or clandestine. This has been the policy of the United States led by four Presidents—President Truman, President Eisenhower, President Kennedy, and myself—as well as the policy of both of our political parties. The record of the actions of the United States over the past twenty years, within and outside the United Nations, is very clear on this point.

The United States has consistently sought to have good relations with all the states of the Near East. Regrettably, this has not always been possible, but we are convinced that our differences with individual states of the area and their differences with each other must be worked out peacefully and in accordance with accepted international practice.

We have always opposed—and we oppose in other parts of the world at this moment—the efforts of other nations to resolve their problems with their neighbors by aggression. We shall continue to do so. And we appeal to all other peace-loving nations to do likewise.

We call upon all concerned to observe in a spirit of restraint their solemn responsibilities under the Charter of the United Nations and the general armistice agreements. These provide an honorable means of preventing hostilities until, through the efforts of the international community, a peace with justice and honor can be achieved.

I have been in close and very frequent contact—and will be in the hours and days ahead—with our able Ambassador, Mr. Goldberg, at the United Nations, where we are pursuing the matter with great vigor and in the hope that the Security Council will act effectively.

REFERENCE NOTES

I

1. David Ben-Gurion, *Israel: Years of Challenge* (New York: Holt, Rinehart & Winston, 1963), p. 15.
2. United Nations, General Assembly, November 26, 1947, pp. 1360–61.
3. Boris Eliacheff, *Le Monde,* June 1, 1967. M. Eliacheff was the first Commercial Councillor representing France in Israel.
4. Walter Eytan, *The First Ten Years* (New York: Simon & Schuster, 1958), pp. 10–12, 138–39.
5. Moshe Pearlman, *Ben Gurion Looks Back* (London: Weidenfeld & Nicolson, 1965), pp. 140–41. In *Israel: Years of Challenge* (op. cit., p. 22), Ben Gurion states that Czechoslovakia and France agreed to sell arms in 1947–48. Much surplus arms had been purchased in the United States beginning in 1945, but the Jewish forces lacked heavy armament, a navy, and planes.
6. United Nations, Security Council, March 30, 1948, pp. 248–50.
7. Raphael Patai, *The Kingdom of Jordan* (Princeton University Press, 1958), pp. 8–10, 48.

II

1. Moshe Dayan, *Diary of the Sinai Campaign* (New York: Schocken, 1967), p. 68.
2. Pearlman, op. cit., p. 147.
3. Dayan, op. cit., p. 3.
4. Ibid., p. 192.
5. *American Foreign Policy: Current Documents 1957* (Washington, D.C.: Government Printing Office, 1957), pp. 944–45.
6. Appendix 2.

7. *The New York Times,* March 19, 1957; *American Foreign Policy,* op. cit., pp. 955–56.
8. *Newsweek,* March 25, 1957, p. 46. This interview was reported on the front page of *The New York Times,* March 20, 1957.
9. The clearest contemporary account of this entire incident appeared in the column, "What Did We Promise?" by Ernest K. Lindley in *Newsweek,* April 1, 1957, p. 47. A perceptive and informed report was also written by James Reston in *The New York Times,* March 1, 1957. Herman Finer, *Dulles Over Suez* (Chicago: Quadrangle Books, 1964, pp. 487–88) seems to have a somewhat garbled version of the essential story.

III

1. Pearlman, op. cit., p. 157.
2. Leonora Stradal, "Entretien Avec les Commandos Al-Fatah," in *Le conflit israélo-arabe* (Paris: Les Temps Modernes, 1967), pp. 214–15. Other sources give the end of 1964 as the date of El Fatah's first operations.
3. *Mideast Mirror* (Beirut, Lebanon), March 5, 1965, p. 5.
4. According to *L'Humanité* (Paris), organ of the French Communist Party, June 13, 1967, Ateyyeh is a member of the Central Committee of the Communist Party of Syria.
5. The first citation is from the *Near East Report* (Washington, D.C.), May 31, 1966, p. 42; the second from *Mideast Mirror,* May 28, 1966, p. 2.
6. *The New York Times,* May 8, May 16, and May 28, 1966.
7. United Nations, Security Council, Provisional Verbatim Record, October 14, 1966, p. 62.

IV

1. *Mideast Mirror,* November 26, 1966, p. 7.
2. Ibid., January 7, 1967, p. 7, and January 14, 1967, p. 2. I have used the original language as nearly as possible. The dates indicate when the alleged incidents took place.
3. Ibid., January 21, 1967, p. 2.
4. Ibid., February 11, 1967, p. 2; February 25, 1967, p. 6, and March 11, 1967, p. 4.
5. Joe Alex Morris, Jr. (Beirut, Lebanon), Washington *Post,* January 8, 1967.

V

1. *The New York Times,* April 8, 1967.
2. *Mideast Mirror,* April 15, 1967.
3. Ibid.
4. Ibid., April 22, 1967.
5. Ibid., April 15, 1967.
6. Ibid., April 29, 1967.
7. Ibid., May 6, 1967.
8. United Nations, Press conference, May 11, 1967 (Press Release, SG/SM/708, p. 13).
9. Appendix 15.
10. Official translation, Press Bulletin, Government Press Office, May 13, 1967.
11. Appendix 11.
12. Editorial in *Renmin Ribao,* June 11, 1967 (English version in *Peking Review,* June 16, 1967, p. 12).
13. Chou Tien-chih, *Peking Review,* September 8, 1967, pp. 24–25.
14. Interview with Prime Minister Eshkol, *Ma'ariv,* October 4, 1967.
15. Speech of May 22, 1967 (Appendix 9).
16. *Le Monde,* May 10 and 12, 1967.
17. Ibid., June 6, 1967.
18. Report of May 19, 1967 (Appendix 5).

VI

1. This account is based on the Report of the Secretary General on the Withdrawal of the United Nations Emergency Force, June 27, 1967 (Appendix 8).
2. From monitored radio broadcasts.
3. Ibid.
4. Speech of May 22, 1967 (Appendix 9).
5. L. Oppenheim, *International Law: A Treatise,* ed. by H. Lauterpacht, 8th edition (New York: Longmans, Green & Co., 1955), Vol. I, p. 508.
6. Report of May 26, 1967 (Appendix 6).
7. Appendix 20.
8. Appendix 10.

9. Michael Howard and Robert Hunter, *Israel and the Arab World: The Crisis of 1967,* Adelphi Papers, No. 41 (London: The Institute for Strategic Studies, October 1967), p. 24.

10. Appendix 11.

11. Appendix 12.

12. Appendix 14.

13. Ahmad Samih Khalidi, "An Appraisal of the Arab-Israel Military Balance," *Middle East Forum* (Beirut), Vol. 42, No. 3, 1966, pp. 55–65.

14. Eric Rouleau, in Eric Rouleau, Jean-Francis Held, Jean and Simonne Lacouture, *Israël et les Arabes: Le 3e Combat* (Paris: Editions du Seuil, 1967), p. 67.

15. Interview with Prime Minister Eshkol, *Ma'ariv,* op. cit.

16. Interview with General Rabin, *Ma'ariv,* May 14, 1967.

17. Speech by General Rabin to Zionist Convention of America, Jerusalem, July 19–26, 1967, in *The American Zionist* (New York), September 1967, p. 9.

18. Speech by General Rabin, September 21, 1967, *The Jerusalem Post Weekly,* October 9, 1967, p. 6.

19. Interview with Prime Minister Eshkol, *Ma'ariv,* op. cit.

20. Ibid.

21. Speech of Prime Minister Eshkol, May 22, 1967 (Appendix 17). General Rabin later stated that the Egyptians had a reinforced division permanently stationed in Sinai and had moved in two more divisions (*The Jerusalem Post Weekly,* October 9, 1967, p. 6).

22. Muhammad Hassanein Heikal, *al-Ahram* (Cairo), October 6, 1967.

23. Rabin, *The Jerusalem Post Weekly,* October 9, 1967, p. 6.

24. Interview with Prime Minister Eshkol, *Ma'ariv,* op. cit.

25. From monitored radio broadcasts.

26. "Pourquoi Moscou a lâché Nasser," *Le Nouvel Observateur* (Paris), June 14–20, 1967, p. 16.

27. Eric Rouleau, op. cit., pp. 102–103.

28. Alexander Werth, "Year of Jubilee: The USSR at Fifty," *The Nation,* October 30, 1967, p. 427.

VII

1. John C. Campbell, *Defense of the Middle East* (New York: Harper, 1960), p. 242.

2. Interview with Prime Minister Eshkol, *Ma'ariv,* op. cit.
3. Speech of June 9, 1967 (Appendix 13).
4. Speech of July 23, 1967 (Appendix 14).
5. Editorial by "Karim" in *al-Hayah* (Beirut), October 10, 1967.
6. Interview with Prime Minister Eshkol, *Ma'ariv,* op. cit.
7. Ibid.
8. Rabin, *The Jerusalem Post Weekly,* October 9, 1967, p. 6.
9. Interview with Hussein, *Der Spiegel* (Hamburg), September 4, 1967, p. 97.
10. David Wood, *The Middle East and the Arab World: The Military Context,* Adelphi Papers, No. 20 (London: The Institute for Strategic Studies, July 1965), p. 5.
11. *Ma'ariv,* op. cit.
12. From monitored radio broadcasts.
13. United Nations, Security Council, Document S/7896, p. 5.
14. Ibid., Provisional Verbatim Record, May 24, 1967 (S/PV. 1342), p. 11.
15. Ibid., pp. 22 and 51.
16. Ibid., May 29, 1967 (S/PV. 1343), p. 16.
17. Ibid., pp. 36–37.
18. Ibid., pp. 87–102 and 121–22.
19. Ibid., May 31, 1967 (S/PV. 1345), pp. 56–60 and 71–75.
20. Ibid., June 3, 1967 (S/PV. 1346), pp. 67–75 and 106–115.
21. Thomas T. Fenton, Baltimore *Sun,* June 15, 1967; Bernard Gwertzman, Washington *Star,* June 15, 1967.
22. Eugene V. Rostow, "The Middle East Crisis and Beyond," *State Department Bulletin,* January 8, 1968, p. 46.
23. *The Times* (London), June 5, 1967.
24. Rostow, op. cit.
25. *The Times* (London), May 26, 1967.
26. *Current Digest of the Soviet Press,* June 21, 1967, pp. 22–23.
27. *Jeune Afrique* (Paris), August 6, 1967, p. 13.

VIII

1. *al-Ahram,* October 13, 1967.
2. United Nations, Security Council, Provisional Verbatim Record, May 24, 1967 (S/PV. 1341), p. 27.
3. Ibid., June 3, 1967 (S/PV. 1346), p. 92.